the architect's house

the architect's house

STEPHEN CRAFTI

PHOTOGRAPHY | NICOLE ENGLAND

INSIDE THE HOMES OF TWENTY ARCHITECTS FROM AROUND THE WORLD

Quadrille

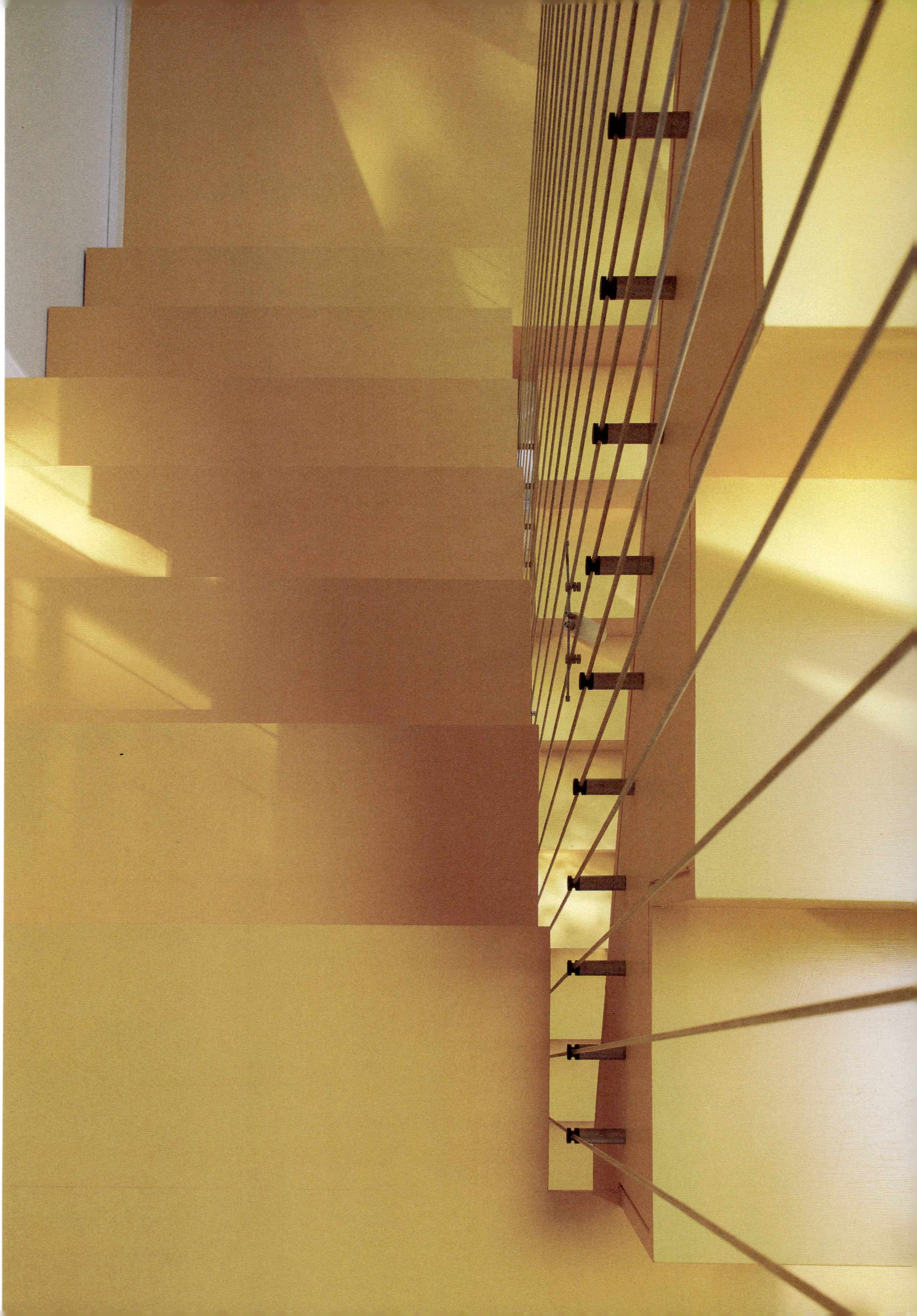

contents

7   Introduction

13   Charles Wu, Polysmiths, London

23   Andrew Piva, B.E. Architecture, Melbourne

35   Ben Ridley, Architecture for London, London

45   Mathieu Luyens & Julie Van De Keere, JUMA Architects, Flanders

57   Jay Bargmann, FAIA, New York State

71   Sam Peeters, Contekst, Antwerp

83   Peggy Hsu & Chris McCullough, Hsu McCullough, Los Angeles County

95   Thomas Gluck, GLUCK+, Upstate New York

105 Percy Weston, Surman Weston, London

117 Mat Barnes, CAN, London

129 Matthew Royce, M Royce Architecture, Los Angeles

141 Jonathan Tuckey, Tuckey Design Studio, London

153 Robert Simeoni, Robert Simeoni Architects, Melbourne

165 Manuel Aires Mateus, Manuel Aires Mateus, Lisbon

177 John Friedman & Alice Kimm, John Friedman Alice Kimm Architects, Los Angeles

189 Ilze Quaeyhaegens & Gert Cuypers, cuypers & Q Architects, Antwerp

201 Jeff Provan, Manuel Aires Mateus, Neometro and MA+Co, Mornington Peninsula, Victoria

213 Zach Fluker & Liz Tatarintseva, ao-fit, London

225 William Smart, Smart Design Studio, Sydney

237 David Leggett & Paul Loh, Leggett Loh Design Studio (LLDS), Melbourne

250 Acknowledgements

252 About the Author

253 About the Photographer

254 Credits for Furniture & Art

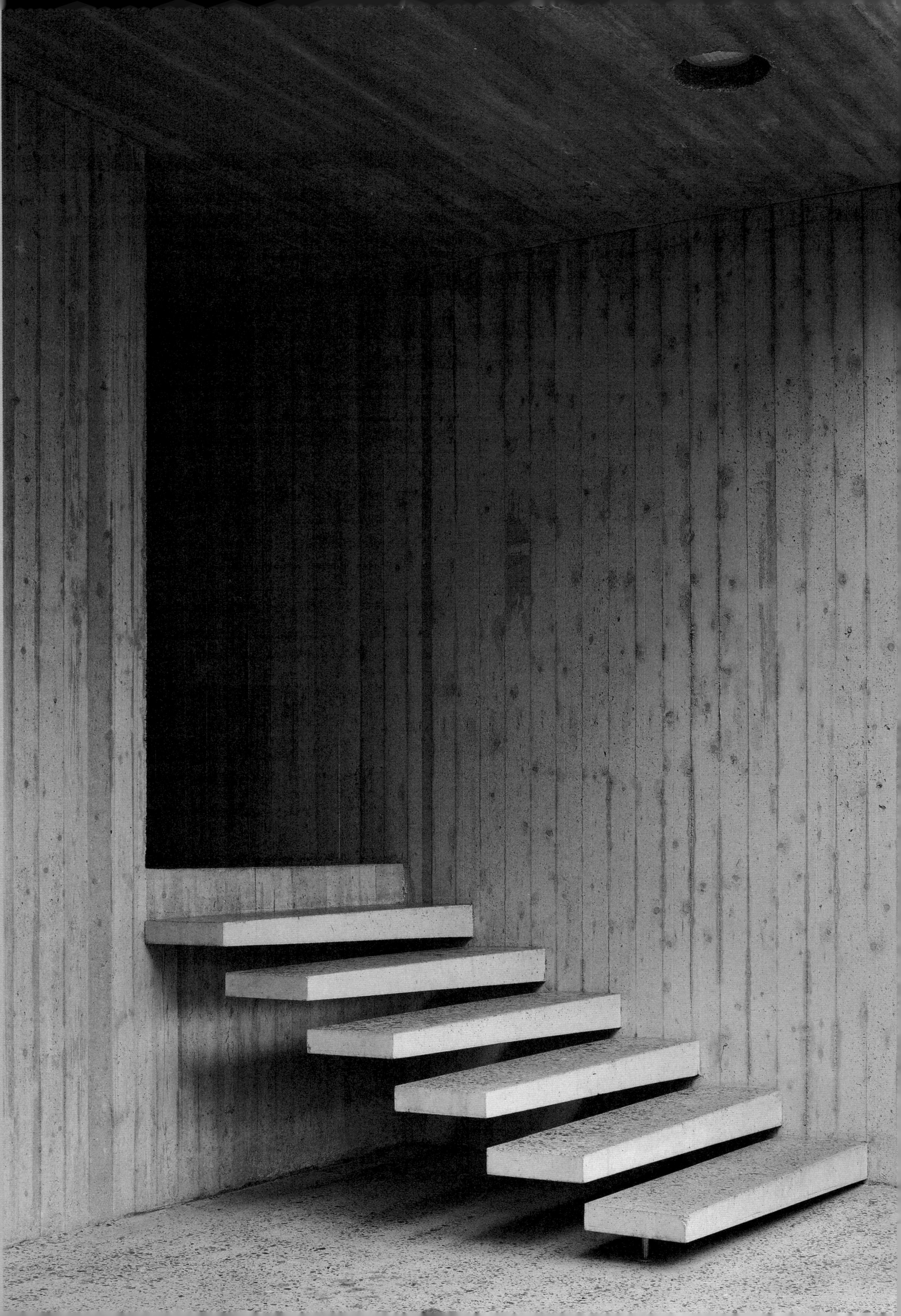

introduction

STEPHEN CRAFTI

An architect generally works to a client's brief when designing a new home or renovating an existing dwelling. However, the opportunity for an architect or a designer to create their own home, without the constraints of a client, must certainly be at the top of their wish list. Even with this freedom, there are always restrictions, be they the dimensions of a given site, the immediate and broader context, the availability of materials and, importantly for most, the budget.

Architects are sometimes privileged to create lavish homes for clients, complete with all the bells and whistles. These abodes might be filled with expensive appliances and pricey fittings and finishes – including an extensive dose of marble. But for an architect's own home, the driver for a design goes beyond surface treatments. There's the chance to explore ideas that may have appeared before on television programmes or in magazines, but not in the way they have been interpreted or expressed for their own design.

It is said that in the 1950s, when adventurous postwar architects heard the phone ring on a rainy day, they'd say 'Just don't answer it!', as there were often leakages from the experimental roofs they designed for their clients. There may be other issues besides leakages today, but with improved technology, there's less likelihood of these occurring. An architect's own home may have a few other issues that might not be fully resolved given that these homes test ideas and push new boundaries. But it's often these new ideas that are refined or reworked at a later time to form part of a scheme for a client's house.

This book isn't the first that's been written on the subject. But it's one that will encourage and also truly inspire those contemplating building a new home or renovating an older style of residence to take on the adventurous spirit shown by the architects featured. At a time when people are being cautious, both in terms of finances and ideas, hopefully they will find inspiration to go beyond the prosaic or not simply to chase the idea of a home with only resale value in mind. Resale is generally the last thing on an architect's mind when they start thinking about their own homes – be it a house, an apartment or a weekender. They would certainly make sure there were sufficient bedrooms for their needs and the number of bathrooms required, but these are simply logistics and standard procedures rather than creating something that's unique, tailor-made for them, their partners and their immediate and extended families.

The homes featured in this book exemplify not just what can be achieved today but also what was achieved in the past. There are houses that were designed as early as 2012, as well as those where 'the paint has just dried'. Ideas can remain fresh and innovative long after they are completed. Thomas Gluck's house, built over 10 years ago, could also have been completed yesterday. Defying gravity, the top-level of the house cantilevers above its majestic site. Fast forward 10 years and architects John Friedman and Alice Kimm's house displays a similar level of gymnastics – integrating a crane into the design gives the home a feel similar to looking at pop art. When it comes to delivering 'gymnastics', there is architect Jay Bargmann's house, with its industrial aesthetic; it also shows what architects can achieve when creating a home for themselves.

While some of the homes featured in this book are generous in scale and on relatively large plots, those located in London or in European cities, such as Antwerp, respond to considerably more constrained sites. Mat Barnes, for example, has transformed a modest Edwardian house into a large family home – adding bedrooms and opening up spaces that were formerly divided by walls. And in the case of architect Charles Wu, a modest garden apartment has been transformed into a magical abode in the heart of London. On the other side of the world, in Australia, one finds solutions just as innovative. Andrew Piva's home in Melbourne is a new build on land that was formerly the backyard of a 1930s semi-detached house. Accessed via a side lane, the new house can't be seen from the wide leafy street and Andrew created an impressive carport/courtyard-style garden upon arrival. William Smart opted for an expansive apartment in Sydney, with an extraordinary barrel-vaulted brick ceiling, that's located above his office.

The homes featured here are diverse – from apartments through to large detached homes surrounded by hectares of native forest. However, what 'stitches' them together is the architects' determination to create homes that perfectly suit the way they choose to live, both in the present and in the future. And because the projects don't follow trends but beautifully capture the 'voice' of the owners, they remain timeless.

After looking through this book, you may decide not to have an open bathroom in your new home or install a crane that is capable of lifting a dining table through a living room window. You may also think long and hard about erecting a mountain scene above your rear terrace. But at least take the time to reflect, admire or even wonder how the ideas presented came to be realised. As with all great architecture, there's a starting point to most homes, be they new or remodelled. The idea could be inspired by a house from the past, perhaps designed by Luis Barragán or Le Corbusier. And without being literal, these eminent architects become a source of inspiration for architects working today – crafting homes for themselves, rather than for others, and looking for new ways to solve problems that have existed for centuries.

I hope you find inspiration in this book – and perhaps explore new architectural territory in the process.

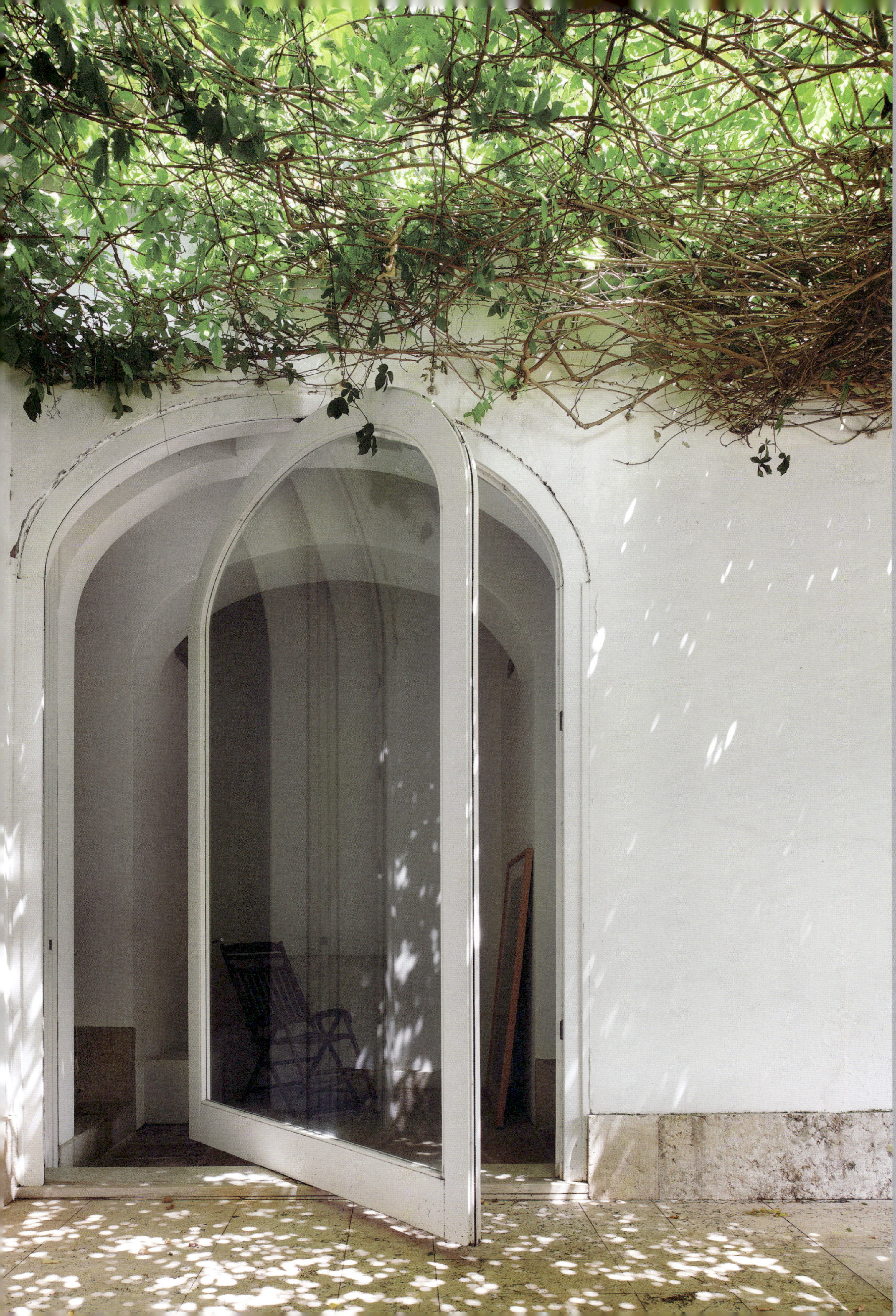

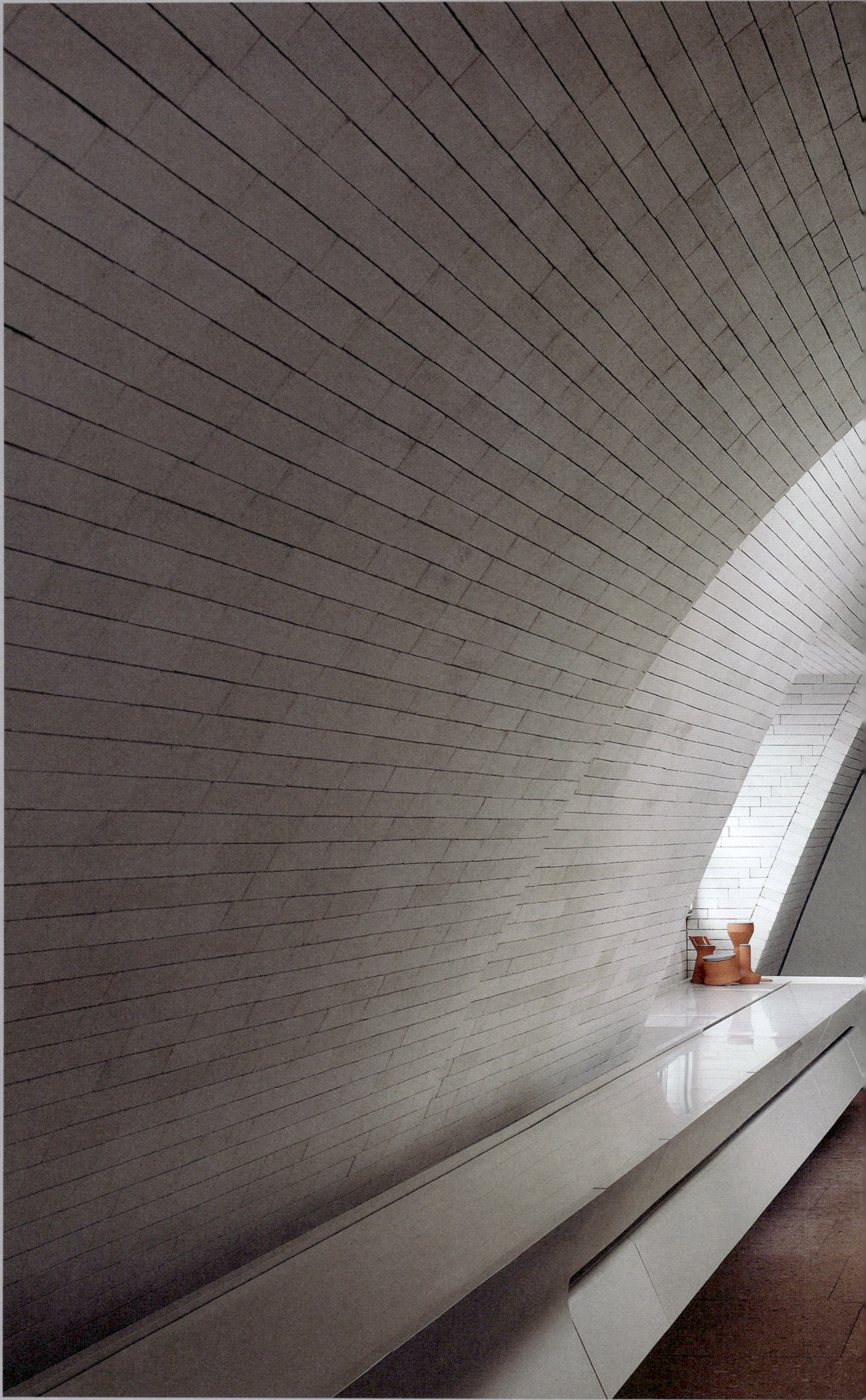

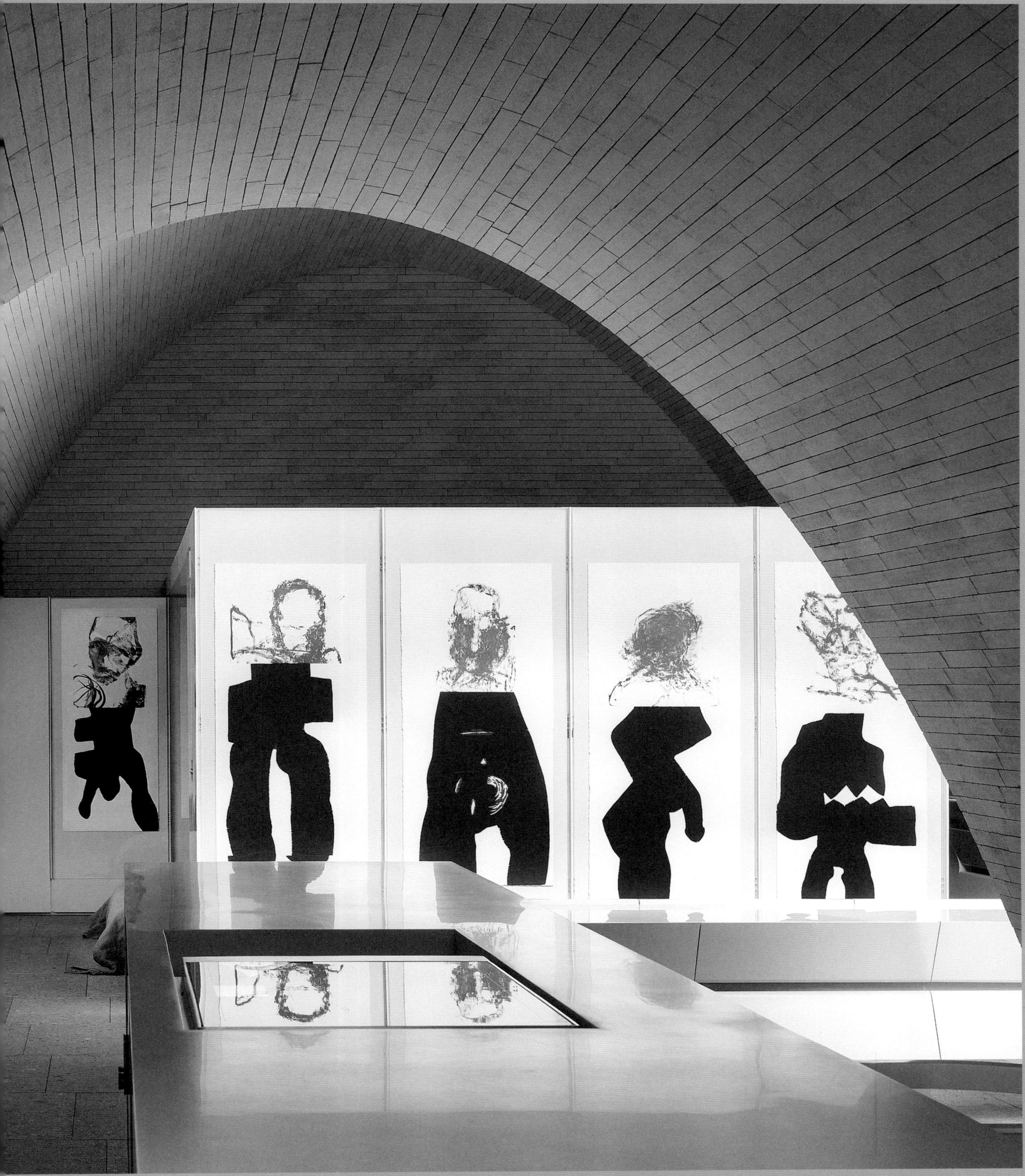

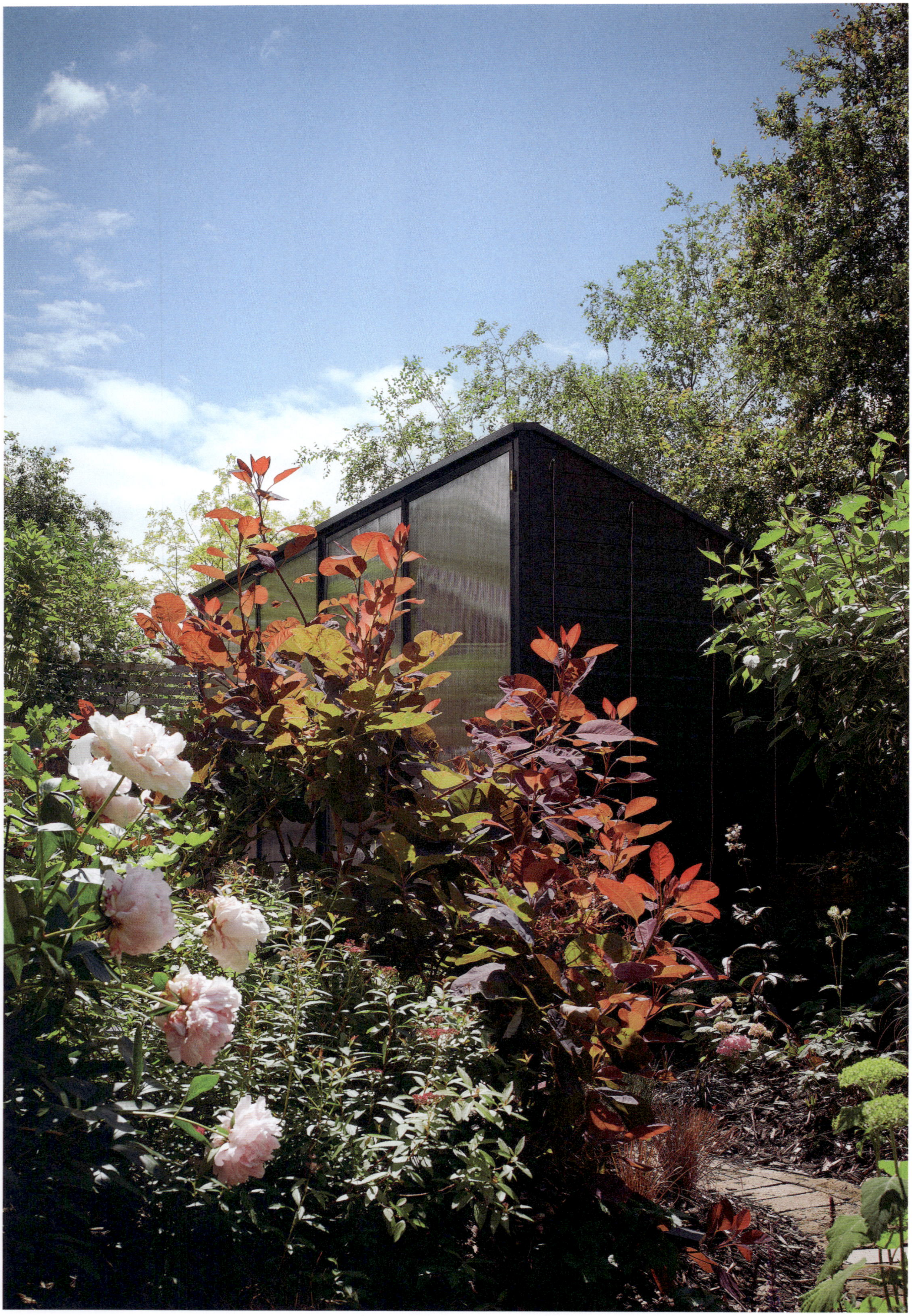

Charles Wu, Director, Polysmiths
WALDEN GARDEN APARTMENT,
HAMPSTEAD HEATH, LONDON

Finding a house in London can prove difficult. While young architects may dream of a grand townhouse close to the city, the reality is that most, even those that are more established, can't afford this scale and opt for more creative housing solutions. Leafy suburbs such as Hampstead Heath (an ancient woodland park in North London) are generally off-limits for most due to their cost. However, this didn't deter architect Charles Wu, director of Polysmiths, from looking in this area, even though it's extremely sought after. 'During the Covid-19 pandemic, we often walked around Hampstead Heath. It's the most magical place in London.'

'We were looking for a home that had great natural light and sufficient outdoor space for gardening and outdoor living,' says Charles, who knew that this was a big ask given the locality. However, he and his husband found a one-bedroom flat on the ground floor of a handsome Georgian terrace built in the 1820s, in a quiet residential street near Tufnell Park. Even though the garden-style apartment hadn't been updated since the late 1980s, Charles was impressed with the 15-metre-long garden and the open sky that surrounded it. 'We used to joke that we bought "a garden that comes with a flat",' says Charles, whose previous home in East London, a three-bedroom detached house that he built himself, was too large and superfluous for the needs of a couple.

From the outset, Charles knew the plan was to renovate and extend the garden apartment so that it could accommodate two bedrooms, a kitchen that was connected to the living room and a separate living area. The other thing at the forefront of his mind was strengthening the connection to the garden. However, with this possible extension, there were practical things that went through his mind – how to extend, insulate, flood-proof and bring light into an apartment while maintaining as much of the precious garden area as possible (the apartment was flooded during an especially wet season in 2021). Charles cites his inspiration as coming from *Walden*, a 1954 novel by Henry David Thoreau, in which he said: 'We want to live in a cabin-like residence bathed in natural light, built using lightweight and natural materials, and enveloped by a lush green garden.' As retrofitting period buildings becomes a more prescient issue in the face of rising energy prices, Charles wanted this project also to serve as an example of a retrofit that is purposeful, sustainable and imbued with character.

The couple inherited a tired and neglected property, with the estate agent's photos making the apartment look even worse – it was a half-sunken and dark flat with low ceilings and small windows that only offered glimpses of an overgrown garden. Still, Charles observed how the light hit the ceiling and imagined himself as a child perched on the windowsill looking up into a garden.

As Charles and his husband are both keen gardeners, they wanted to preserve as much of the garden as possible; stepped double- and triple-glazed windows were inserted following its contours. The extension to the roof, with three angled skylights, lets natural light deep into the floor plan. A Siberian larch slatted trellis completes the rear elevation, allowing for climbing plants and dappled light through the skylights. The extension now accommodates a light and airy living and dining space, while an open kitchen leads to two bedrooms at the lower ground level on the north side of the apartment. And although the bathroom, adjacent to the living area, does not benefit from direct light, it receives borrowed light via a wall of glass bricks.

To prevent a recurrence of the flooding that occurred in 2021, limewash was used throughout to enable the walls to remain breathable from any residual damp. All the external walls were treated with damp-resistant slurry. Channel drains were also laid around the extension that connects to an oversized basement water-pump system in case of a storm surge.

As well as increasing the light via new windows and a raked roof with skylights, Charles used natural and recycled materials to create both texture and a lighter touch. A lightweight timber structure was used for the extension, with pale grey Valchromat (panels made from wood fibre that is moisture resistant) lining the ceiling. Hand-sawn oak tongue and groove boards appear on the floors. In contrast to the muted palette used for the dining and living areas, the bathroom is dark and moody with black ceramics on the floor and walls; it is described as a 'luxury cocoon'. The ceiling is lined with reflective acrylic boards that soften the bathroom's relatively low ceiling.

The kitchen is considered the 'heart of the house', connecting all the rooms. In contrast to the lighter palette of materials used in the dining and living areas, the kitchen, like the bathroom, is darker in its treatment. Walnut veneer was used for the joinery and slate tiles for the splashback. These darker hues can also be seen in the bedrooms that feature dark green walls.

While the garden apartment is relatively modest in size, it feels spacious not only by London standards, but also in comparison to Hong Kong and Sydney, where Charles grew up before moving to London 20 years ago. When friends visit, they often comment that there's a 'bit of the curious "Aussie" and "Japanese" touch to the place – the proportion, sequence of spaces, materials and its connection with the outdoors'. And although the couple is well ensconced in their new abode (Charles' partner is not an architect), Charles doesn't rule out another move down the track. 'I love sitting in our living room and seeing the bands of shadow through the pitched roof ceiling in the morning, with flickering shadows of flowers and leaves on the ceiling,' says Charles.

TIPS

Don't be driven by trends. They are there to sell advertising and trends fade, or you'll fall out of love with that pink tub as soon as the Barbie fad subsides!

Don't be afraid of darkness when there is daylight. I was inspired by Jun'ichirō Tanizaki's *In Praise of Shadows*. Sunlight glows brighter on a dark textured surface and I used a dark green limewash for the bedroom walls.

Good architecture is about problem-solving – in an elegant manner.

charles wu

the architect's house

charles wu

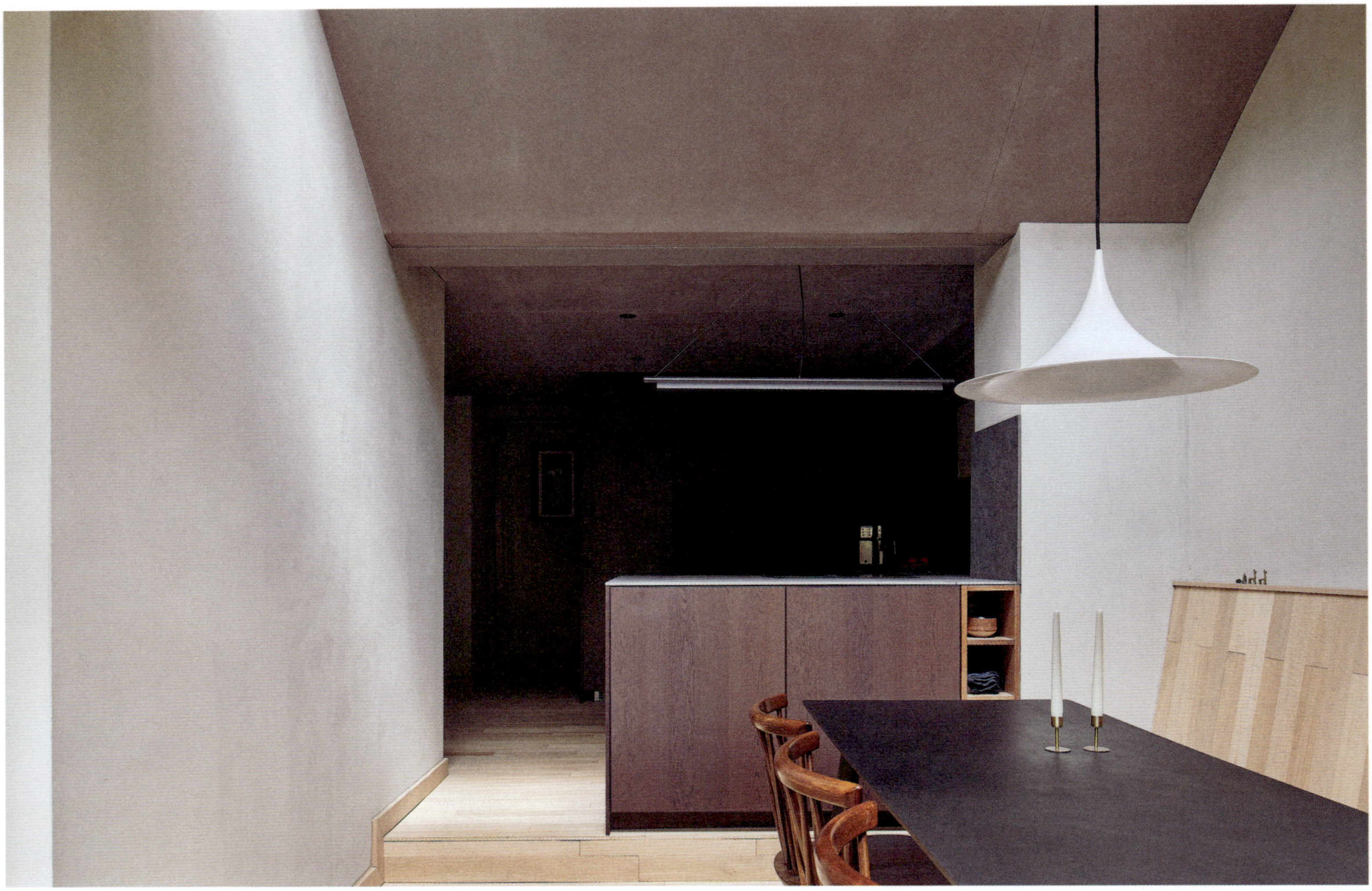

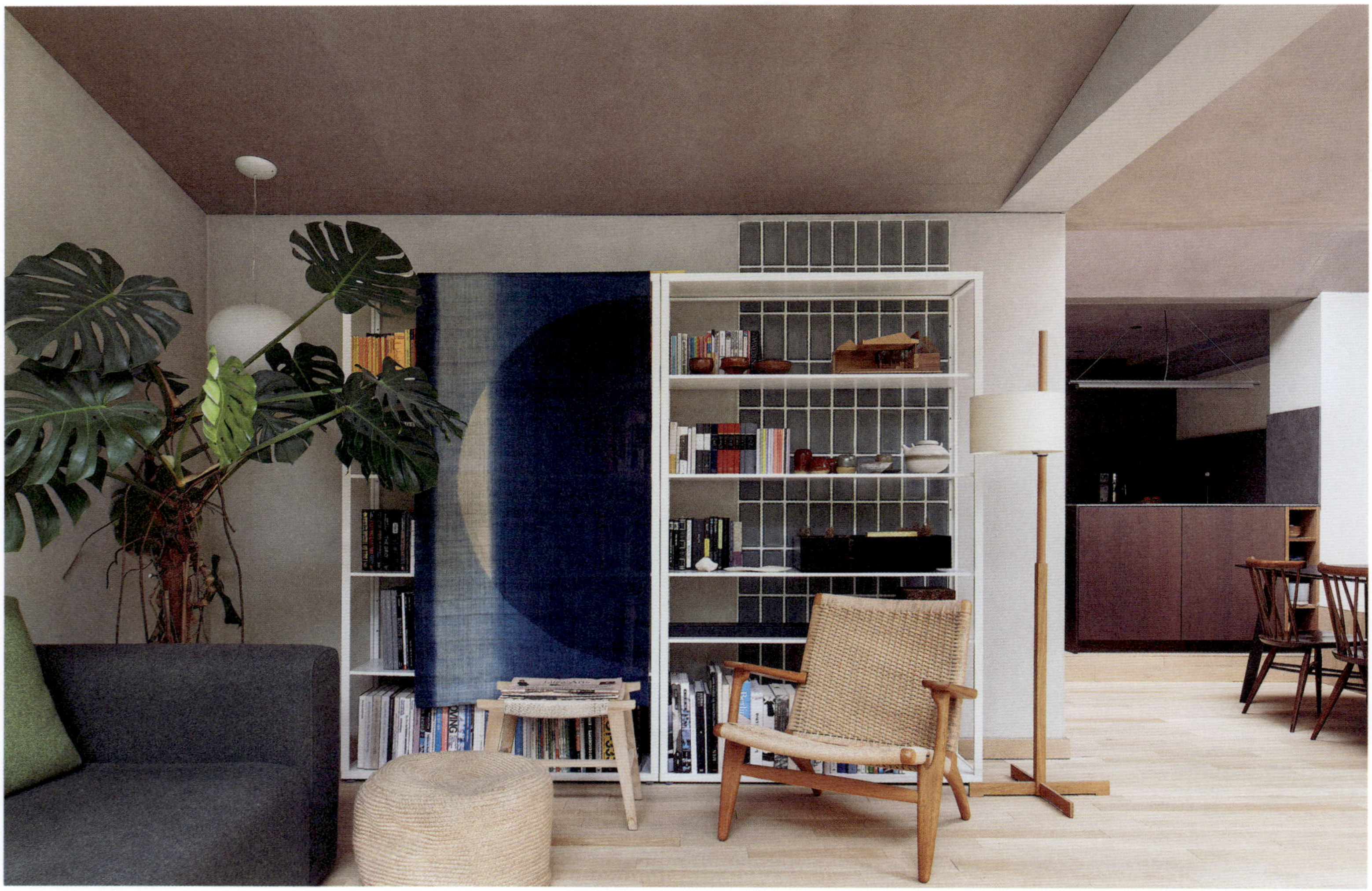

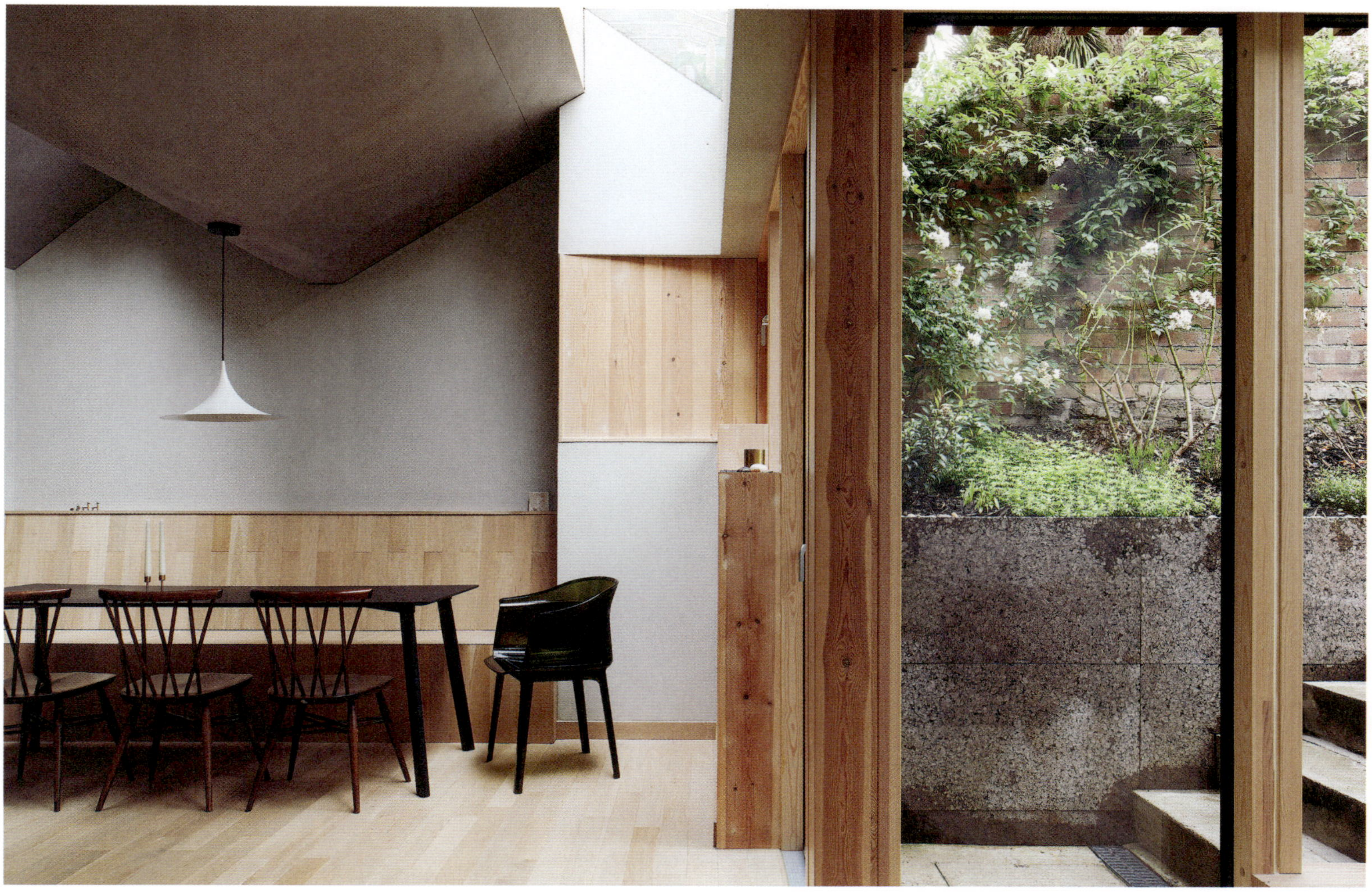

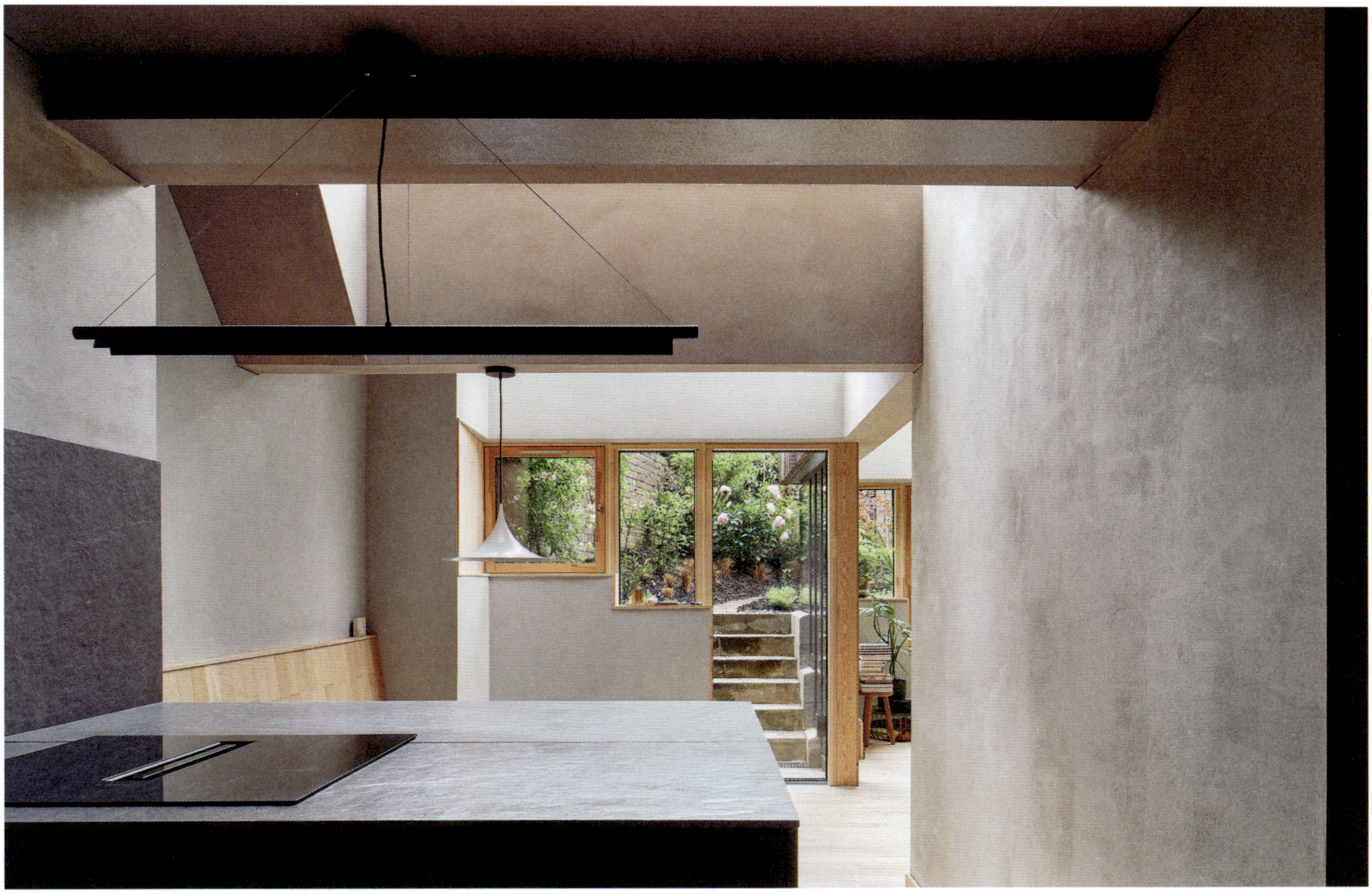

the architect's house

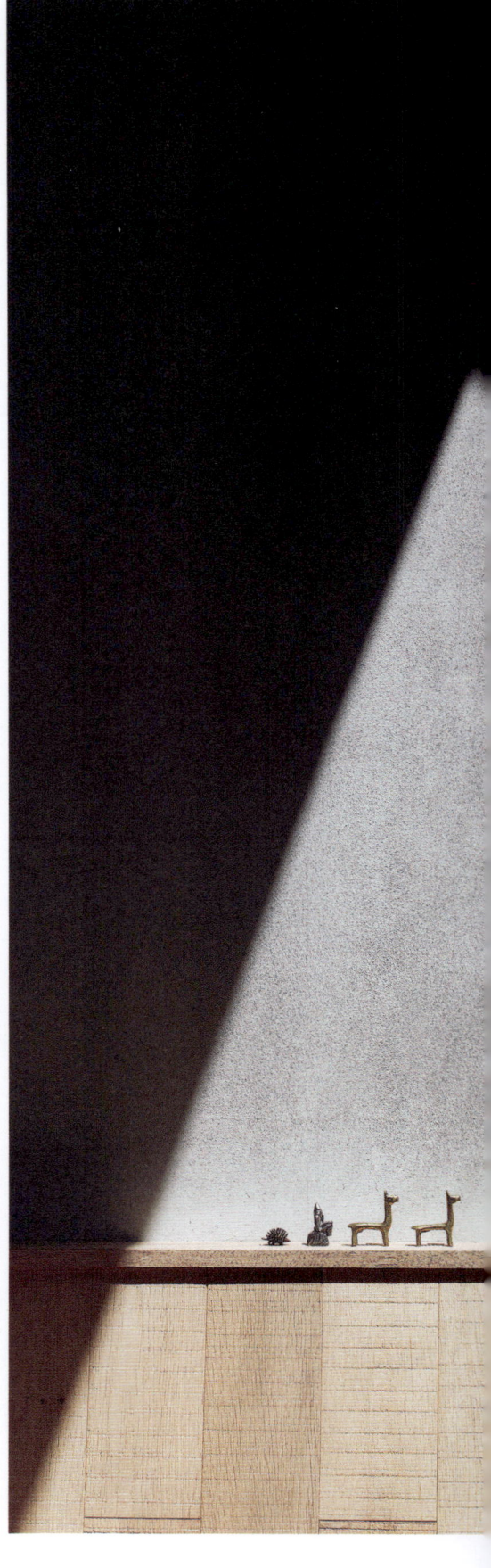

charles wu

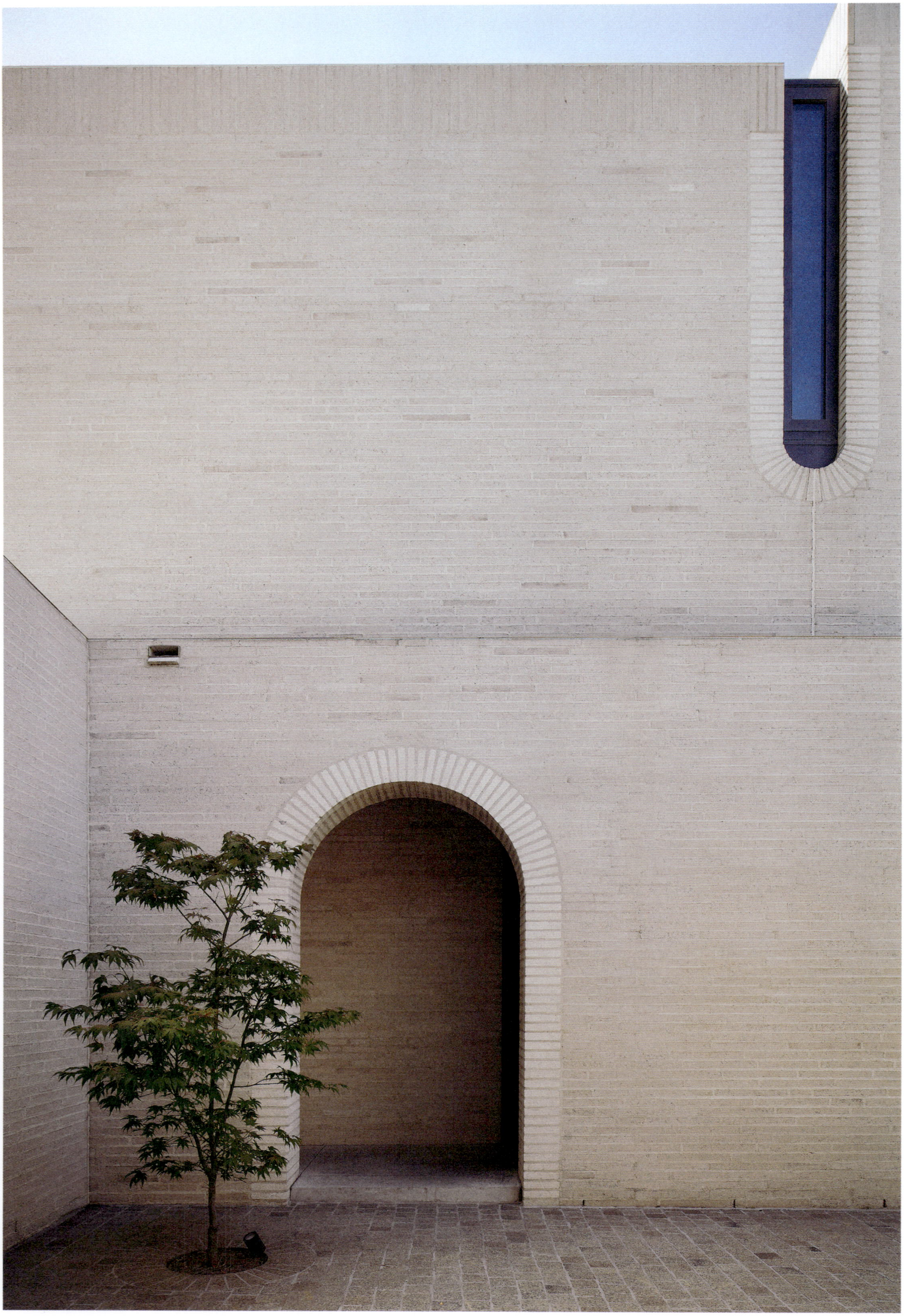

Andrew Piva, Director, B.E. Architecture

EAST MALVERN HOME, MELBOURNE

There are few signs, if any, of this home from the street. Set behind a 1930s semi-detached dwelling, this new house, designed by architect Andrew Piva, is accessed from a laneway. Andrew, a director of B.E. Architecture, purchased the property nine years ago, attracted to the location as much as the generous plot of land (approximately 470 m²) behind it. The 1930s house is still owned by the family and leased out.

'When we attended the auction of the house, very few people knew what could be achieved – putting it in the "too hard basket" given the property is located in a heritage-listed streetscape,' says Andrew. So the family – comprising Andrew and his wife Laura, their two teenage children, Ingrid and Alex, and their ragdoll cat, Bottas (named after the Formula One racing driver Valtteri Bottas) – lived in the modest semi, knowing eventually they would build a new family home directly behind it. 'We'd renovated the semi but it was only about 80 m² [the size of an apartment] and was far too small,' he adds.

Although Andrew and Laura weren't sure of what the 470 m² of land could become, they knew they needed spaces that worked for a family as well as for teenage children. The spacious 300-m² house now covers almost 70 per cent of the site, with a series of courtyards making the living areas feel considerably larger. Even the entry courtyard, which can accommodate up to three cars, feels generous and doubles as an additional outdoor area when the cars aren't there. And rather than being fully enclosed, there's only a partial roof over the carport that makes it a place to enjoy.

Andrew drew on their Italian heritage (Laura also comes from an Italian family) when it came to the selection of materials for the two-storey home. Slim-lined concrete bricks, with detailed corbelling around the entrance and windows, create a slightly Tuscan feel. 'I wasn't particularly conscious of trying to create a slightly Tuscan villa. Our practice, B.E. Architecture, is known for creating contemporary but classical homes, something that will stand the test of time rather than following trends – having a timeless quality,' says Andrew. 'The house was also designed around how we live,' he adds.

Part of this timeless quality can be traced to the restrained material palette used – concrete bricks for the exterior, including walls that frame the courtyard, and Tuscan oak walls throughout the home. Sawn travertine-tiled floors feature in the kitchen, dining area and the separate living area, with oak joinery making an appearance in most rooms, whether in the form of built-in cupboards in the bedrooms or the customised credenza in the dining area. An L-shaped bank of built-in cupboards in the living area functions as storage for the couple's extensive record collection, a display area for objects and as additional seating when friends and family come over. Andrew singles out the kitchen as being the heart of the house, with the couple enjoying preparing meals (Laura works in the wine industry). As a result, the kitchen centres on a large stone table/island (2.5 x 1.5 m) with stone benches and a stone splashback. And given there's a preference for uncluttered spaces, many appliances, such as the fridge and freezer, are concealed behind timber doors. A butler's pantry assists in keeping the kitchen free of disorder and appliances. Given the home's location adjacent to the laneway (used by other neighbours), translucent glass was used creating soft and diminutive light.

In contrast, the living area, separate from the kitchen and capable of being enclosed by a cavity glass door, is bathed in full light. For Andrew, it's one of his favourite rooms in the house. 'The kitchen and dining area have a more introverted feel, while the lounge feels like it's an extension of the courtyard,' says Andrew, pulling back the large sliding glass doors. He often gravitates to his Eames Lounge Chair and Ottoman at the end of a day or to one of the lounges covered in vintage Missoni fabric. And rather than being surrounded by art, there are just a couple of drawings by artist Mike Parr resting against a wall. While the focus is on the courtyard during the warmer months, during the peak winter months, it's all about the Cheminées Philippe pot-belly fireplace.

Although this is a four-bedroom house, including the main bedroom suite and the two children's bedrooms all located on the first floor, the fourth bedroom, located at ground level, is multifunctional, acting as a second living area, a study/library and also a guest bedroom with a fold-down bed concealed behind a timber veneer wall. For Andrew, the idea of creating a fourth bedroom dedicated solely to guests didn't stack up. Complete with the borrowed view of an established willow tree in a neighbour's backyard, this sunken space (there's a fall of 1.5 m across the site) is cocoon-like.

There's a sense of generosity in Piva's home, from the broad timber staircase with light captured from a highlight window, to the curated sightlines achieved by the kitchen/dining joinery that falls short of the ceiling, allowing light and one's perspective to be extended. And rather than try and make every space a primary one, there's an appropriate hierarchy of spaces, including a modest-sized music room adjacent to the garage that's used by Andrew to practise his drums. 'I'd like to say that the house as a whole has quite a classical design and is extremely comfortable – a bit like my Eames chair that I've had for over 20 years,' adds Andrew.

TIPS

There's often FOMO (fear of missing out) when people either build or renovate. You really can't expect to realise every possible idea – some things are best left out even if they have been on your wish list.

Architecture and design are about problem-solving. This could be as simple as making sure you have a drying room in a house in an area that has a fairly wet climate or, similarly, something as simple as having a nook or shelf on which to drop your keys when you come home.

B.E. Architecture also designs furniture and lighting. In this home there are built-in low-level lights in the timber walls that are particularly useful at night when you're going to the bathroom. These things are small details but improve the quality of your life.

andrew piva

the architect's house

andrew piva

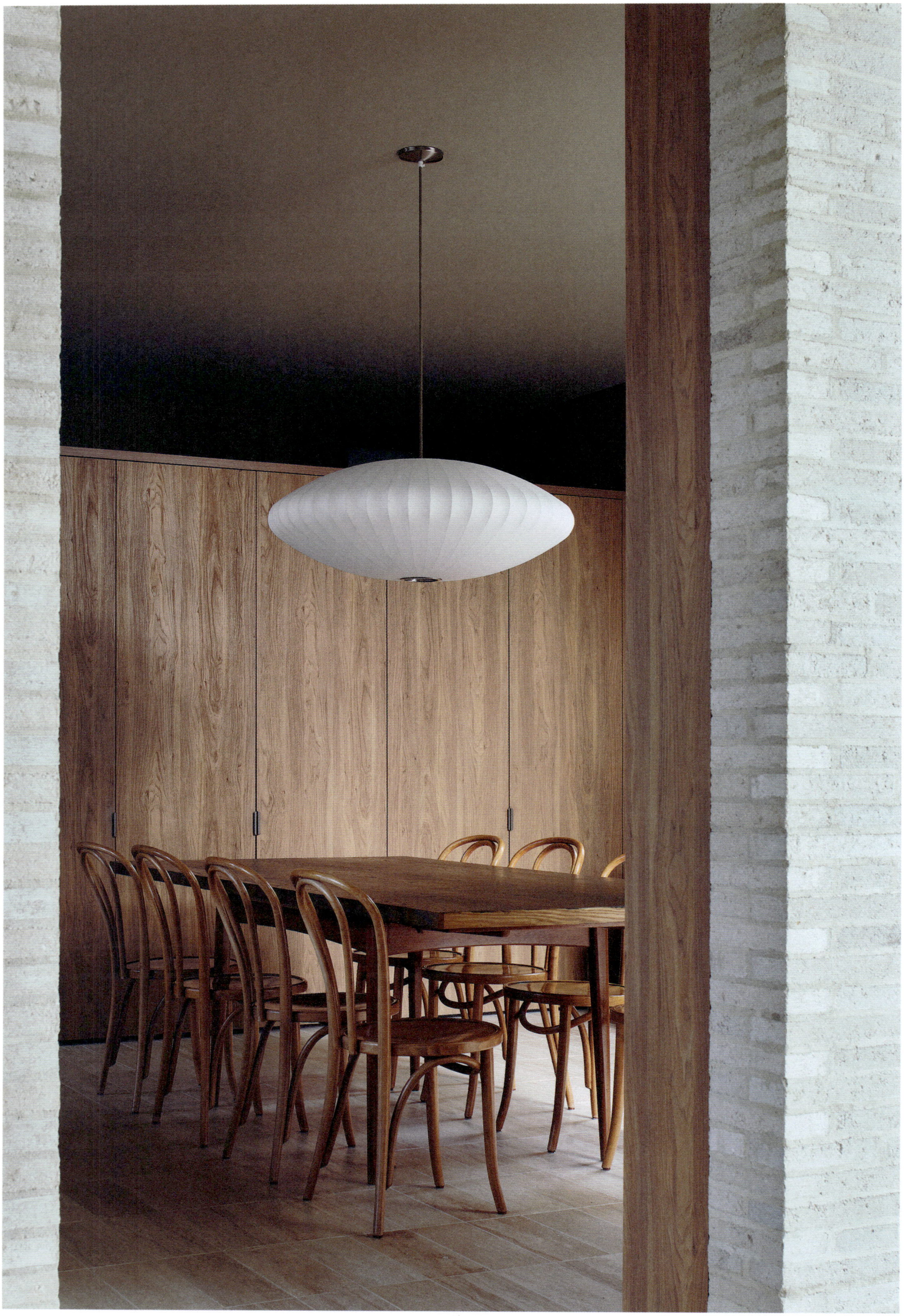

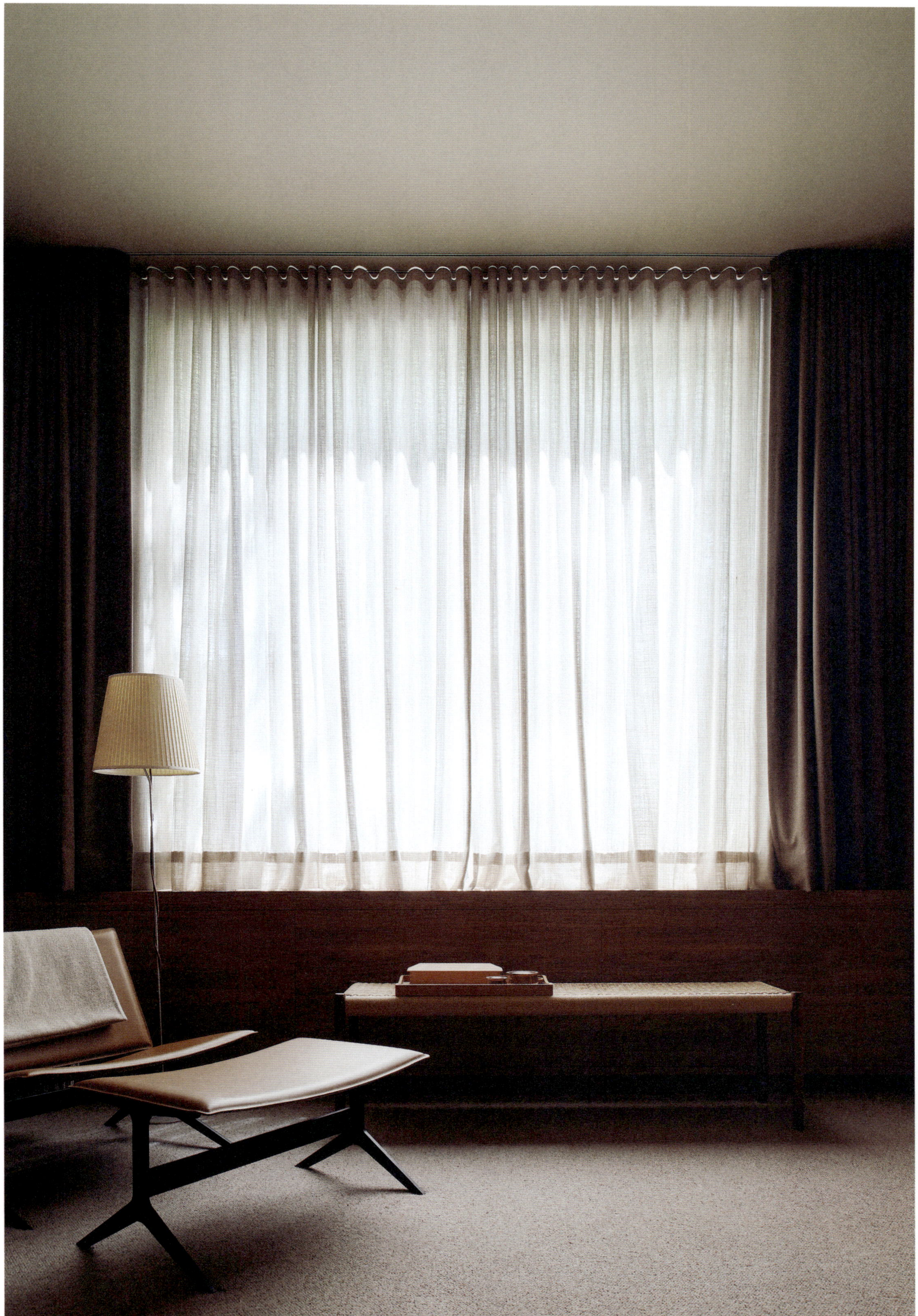

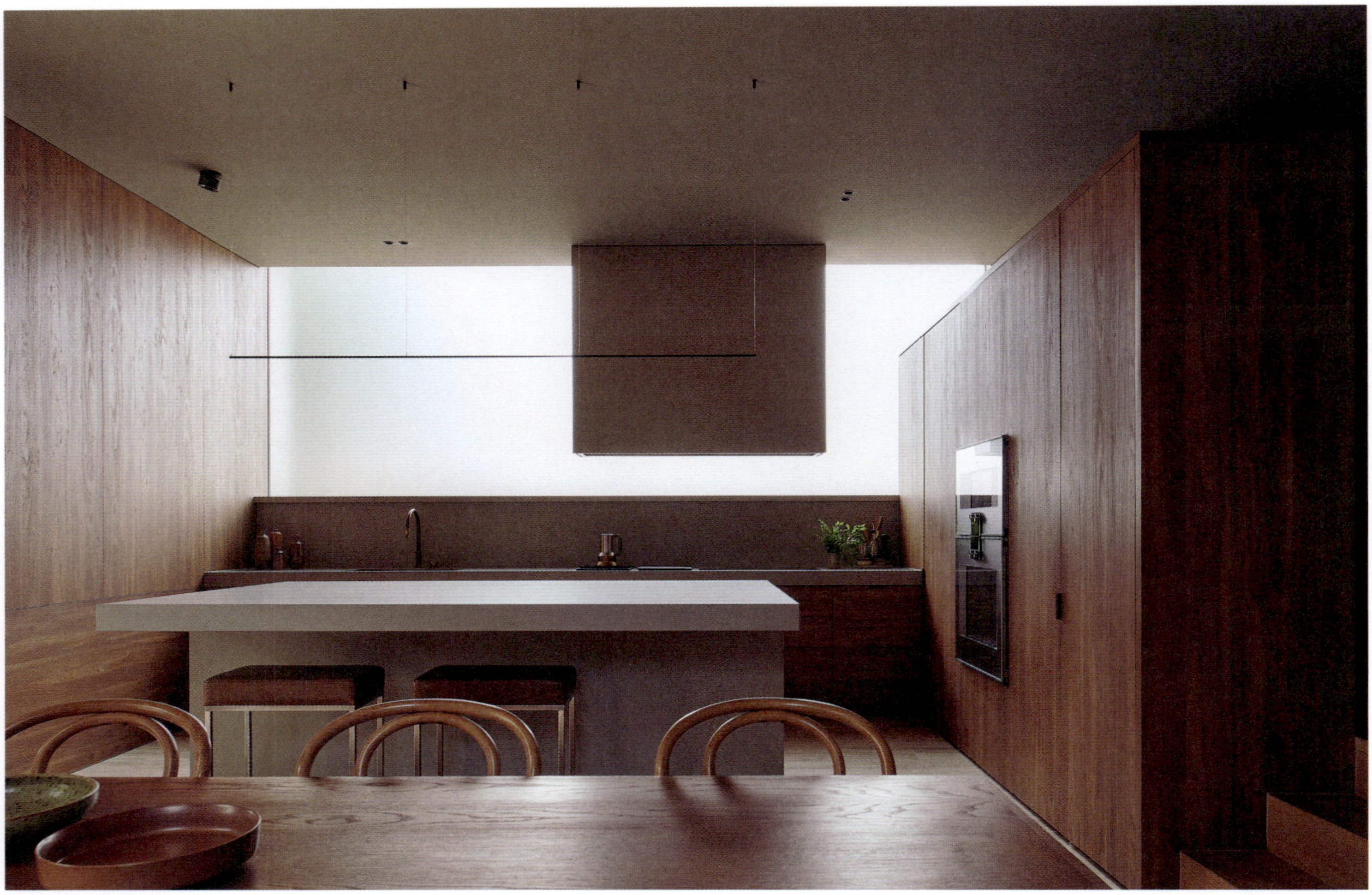

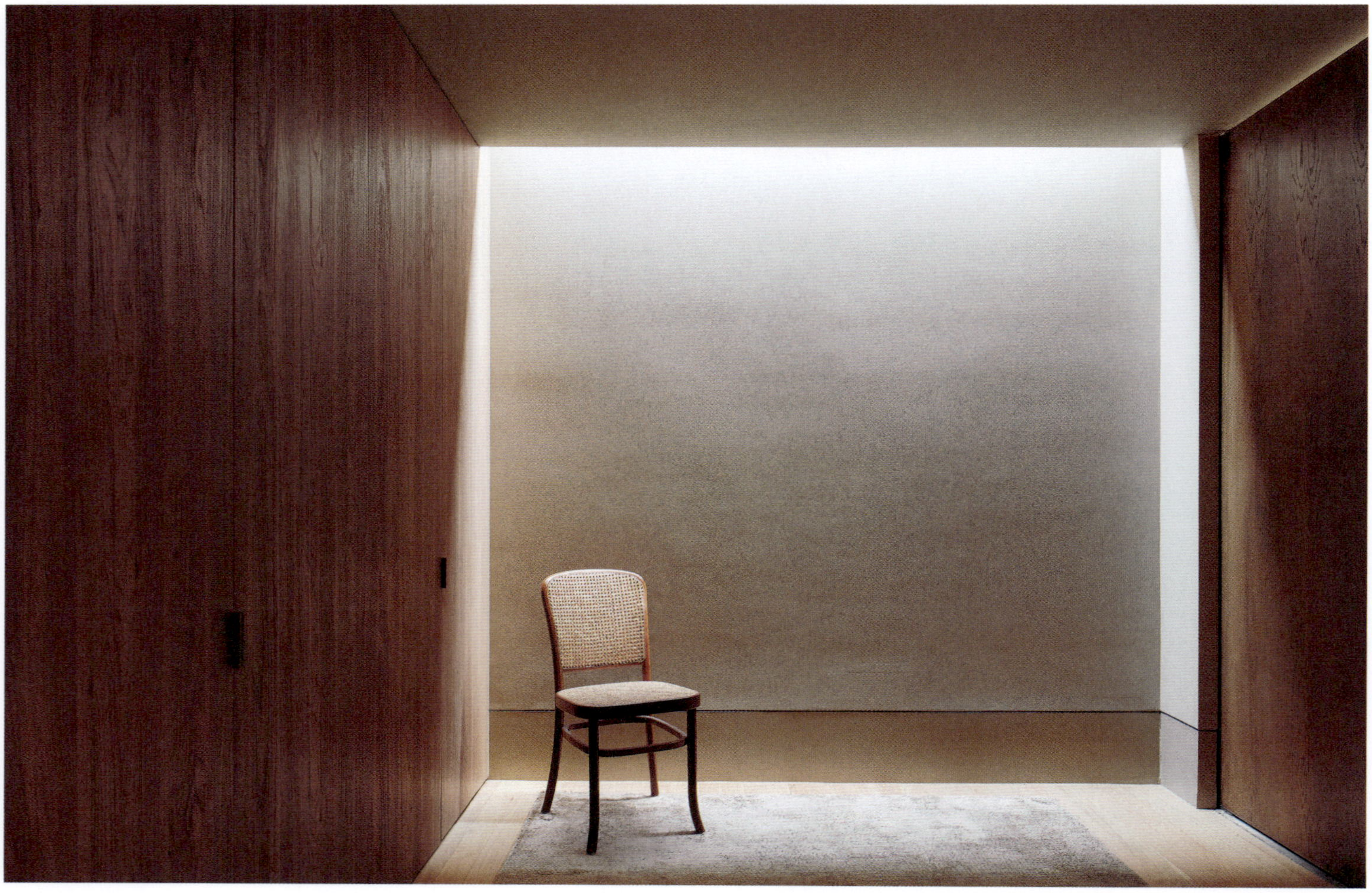

andrew piva

the architect's house

andrew piva

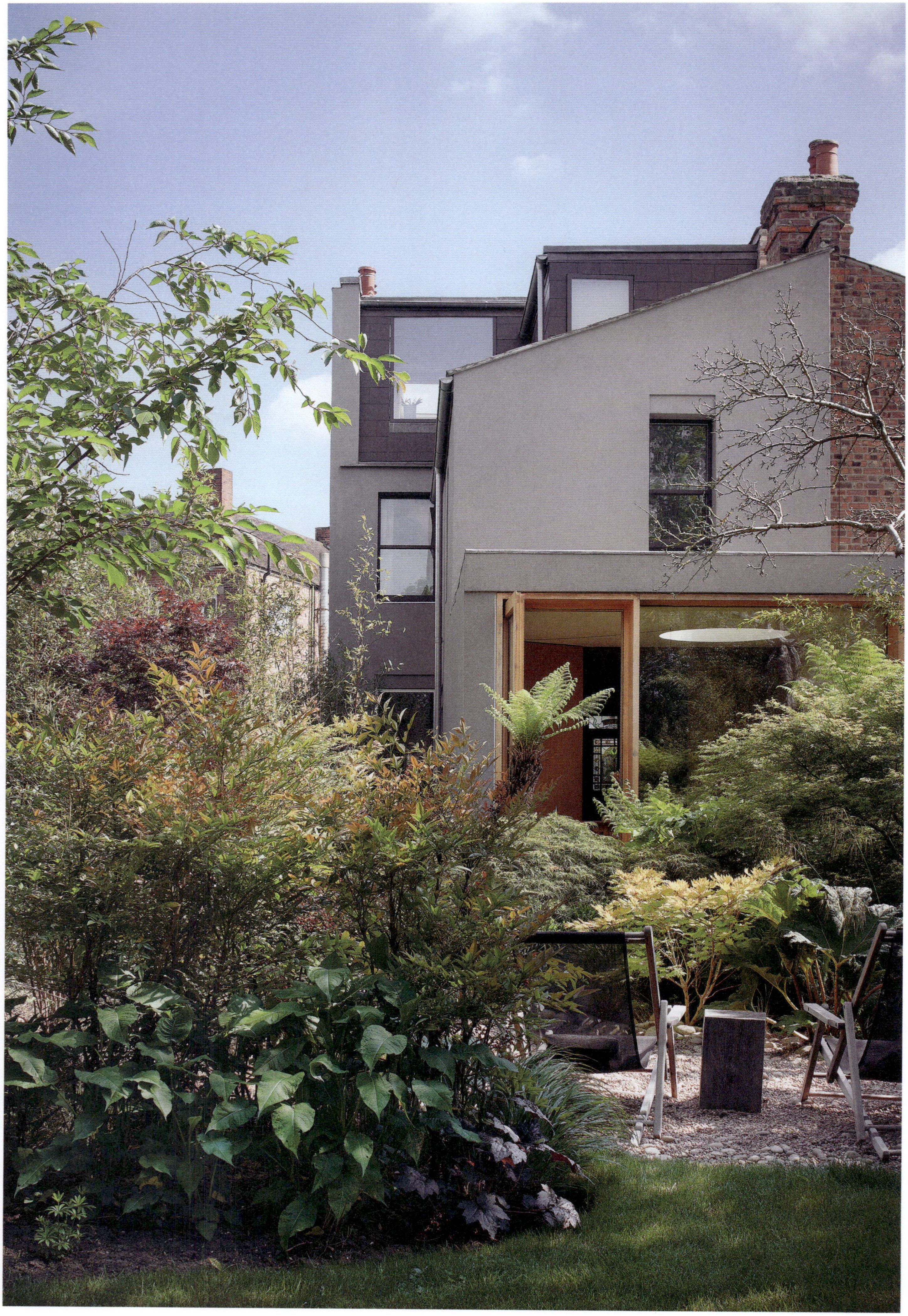

Ben Ridley, Founder, Architecture for London
LOW-ENERGY HOUSE, MUSWELL HILL, LONDON

There are numerous, almost identical, Edwardian homes to be found in North London, complete with low brick fences, front bay windows and relatively intact leadlight doors. This home in Muswell Hill is slightly Gothic in feel and retained many of its original features, but there were numerous ad hoc additions, with many of the rooms plastered with garish wallpapers from the 1970s. While the dark and damp house, which hadn't been touched in over 40 years, would have deterred some from buying it, architect Ben Ridley, founder of Architecture for London, saw it as an opportunity that would lend itself to a complete retrofit and modest extension. 'I'd worked on a number of similar refurbishments and extensions for clients, but this was the first time that the practice and I made a commitment to a low-energy design from the outset,' says Ben, who lives here with his ragdoll cat Astrid.

Spread over three levels, and approximately 190 m² in area, the house has been virtually gutted, with the 'bones' retained but a number of walls removed. In contrast, the facade has been sensitively restored. 'It felt like an unloved house, suffering from considerable damp and condensation issues, with mould on some of the walls,' says Ben, who was keen to remove the floral carpets and flock wallpaper. But on the positive side, the house benefited from having a side garage and large garden, both a rarity so close to the centre of London. The size of the land would also provide the opportunity to build an additional house on the site if it were needed in the future.

As well as damp and a dated 1970s interior, the front reception area received very little natural light in spite of its bay windows. To address this, the front living area was opened up, allowing sunlight to permeate through to the new floor-to-ceiling windows and doors at the rear of the property. The plaster ceiling at ground level was also removed, exposing and celebrating the original timber structure of the house while at the same time providing a heightened sense of volume and space.

Given most people expect a 'shotgun' corridor running alongside a series of enclosed rooms in period homes of this type, they are generally surprised when they pass through the ornate leadlight front door and can see through the open-plan space to the verdant garden at the rear. 'People usually expect to see a decorative Edwardian hallway with fretwork arches rather than one continuous volume,' says Ben.

The island bench in the kitchen extends to the living area, given the change in floor level. 'As a busy architect working in the city, I enjoy clean and minimal spaces. They help calm my mind at the end of a day,' says Ben.

The palette of materials used is also restrained – stone, timber and lime plaster rather than cement-based products that often need to be painted. 'Materials with low embodied energy add no additional cost,' says Ben, who is mindful of the need to reach net zero by 2050. 'The homes we refurbish now will not be updated again before this time,' he adds. Ben also included triple glazing, a continuous airtight layer and insulation to the entire building envelope. Walls were insulated externally, both at the side and rear, and at the front with wood fibre, the latter allowing the original Edwardian facade to be preserved. Ben also used a mechanical ventilation with heat recovery system (MVHR), which provides pre-heated fresh air that creates a warm and comfortable home – something that's often lacking in unrenovated period homes. Natural limestone floors appear throughout the ground floor (sensible when one has a ragdoll) with a plush rug adding a bit of cosiness during the colder months.

While the house appears relatively imposing from the street and is spread over three levels, it is relatively modest in scale. At ground level, there's a more formal sitting area at the front, which connects to a kitchen and dining area at the rear. And aligned with the kitchen bench is a built-in window seat that allows guests to have a conversation with Ben while he's preparing a meal. There are three bedrooms, a bathroom and a laundry – with a rooftop terrace that takes in views of the leafy neighbourhood. While Ben and his friends gravitate to the terrace on warmer evenings, he regularly moves to the limestone kitchen bench when he's on his own, or relaxes on the deep window seat. And rather than display too many fussy details, the timber joinery is flush with the walls and the island bench is void of any cupboards – appearing as a 'solid' block of stone in the space. Having stairs on both sides of the island bench also reduces a 'tunnel' effect when family and friends come over.

Ben also opted for a light option in his choice of materials for the bedrooms, located on the first floor. Timber walls, timber floors and soft putty-coloured walls feature, along with trusses painted white, some of which allow for glimpses of the level above, including a modest sitting area.

Though the design appears seamless and relatively straightforward for those who only see the end results, it was one of the projects in the practice that took place during the pandemic and issues cited by Ben include material supplies, labour shortages and neighbour relationships. 'We couldn't source some materials such as the special roof slates, so we ended up having to use a more common product,' says Ben.

While the Muswell Hill house still appears to be in its original state, the front garden, like the back, is densely planted with ferns and creepers rather than presented with old-fashioned climbing roses, as would most likely have been the case during the Edwardian period when the original house was built. However, once past the front door, the 'language' is clearly contemporary with less being considerably more.

TIPS

Sustainability is always at the forefront of our design ethos. There are so many changes one can make even in the smallest projects that create a calming, low-energy home.

During my studies to become a certified Passivhaus designer, my teacher would remind me of the importance of 'going for the low-hanging fruit first'. I keep this simple sentiment in mind for many projects so that sustainable choices can be made minimally or incrementally to improve overall energy performance. One simple example for this house was to fit an internal insulated magnetic letter box flap that can significantly reduce cold draughts.

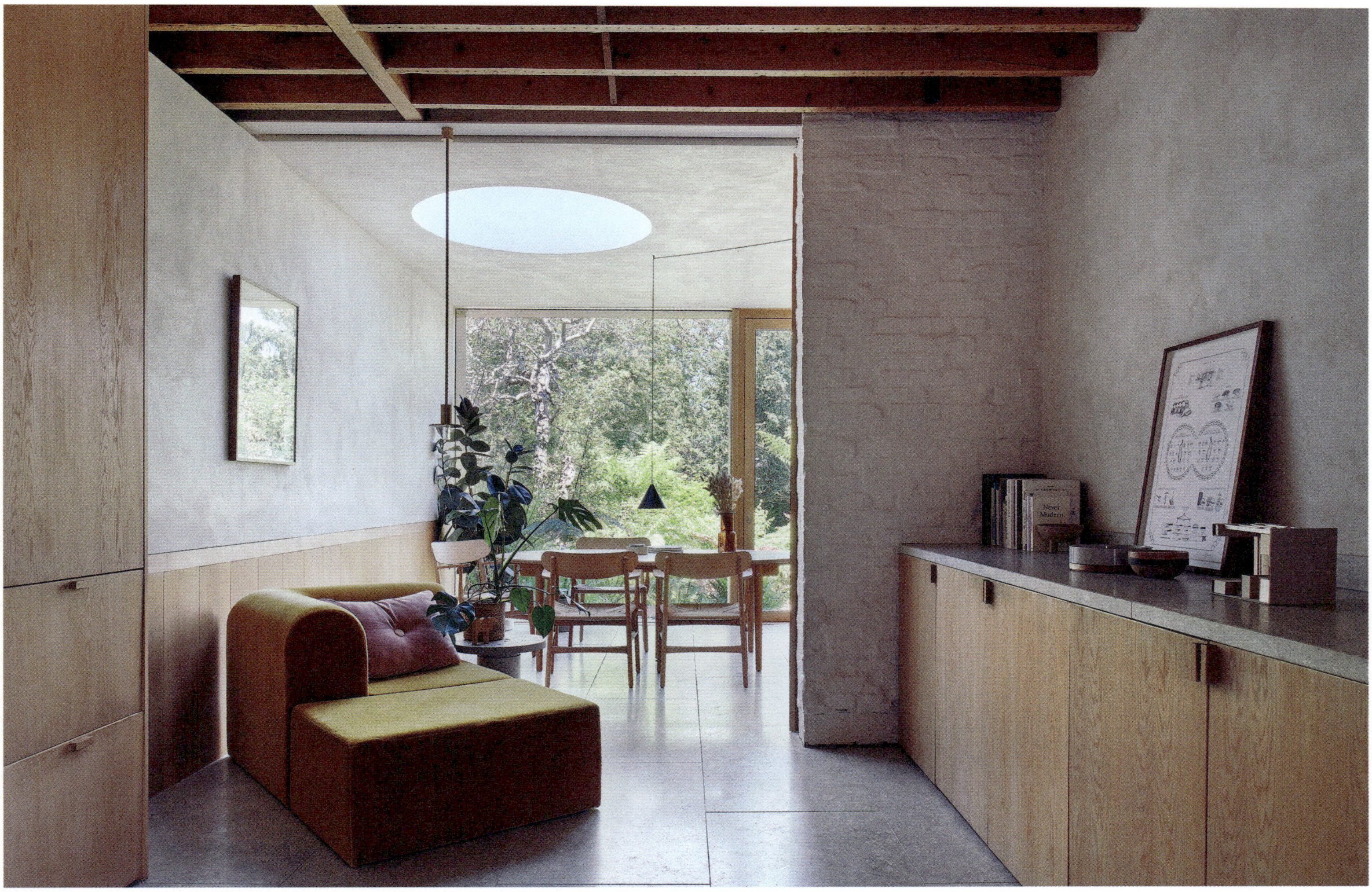

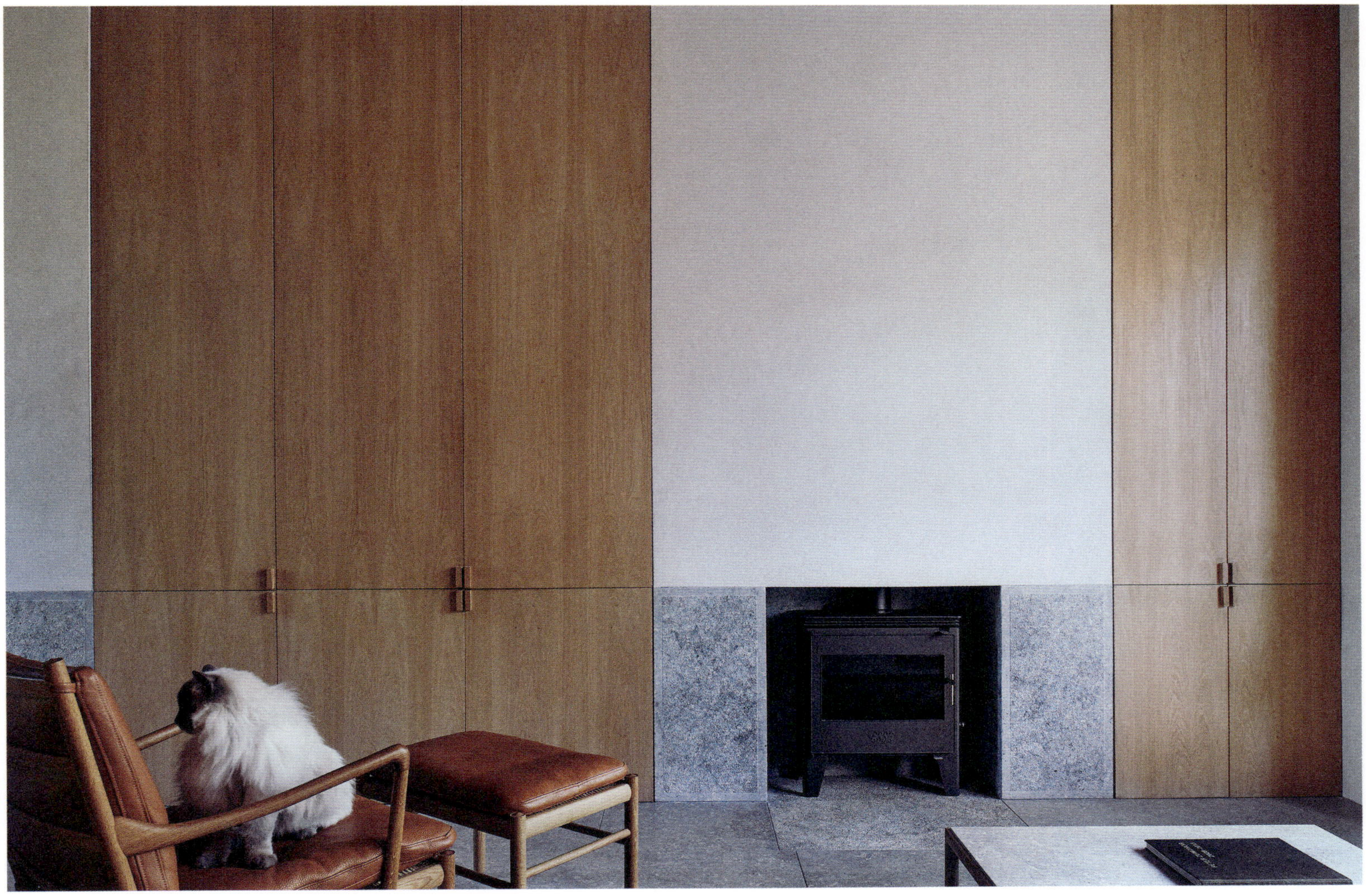

the architect's house

ben ridley

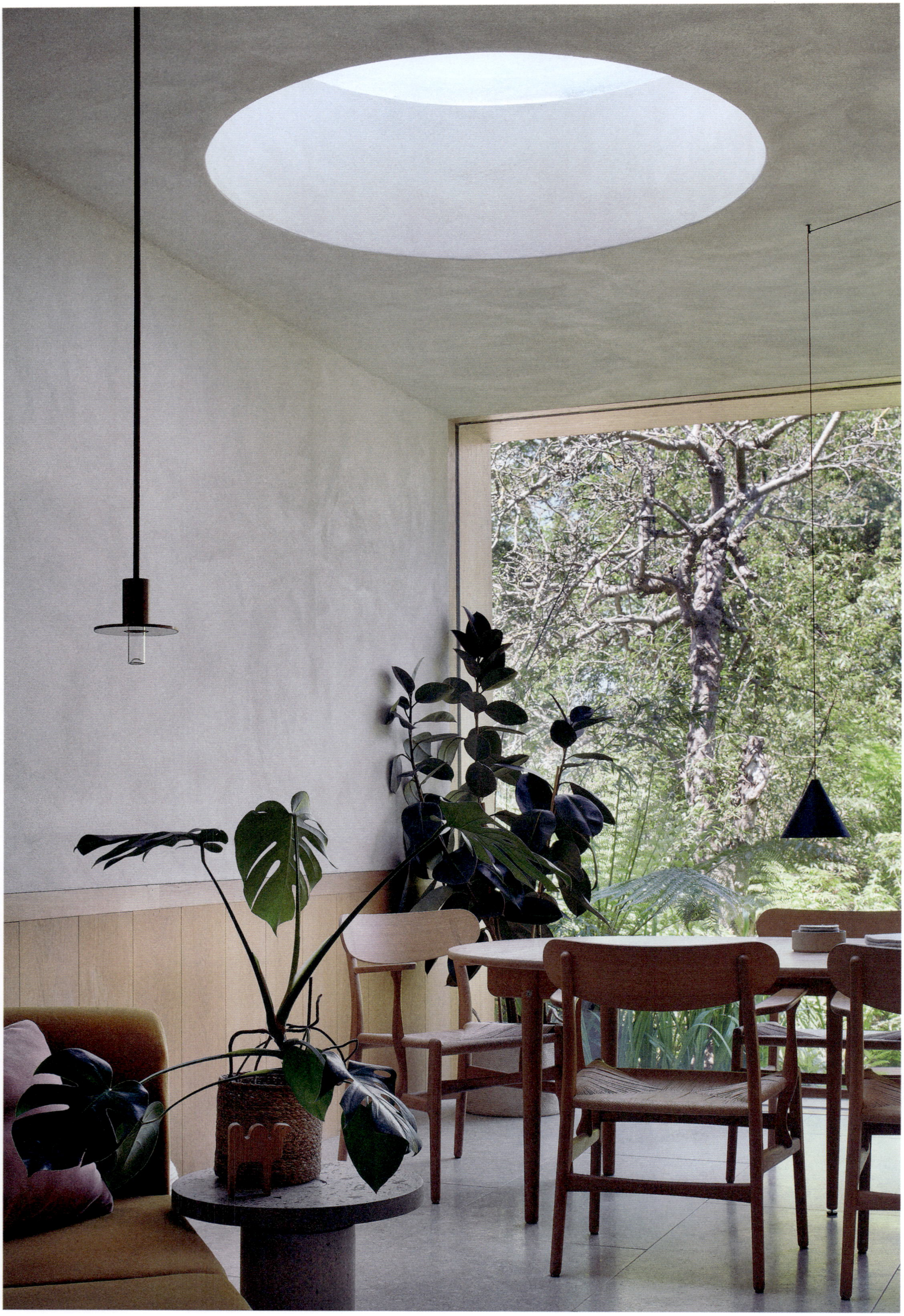

ben ridley

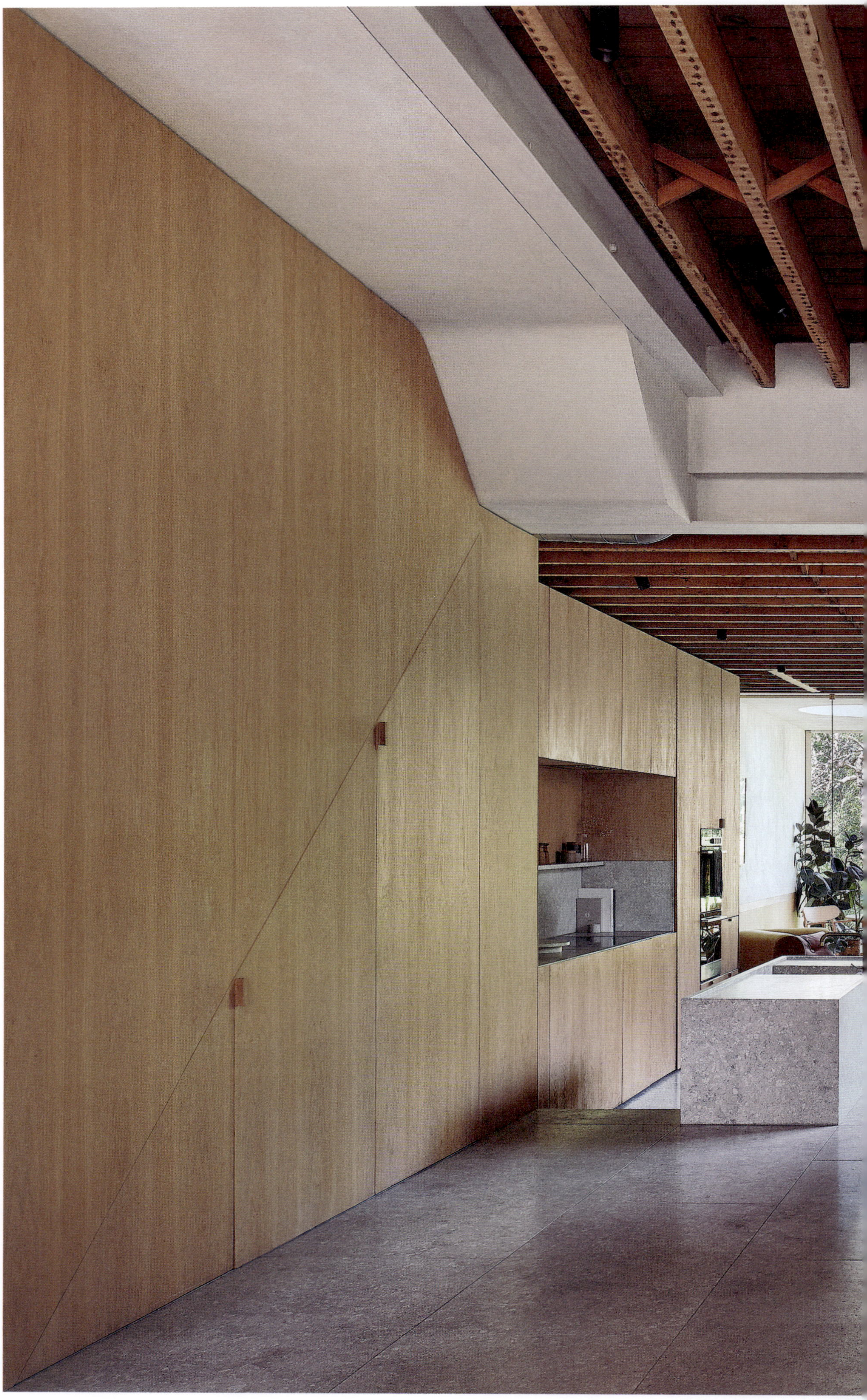

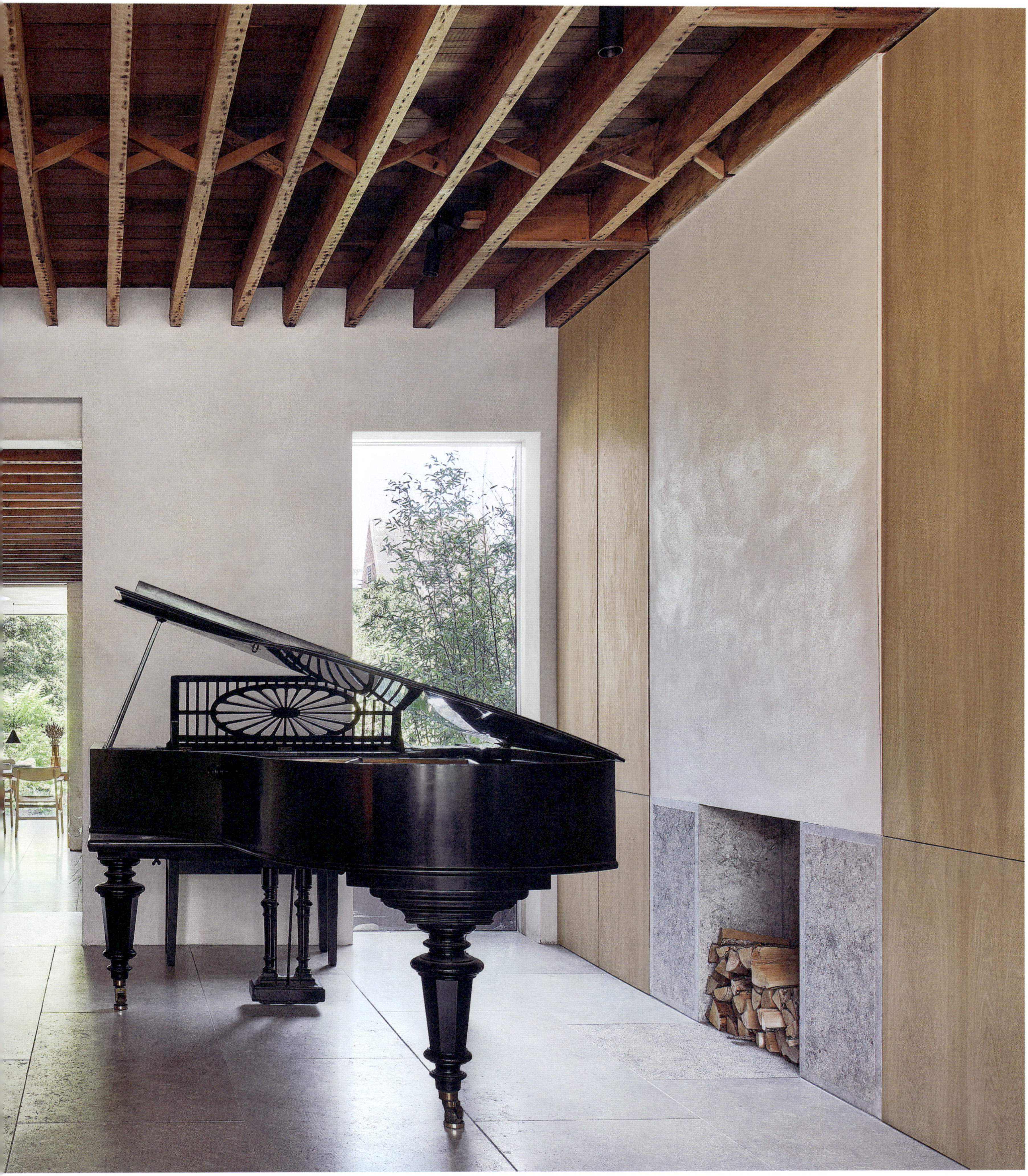

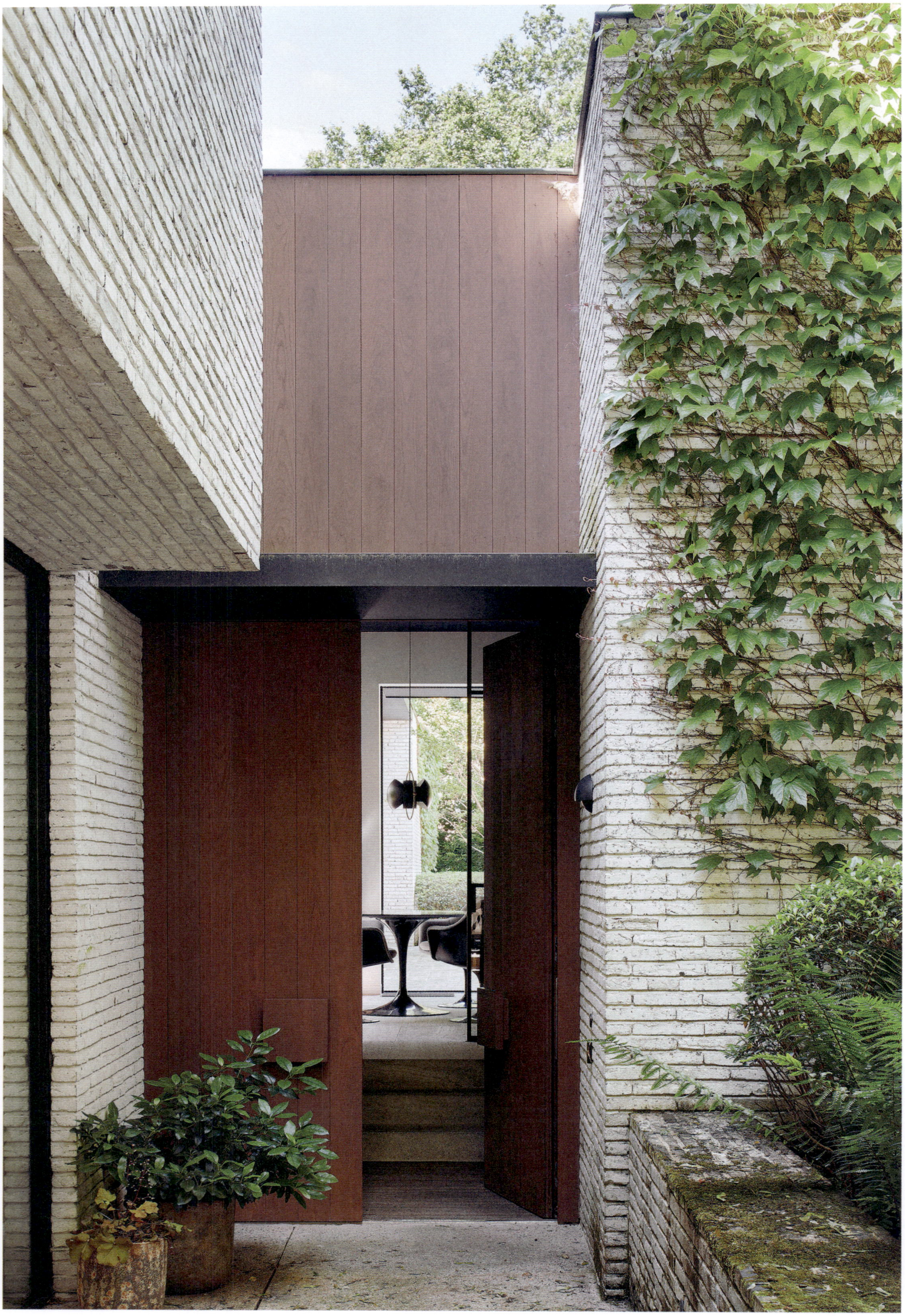

Mathieu Luyens & Julie Van De Keere
Founders & Directors, JUMA Architects

VILLA BB, SINT-MARTENS-LATEM, FLANDERS

The place where Mathieu Luyens and Julie Van De Keere decided to build their home is steeped in memories. Julie's mother still lives next door in the family home she grew up in and this plot was carved off from a neighbour's property. 'This is a very special place for me. I grew up with these surrounding trees and am familiar with most of the houses in the village,' says Julie. So, it just felt right for the couple to move from the centre of Ghent, where they'd lived for 10 years in an Art Nouveau-style house near the majestic St Bavo's Cathedral, to the lush and creative environment of Sint-Martens-Latem, a township that attracts many creatives, including poets and painters.

Though living in Ghent, a student town intersected with canals, came with the proximity of shops and restaurants, the disadvantages became more evident after having their first child. 'The apartment, a duplex, only had two bedrooms, one of which was used as an office. We eventually rented the apartment below to accommodate our expanding office,' says Mathieu. The duplex also suffered from not having any outdoor space and the lift was in constant use ferrying groceries up to the other apartments. So, when the couple's second child arrived, they decided to look for a place on the edge of the city (Sint-Martens-Latem is approximately 12 km from Ghent).

The property is well endowed with large mature trees on a long narrow block and the neighbourhood also benefits from being close to local amenities, such as a bakery, cafes and other speciality shops. And unlike their previous abode, where it was often challenging to find a spot to park their cars, here there's more than sufficient parking with the garage accommodating up to two vehicles. 'Even before we saw the sale sign go up, we were attached to it,' says Julie, and she and Mathieu acted quickly to purchase the property.

The new brick house was conceived as three connected volumes. One of the volumes, or pavilions, comprises the garage. Another is JUMA Architects' office, with its own separate access, while the third volume is given over to the family home. The three volumes' varying height can be easily 'read' from the garden. And while many people living in Belgian cities, be it Antwerp, Brussels or Ghent, have homes directly aligned to the pavement, which often lack privacy, both Mathieu and Julie appreciate their new sanctuary-like environment, complete with a raised swimming pool and generous wraparound terraces. 'We've never quite understood why so many people choose to live so close to a street,' says Mathieu.

Although the design of this house responds to the site and its verdant surrounds, it is 'loosely inspired by the architecture of Ibiza [solid brick homes with a strong dose of limestone],' says Mathieu, who engaged landscape architect Duo Verde to create the effect of a well-established garden.

JUMA is recognised for its low forms and the elongated floor plan of the home reflects this aesthetic. The ground floor also accommodates the children's bedrooms, while the main bedroom, dressing area and bathroom are located on the first floor and lead to a terrace – the effect is not dissimilar to a hotel suite. By locating the children's bedrooms next to the living space, the children can always be nearby and easily supervised. 'A separate play area in an attic might seem like a good idea but when children are young, you need to be able to keep an eye on them. And by having their bedrooms next to the living area, the lounge doesn't get overrun with toys,' Julie adds.

Practicality was always at the forefront of the couple's minds, with an acoustic ceiling in the kitchen allowing the space to feel welcoming, even when family and friends are visiting and it's noisy. There are other practical features, including only having the one dining area adjacent to the kitchen rather than a second more formal dining area. Instead of having a guest bedroom that is only used occasionally, this additional room can be used for a variety of purposes, including as a second living area for the children. Part of the home's charm comes from the selection of natural materials, which gives the interiors a certain roughness that in turn adds character. 'We've also used slightly different materials in every room to change the atmosphere in each one,' says Julie, pointing out the timber veneer cabinets in the living areas. 'In the kitchen, we've used a dark larch veneer with natural stone as well as some Tadelakt [a type of Moroccan plaster]. The kitchen has a continuity of materials – limestone benches and dark-stained timber joinery. The glazed portico between the kitchen and the living area creates an in-between garden/patio. Another strategic move was to raise the level of the garden where the pool is located to ensure strong sightlines through the home's large picture windows and floor-to-ceiling doors.

The house is also filled with furniture and objects that come with a history and a back story. Some pieces were collected on the couple's travels to Iceland and Africa, while others are family heirlooms. There's a cabinet in the living area from the Rimadesio showroom that's filled with objects and artefacts that are imbued with memory. Some of the living room furniture was from Mathieu's late mother. 'She always had an eye for beautiful design and would regularly purchase vintage items, such as these Barcelona chairs and the Scarpa sofa,' says Mathieu, who has added a coffee table designed by Charlotte Perriand.

This new home is more of an oasis than Mathieu and Julie's duplex in Ghent. But, like in Ghent, where the office was just a flight of stairs or lift ride away, JUMA Architects' new office is only a few steps from home, with the house doubling as a case study for potential clients.

TIPS

Many people focus on having lots of windows and are keen to have as much light as possible. But while this is important, windows must be appropriately positioned and orientated.

If you do decide to work from home, make sure you have a separate entrance and a clear delineation between home and work life.

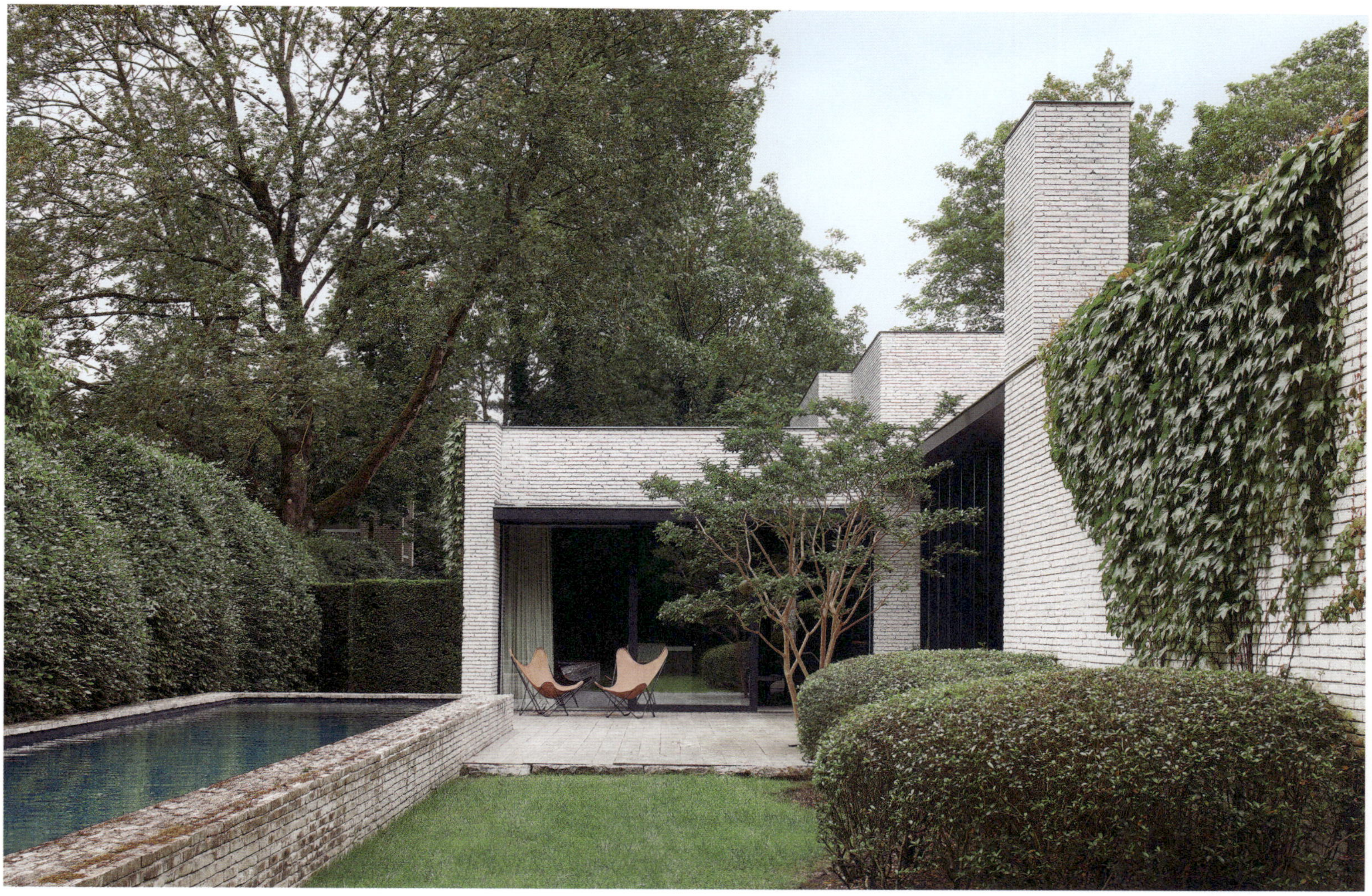

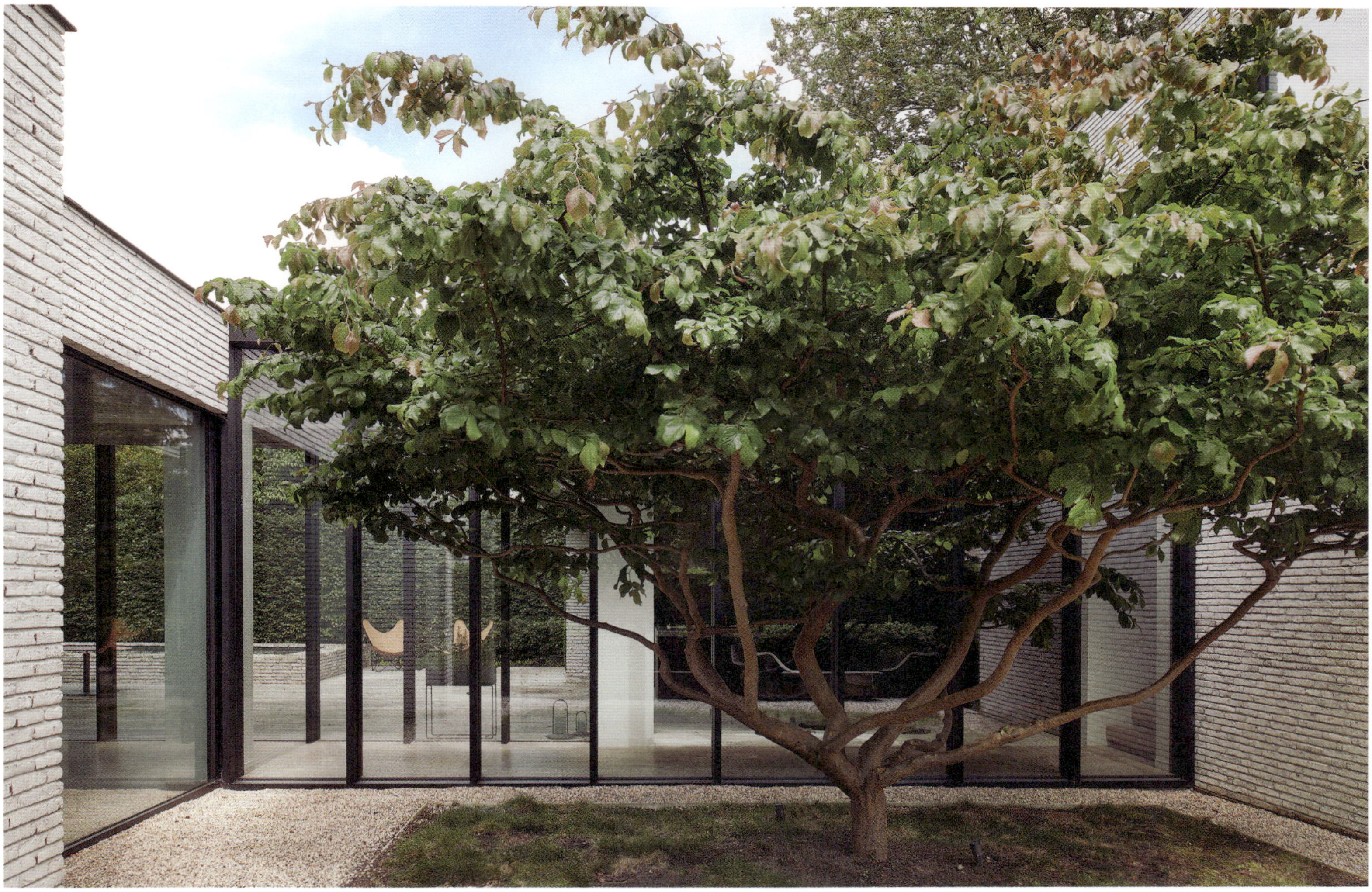

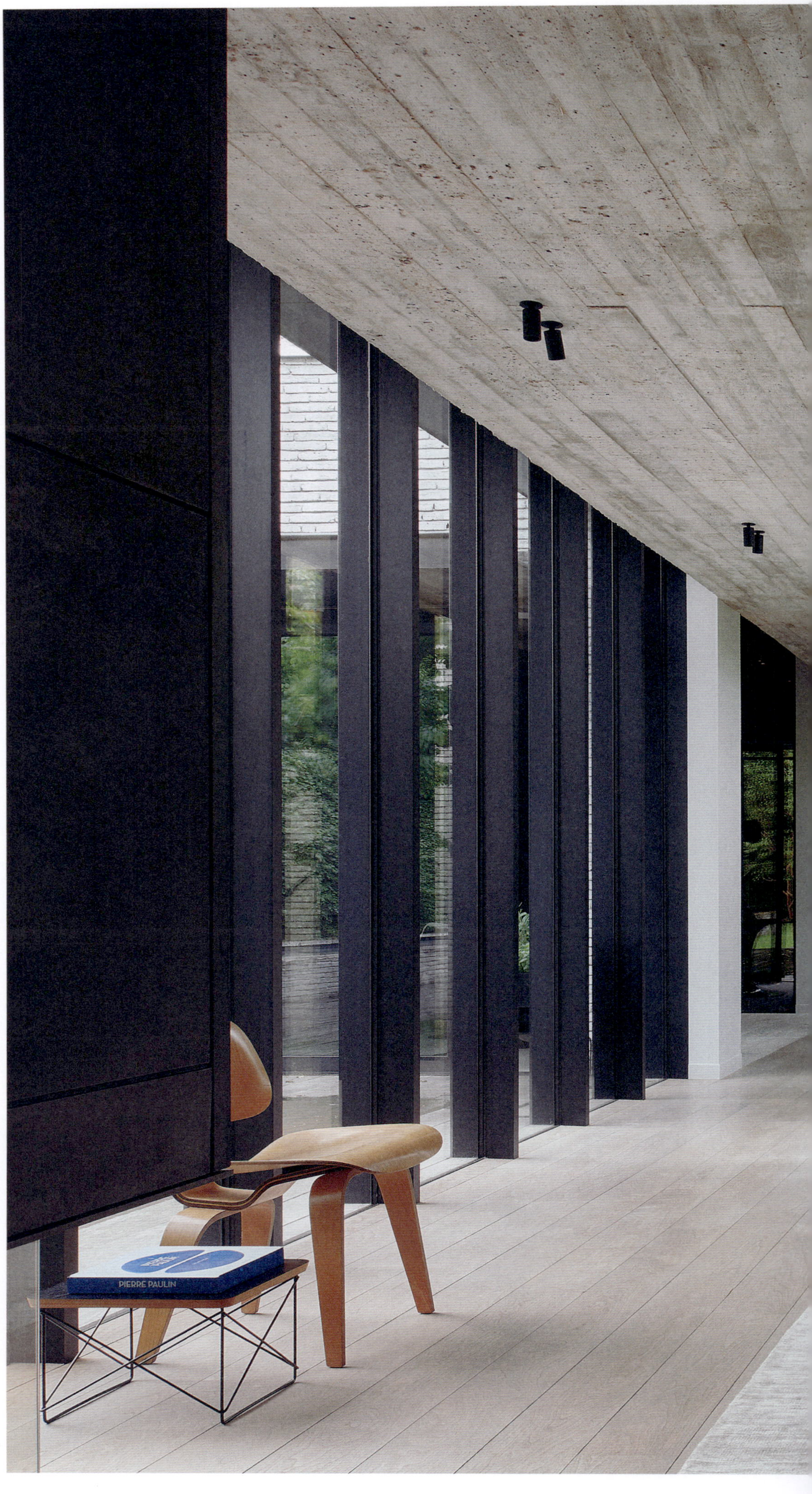
PIERRE PAULIN

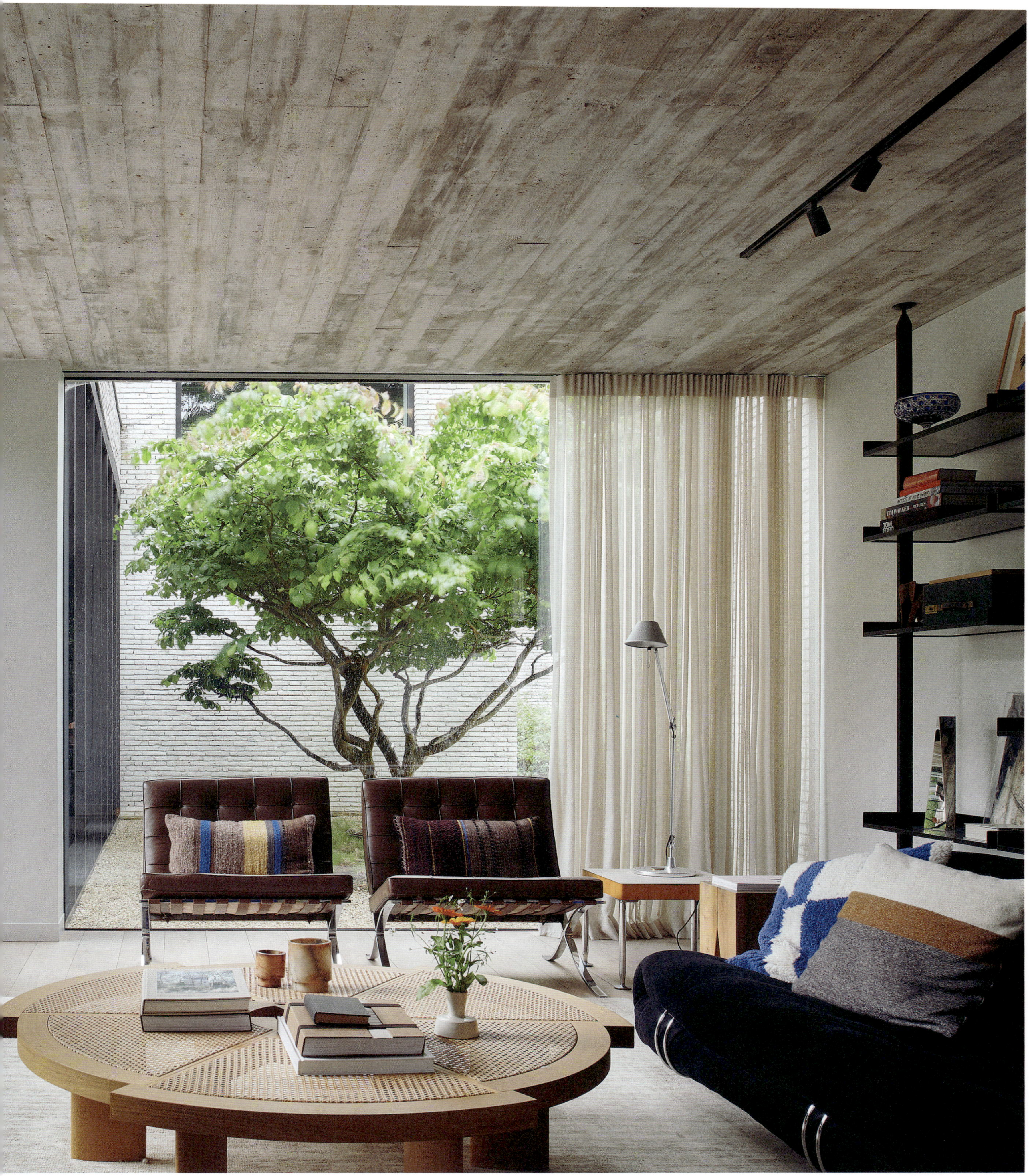

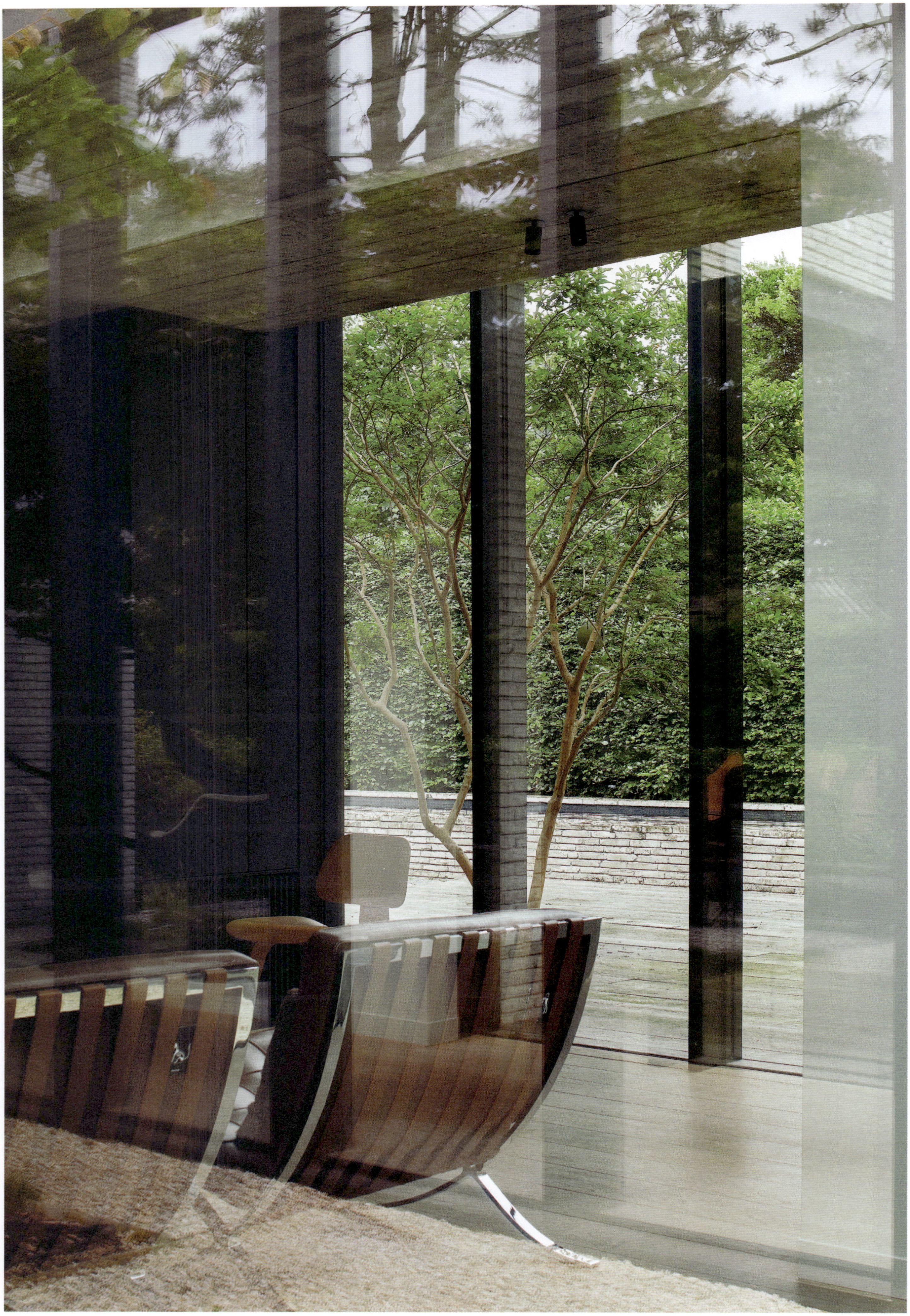

mathieu luyens & julie van de keere

the architect's house

mathieu luyens & julie van de keere

the architect's house

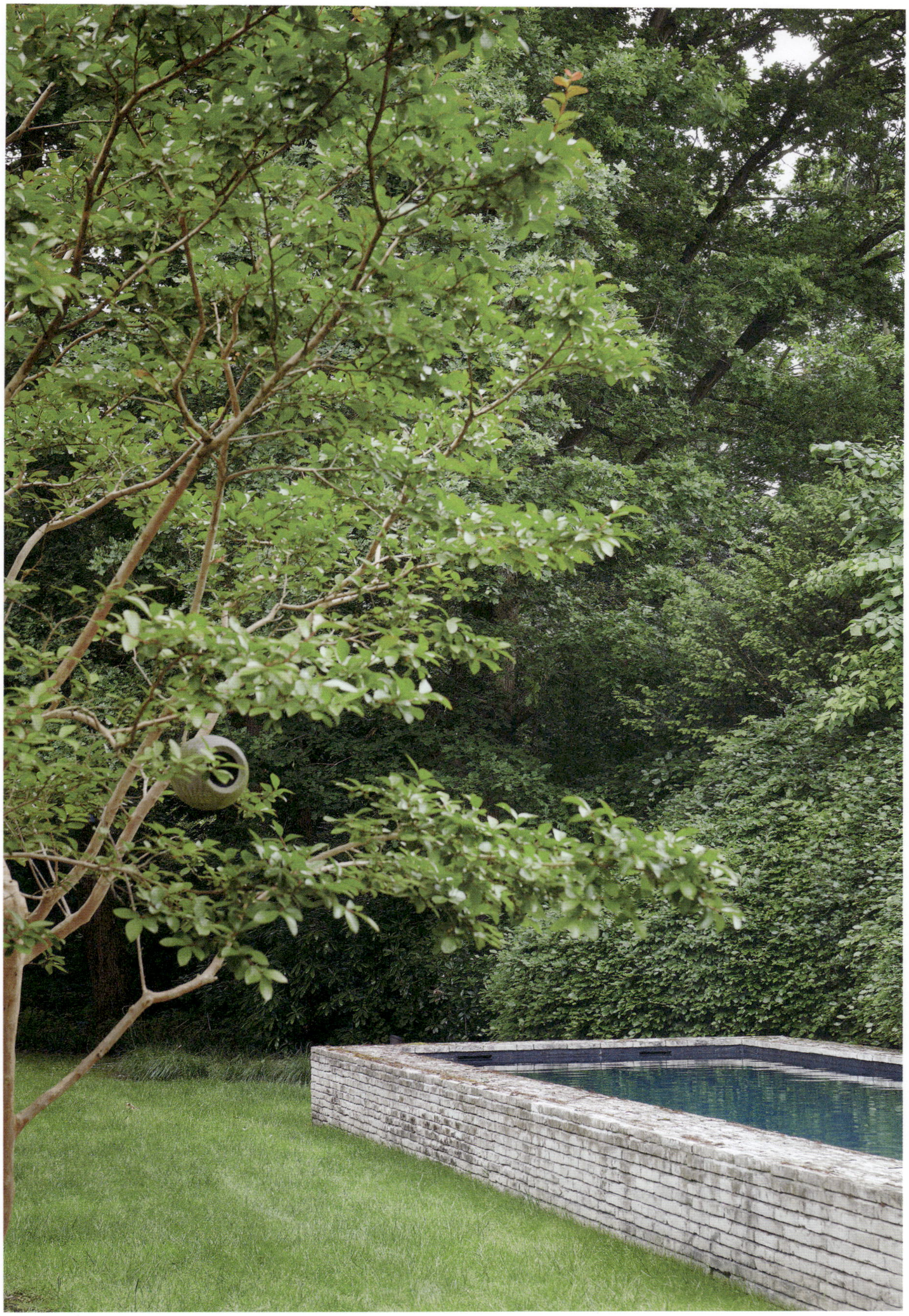

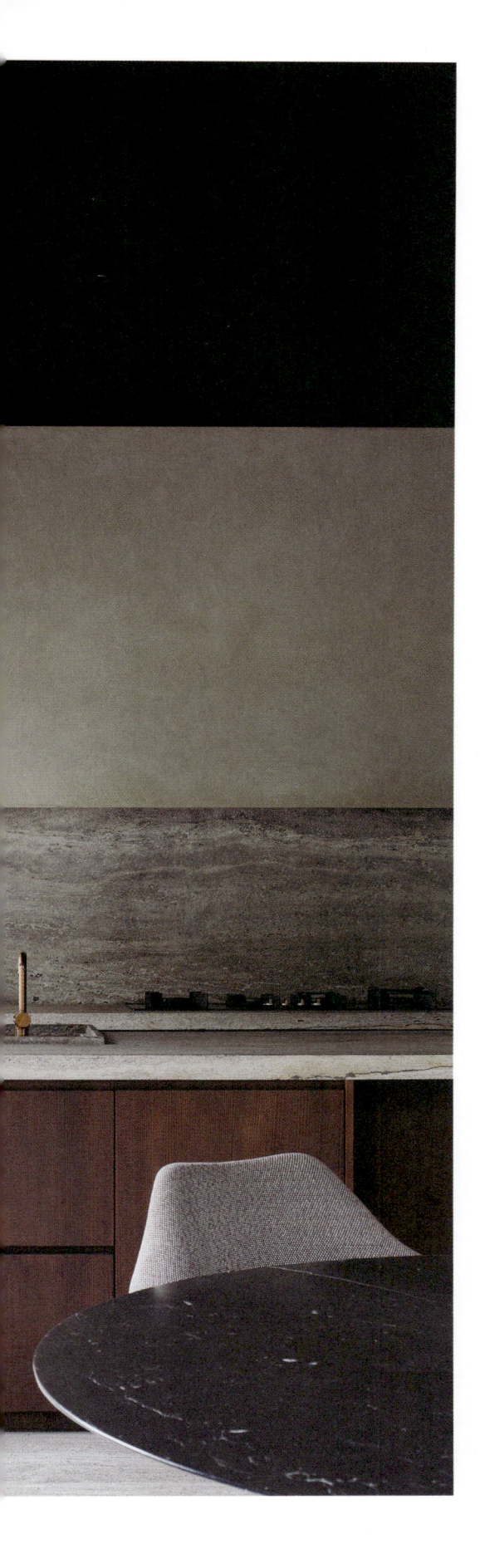

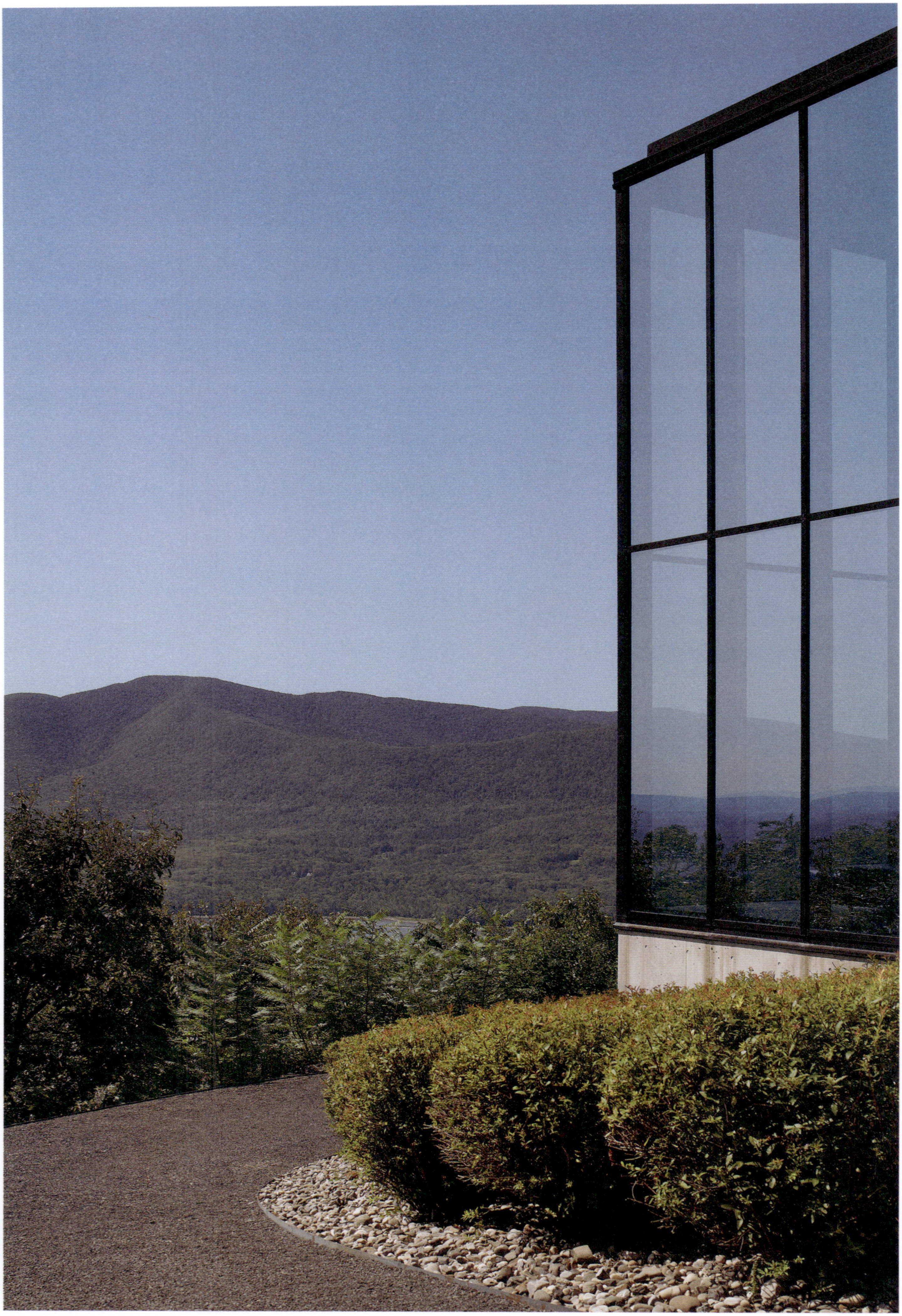

Jay Bargmann, FAIA
SHOKAN HOUSE, CATSKILL PARK, NEW YORK STATE

Some architect-designed houses are timeless, presenting as strong and contemporary years after they were built. The Shokan House, completed well over 10 years ago (construction commenced in 2012), could have been erected yesterday. Fabricated in steel, glass and concrete, the house can be spotted just below the summit of one of the Catskill Mountains. For owner Jay Bargmann, it is a place where friends and family come together.

Jay's permanent residence is in Pelham, New York, just north of Manhattan, and while he was open to suitable locations to build a house, he was looking for a large plot relatively close to New York City – within 150 km or two-hour drive. 'We saw this eight-hectare site at the top of the mountain and were captivated by the views of the Ashokan Reservoir and Kingston (the latter being the first capital of NewYork State),' says Jay, who knew instantly that it would be the perfect spot. He also saw this project as a house that would be an ideal retreat in his retirement years. As well as an opportunity to cycle and play tennis, the Catskill Park's 280,000 hectares is endowed with an endless number of walking trails, waterfalls, cliffs and forests, with diverse wildlife and a history that dates back thousands of years. Occupied by the Lenape people for hundreds of years before the first Europeans arrived in the 1600s, there's a logging trail from this time that passes through the centre of the Shokan House. Jay built a gazebo at the top of his property to acknowledge the end of this trail. While the name Shokan sounds Japanese, it was the name of the original colonial town that remains submerged at the bottom of the reservoir.

Unlike many rural locations that are dotted with weekenders, there's a sense of privacy here. Jay also benefited from working with a clean slate, with the site and surrounds free of other buildings. 'We developed the concept for this house in the first week and started construction just four months later,' says Jay, whose first task was to construct a road, just under a kilometre in length, to be able to reach the new house.

From the outset, Jay was mindful of both the form and the siting of the new house, focusing not only on the views but also wanting to create a level of privacy for areas such as bedrooms. The Shokan House is constructed with only a few materials – concrete, glass and steel – with no applied finishes, and the concrete foundation clearly expressed both inside and out. The aluminium and glass enclosures are connected to slender steel columns and open web joists. And in contrast to the steel, the open-plan interiors are delineated by American walnut. While the sightlines through the more public areas in the home are fairly transparent, the design includes three white volumes made from sheets of Corian that enclose the showers and water closets. While the materials are used sparingly, they are much more than simply functional. All the horizontal working surfaces, such as the kitchen bench, are made from brushed stainless steel, reflecting the sunlight and picking up on the same hues as those found on the surface of the reservoir.

As clearly defined is the soaring ceiling, which is constructed in galvanised sheets of steel over the double-height living area at the lower level. And to allow the architecture to be fully visible, Jay kept the art and furnishings to a minimum. The only art displayed in the house is a black and white photo of Thelonious Monk, taken by William Gottlieb in 1947. When it came to the furniture, including the beds, dining tables, desks, shelves and cabinets, the designer is Jay himself. 'There are a few sofas and chairs that I've always admired,' says Jay, singling out the two Ray and Charles Eames Lounge Chairs and Ottomans found in the living area as well as the couple's aluminium and leather desk chairs. There's also a Jean Prouvé Standard chair in a guest bedroom, as well as the Cité lounge chair in the study that benefits from the late afternoon light.

While the word 'design' is often overused by creatives, Jay refers to the word 'built' when describing his home. 'I wanted to express each material and every connection, making this house with "ornament but with no decoration",' says Jay, who saw the house in terms of solids and voids, with solids that one walks between – the house has no doors. Every room is as important as the clarity of the circulation; there's an absence of hierarchical spaces. But each room has its own sensibility. The living room, for example, is quite grand, while the study, surrounded by books, feels intimate. And to create another sense of intimacy, the main bedroom and the guest room are built into the side of the mountain.

'I saw the exterior and the interior as a "dialogue", but one that's continuous,' says Jay, who was also interested in creating an element of surprise. When one opens the solid door to the shower, there's a glass ceiling drawing in light. While Jay spends a considerable amount of time exploring the parkland, he also enjoys simply looking at the forest from the dining area and kitchen located on the first floor – watching the rising sun as he contemplates what's on the agenda that day.

Although the house has been fine-tuned over the 10 years since its completion, one of the greatest challenges was the construction and installation of the two garage doors which measure 2.4 x 11m. 'We fabricated these from airplane hangar doors that are hydraulically operated,' says Jay, who appreciated the many talented craftspeople who worked on the house, many of whom remain friends and see the quality of their workmanship a decade later. These talented people have made even the most challenging aspects of the design appear relatively simple, in spite of their complexity.

TIPS

Don't be afraid to start building. Start with a solid intention and adjust to the site. Sometimes, you need to improvise and allow for changes, but stick to the design's fundamental intention.

When building in fairly remote areas, you need to factor in the passing wildlife. We'd ordered a package to be delivered and, through the camera positioned at the front gate, we saw that it was picked up by a black bear as he continued his way up the mountain!

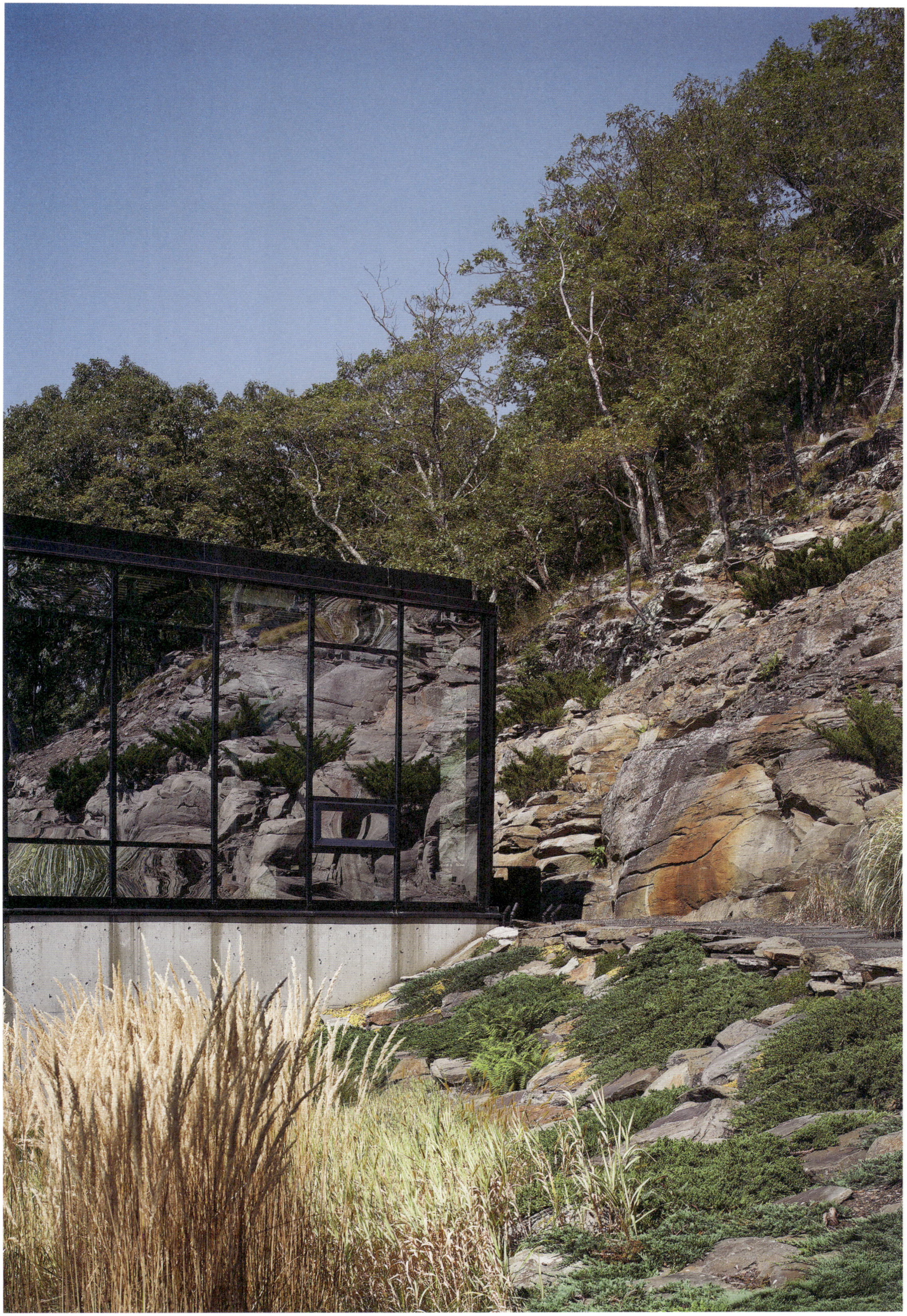

the architect's house

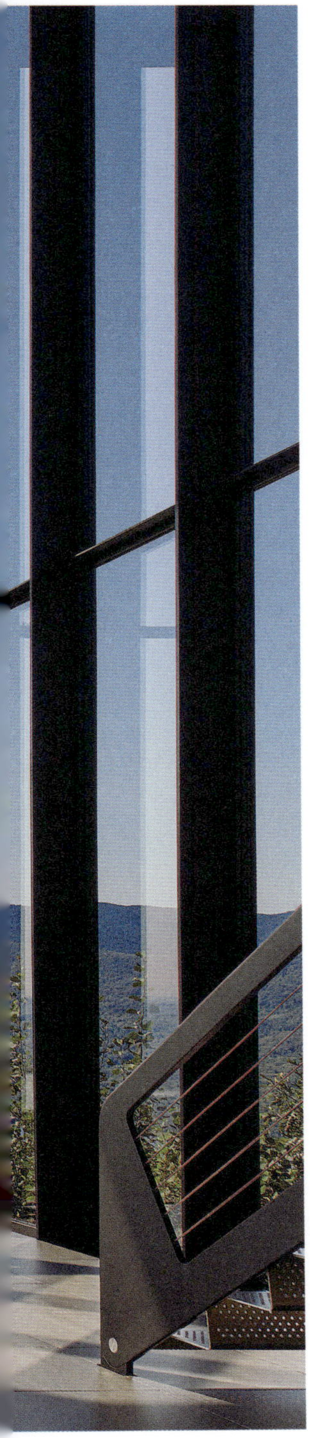
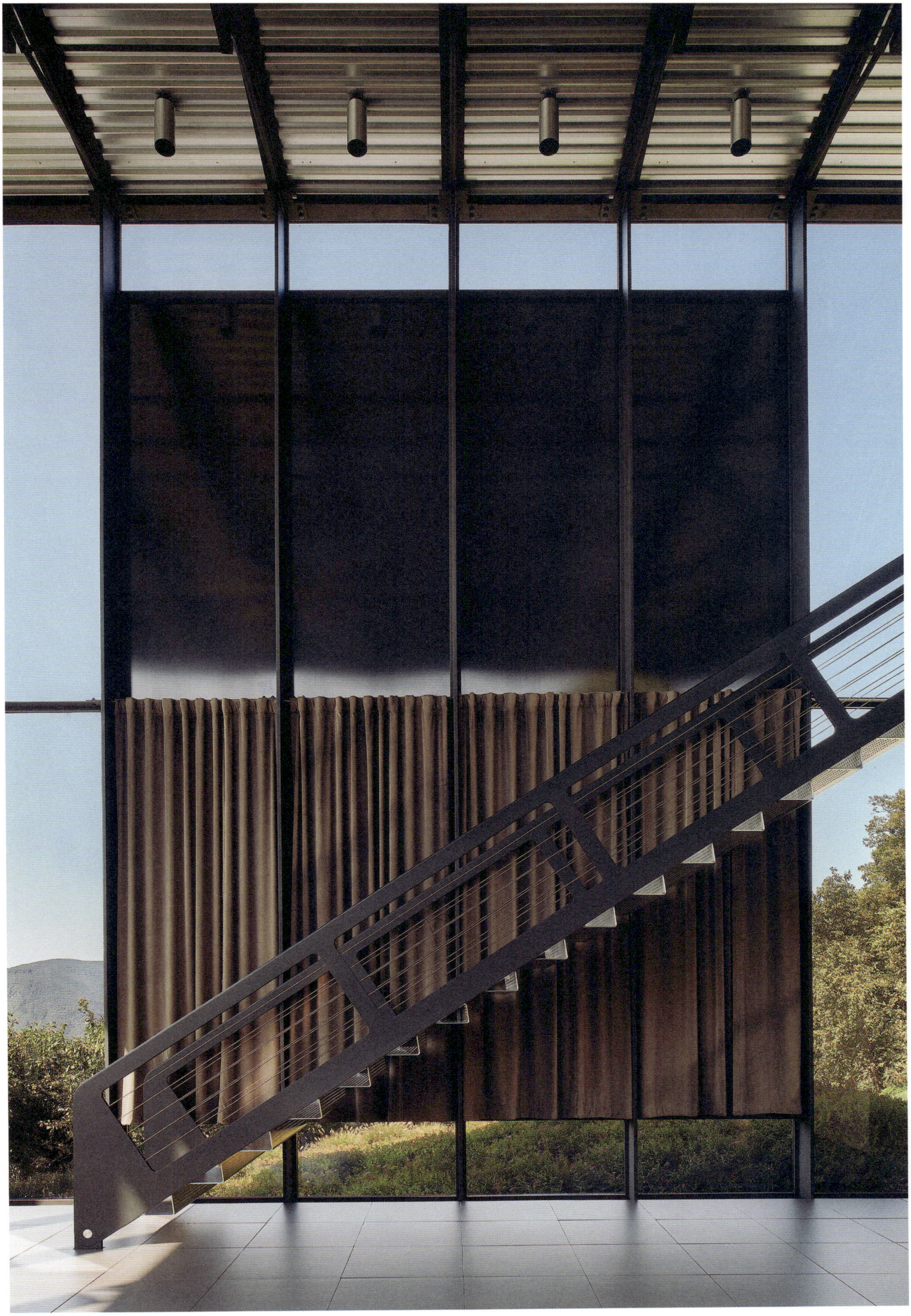

the architect's house

jay bargmann

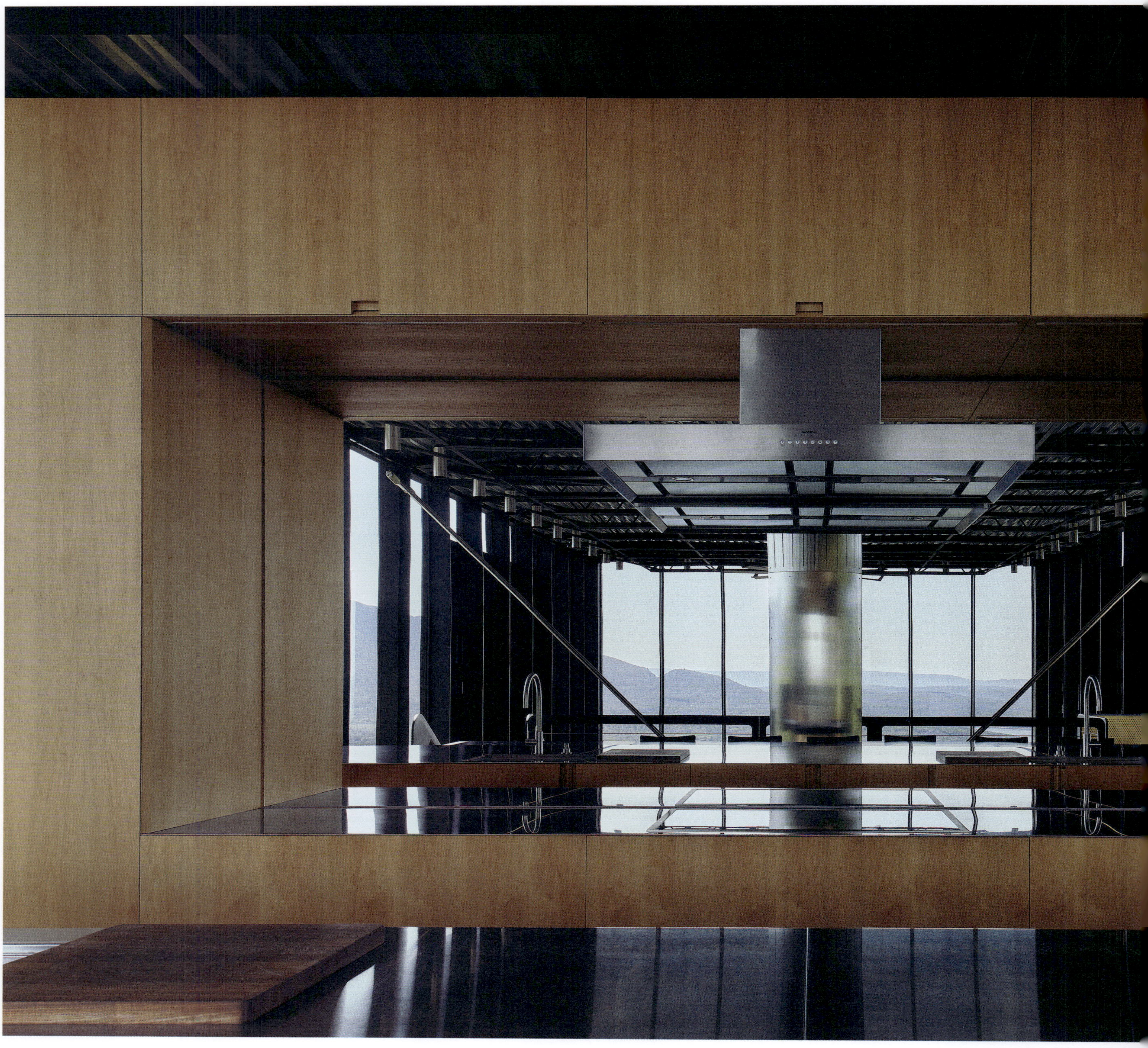

jay bargmann

the architect's house

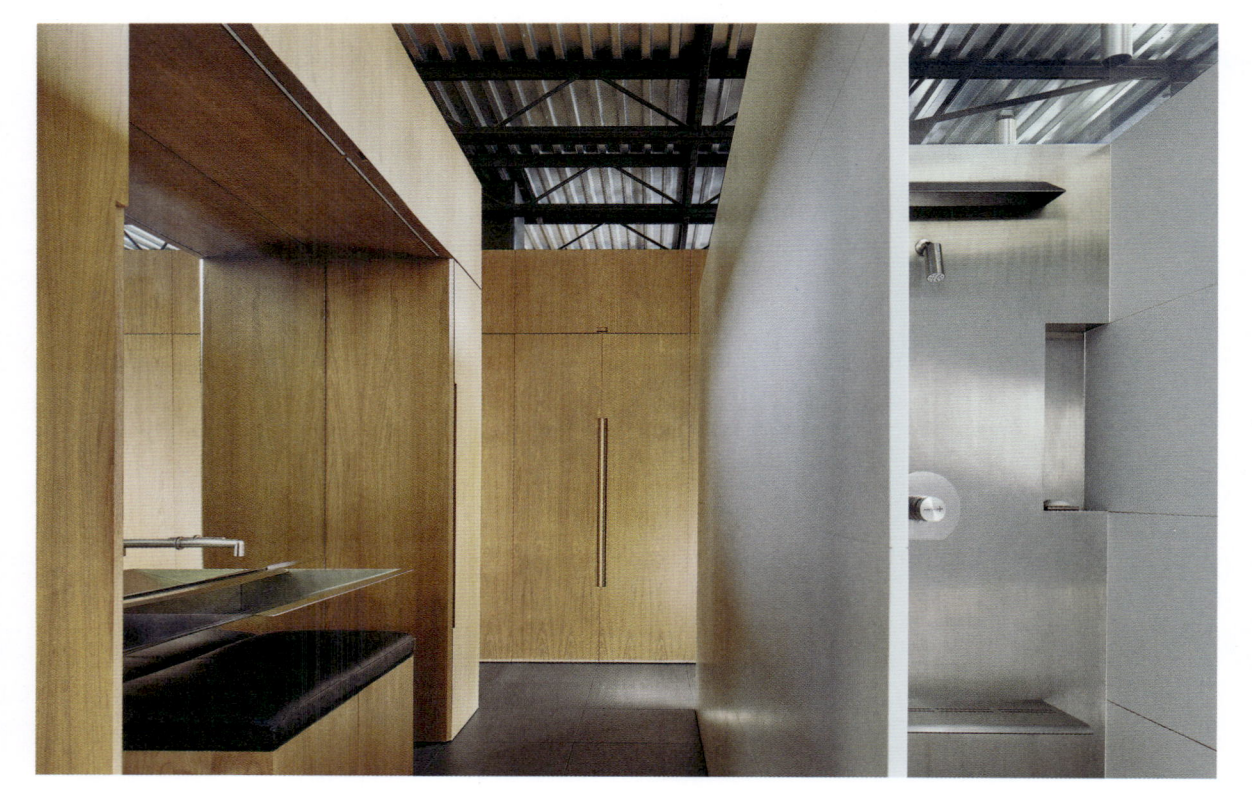

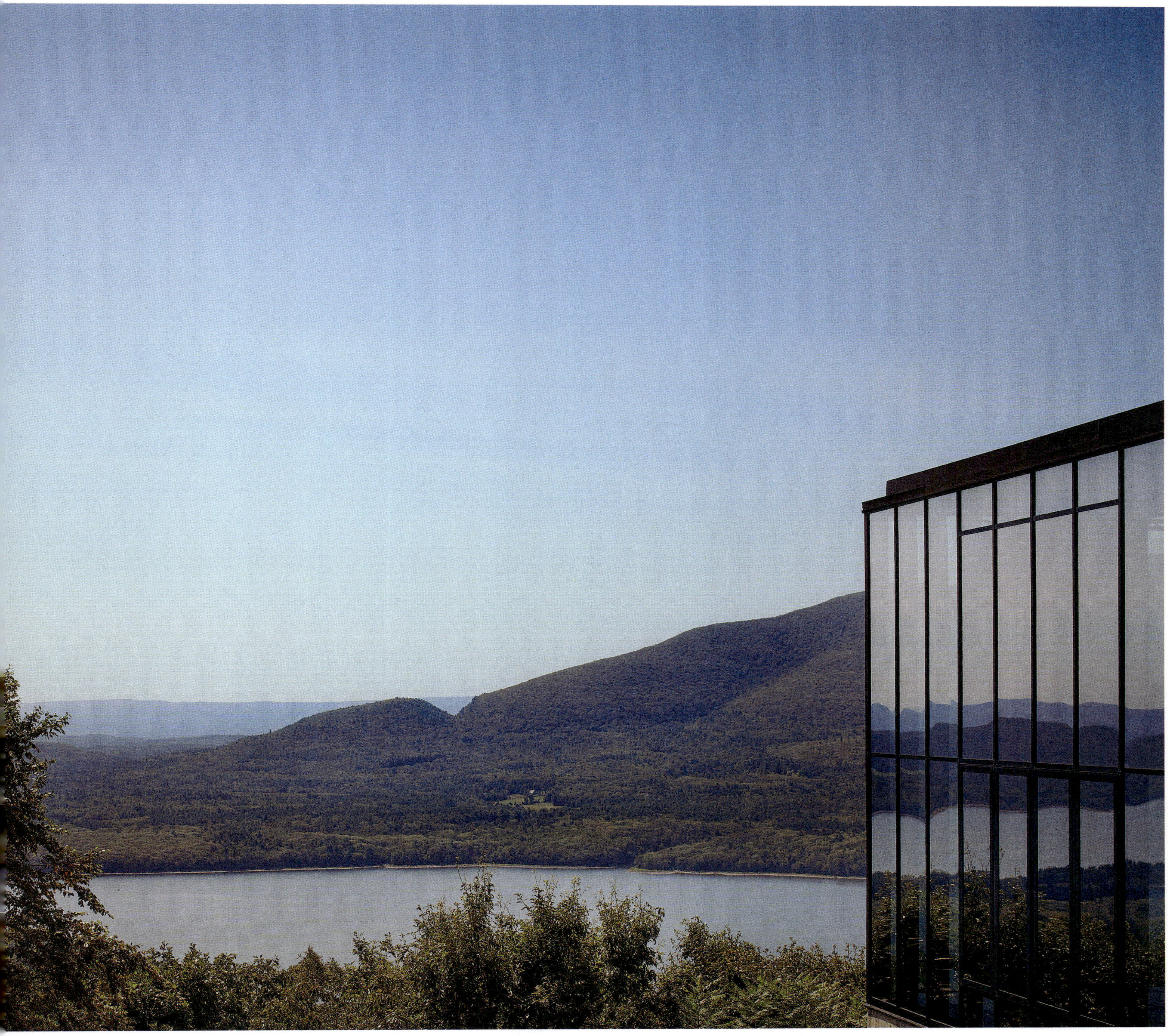

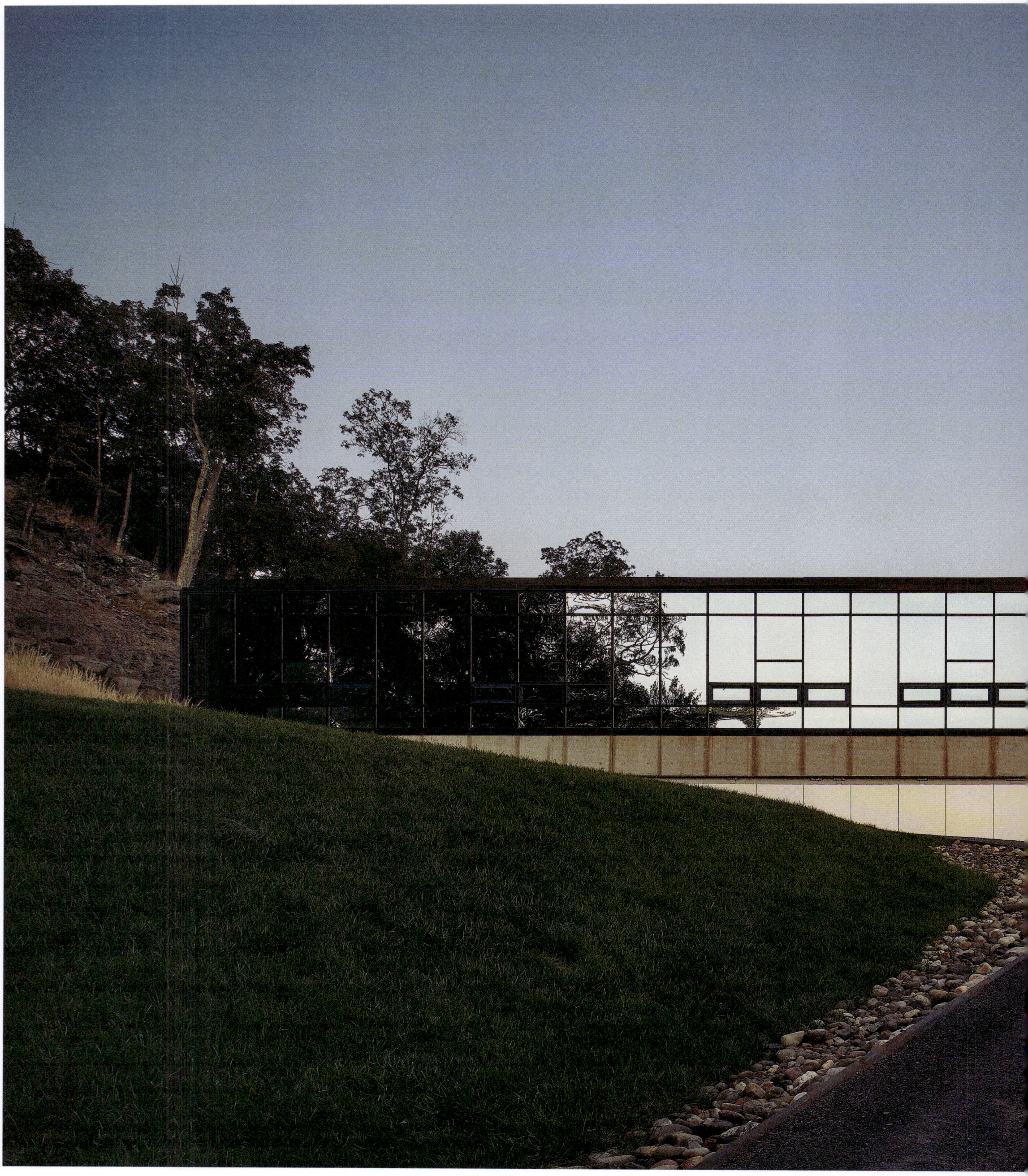

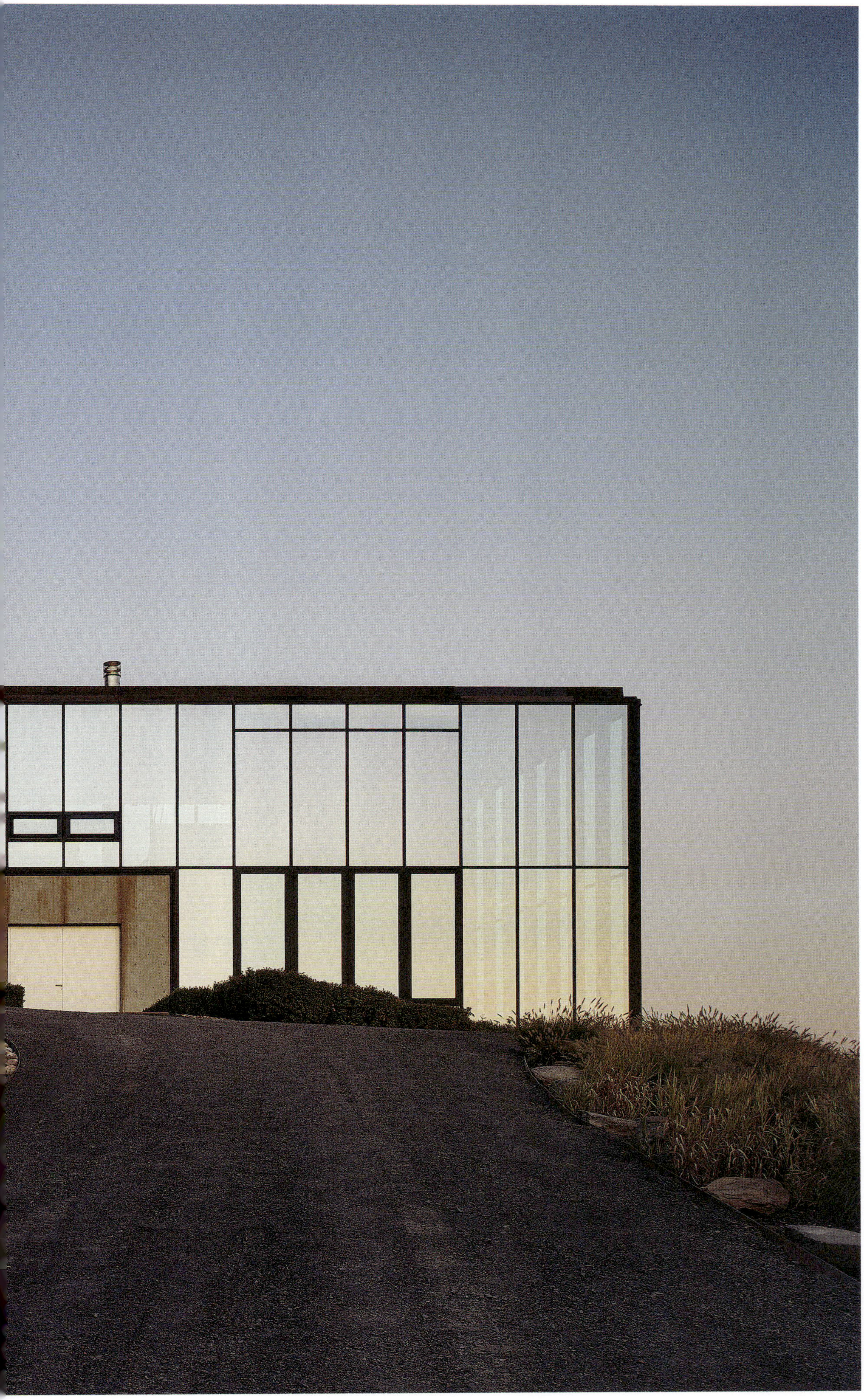

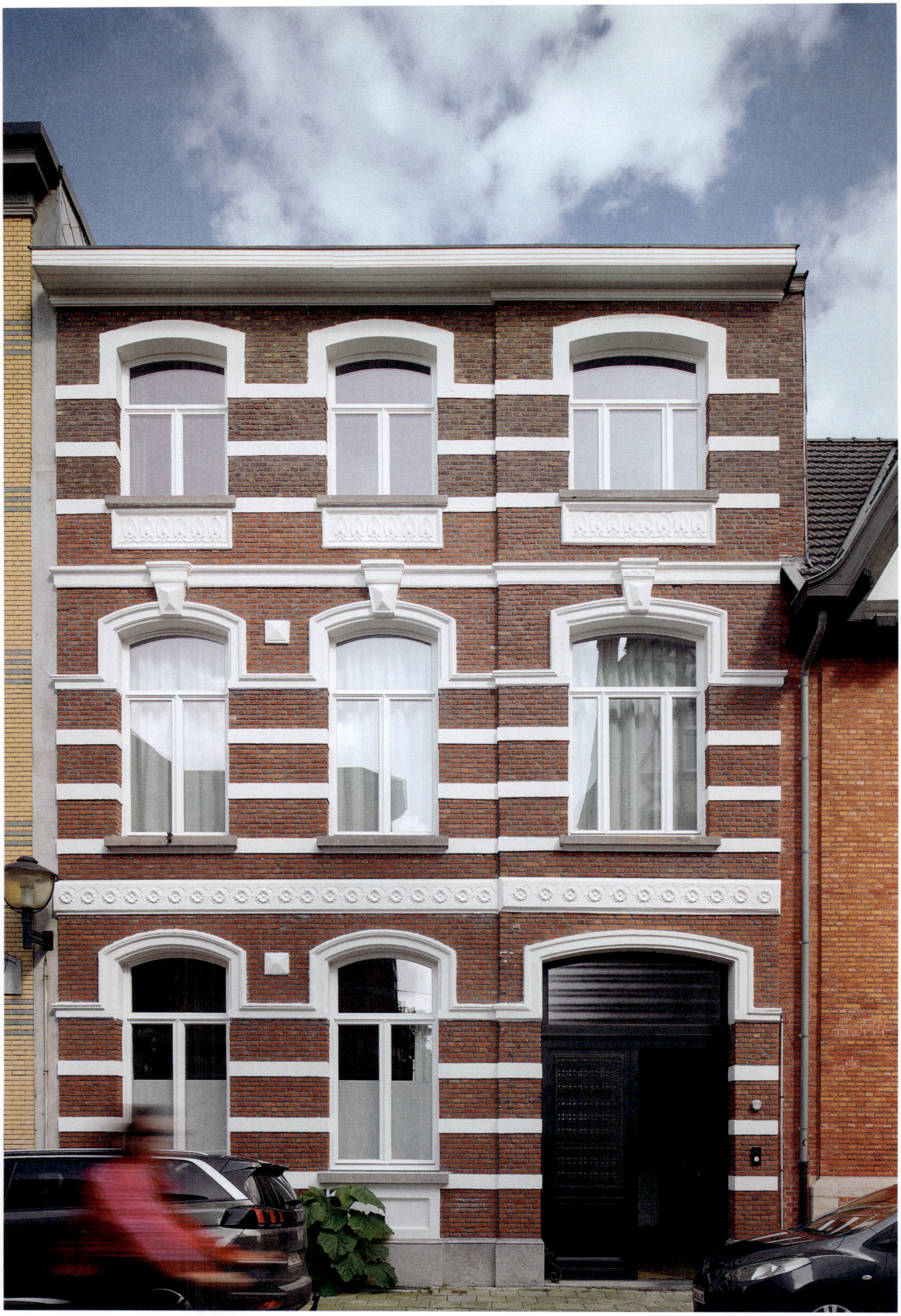

Sam Peeters, Director, Contekst

ANTWERP HOUSE, ANTWERP

There are a number of narrow homes that line the streets of Antwerp. Many abut the street, their front windows up against the pavement. Usually curtained for privacy, there's a sense of mystique about what lies behind the facade. For interior architect Sam Peeters, who founded the practice Contekst with Toon Martens, his preference was to 'look for a house that had undergone "bad" interventions over the years' – something that is diametrically opposed to what most people are looking for. 'This type of condition allows you the freedom to work a little more radically as a designer,' says Sam.

Part of the pleasure that comes from buying a house that's far from perfect is the opportunity to identify more salient qualities before renovating. Although the house came with a number of 'blemishes', it benefited from being in a coveted Antwerp neighbourhood. Sam was used to living on relatively modest footprints – his previous home, renovated eight years prior, was even smaller and without a garden. But, after having a child, he thought there was a need for something that was a tad larger and with a garden, however modest in scale that was.

So, with his husband Christophe and their daughter Scottie, the hunt was on. The couple chanced upon this townhouse in the district of Zurenborg, whose most famous street, Cogels-Osylei, is known for its Belle Époque mansions, including a rare architectural gem designed by Josef Hoffmann. 'Our street is far less known and much quieter – Cogels-Osylei regularly has buses and tourists marvelling at the eclectic architecture. Christophe and I fell for the house immediately. We could see its potential and, like all the tourists, we were attracted to the neighbourhood.'

The first traces of the period home, as discovered in the city archives, date from 1888. (Art Nouveau came to Belgium with the legendary Victor Horta in 1892 when he built the Hotel Tassel in Brussels.) At that time, the two-storey building was semi-detached and there was a passage on the side that led to a coach house in the back garden.

Over the years, the side entrance was enclosed and a second floor was added. 'The last renovation was done without any permission, which saw the coach house turned into a warehouse,' says Sam.

Designed in the neoclassical style, the house is characterised by red brick walls with white bands (referred to as 'layers of bacon') and natural stone window tablets. However, the home's facade was in poor condition and required restoration, including the replacement of missing ornamentation. 'The place was virtually uninhabitable,' says Sam, who recalls inspecting it for the first time, when the ground floor was used as a storage space and an office, and the upper two levels given over to an apartment.

Sam took inspiration for his design from mid-20th-century American homes, where spaces are allowed to flow into each other and there is limited use of doors. He was also keen to retain as much of the original fabric as possible, using this as a basis to create new contemporary interventions. The dining room, located at the front of the house, exemplifies this approach. During demolition, Sam and Christophe discovered a beautifully painted ceiling which they restored with the assistance of Sam's mother. The colour of the ceiling's rosette and cornices also served as a design cue for the colours of the floors and the new joinery.

Some of the spaces are open and fluid, while others, such as Scottie's playroom, are tucked away behind a mirrored door. Although the space is relatively small, it was perfect for a playroom and ideally located next to the kitchen.

Sam was also keen to express both the past and the present in an honest manner, which meant that some materials were reused. The wooden and steel beams of the space formerly used as a storage area at ground level were reused for the roof of the new extension as well as for structural interventions. 'We left these elements exposed to allow the house to have a rich patina,' says Sam, who was also keen to reveal the timber ceiling structure in the bedrooms to increase the height. The brick walls in the kitchen also remain raw.

As the couple had their art collection in mind, including a painting by Christophe, the walls are predominantly white with the dark-stained timber floors adding a sense of warmth. Pigmented polyconcrete was used for the ground floor and a dark stain for the solid wooden parquetry. 'My preference in a home is for functions to have no clear separation,' says Sam, pointing out the living space next to the kitchen, with the dining table also serving as a meeting room. Scottie's playroom doubles as a fitness room and other spaces are used freely and for a variety of purposes – from working to reading or watching films. Sam also sees the paintings as being as important in the 'conversation', whether a portrait of a boy by artist Marc Bauer or a portrait of a woman by Kati Heck. Other paintings hold more sentimental value, such as the portrait of Sam's great-great-grandfather painted by Ernest Albert. Books are also held dear to the couple, with many bought over the years. But rather than having them 'displayed' in a classic bookcase, they lie on a sill on a raised floor.

Although the house is important for Sam, it's the garden he designed to which he gravitates. 'I wanted to create an urban garden, with sufficient space to sit and relax, as well as to have meals,' says Sam. He also enjoys the transparency and the sense of openness that the renovation has achieved. 'We can hear each other wherever we are in the house, whether someone is cooking downstairs and the others are upstairs,' he adds.

TIPS

It can be challenging converting a period home for contemporary living, particularly using sustainable methods. You need to think about how to conceal things like solar panels, heat pumps and areas for recycling water.

We often say to clients who want to renovate period homes to 'preserve the magic' but be open to changes and keep evaluating things during the process of the renovation.

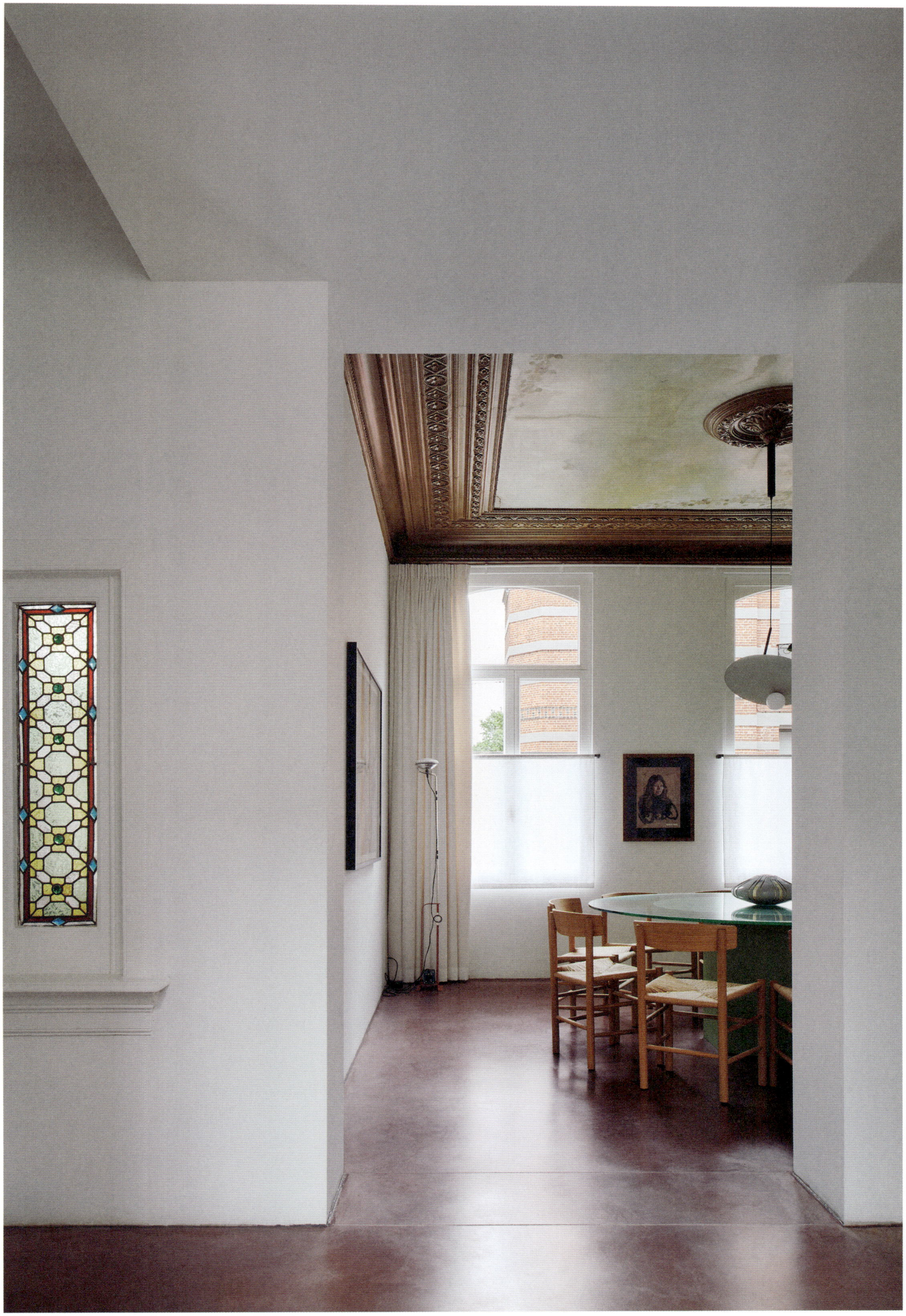

the architect's house

sam peeters

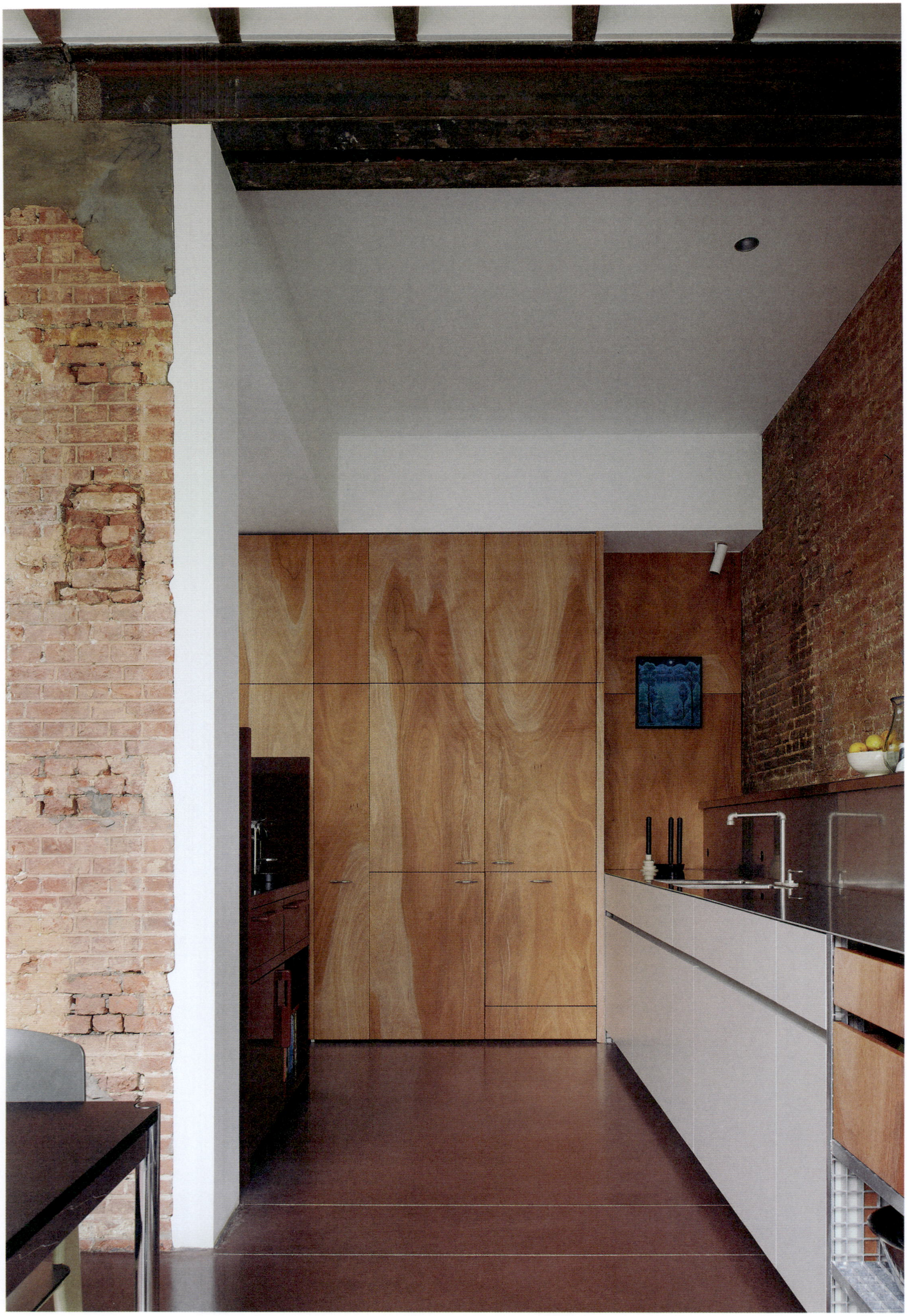

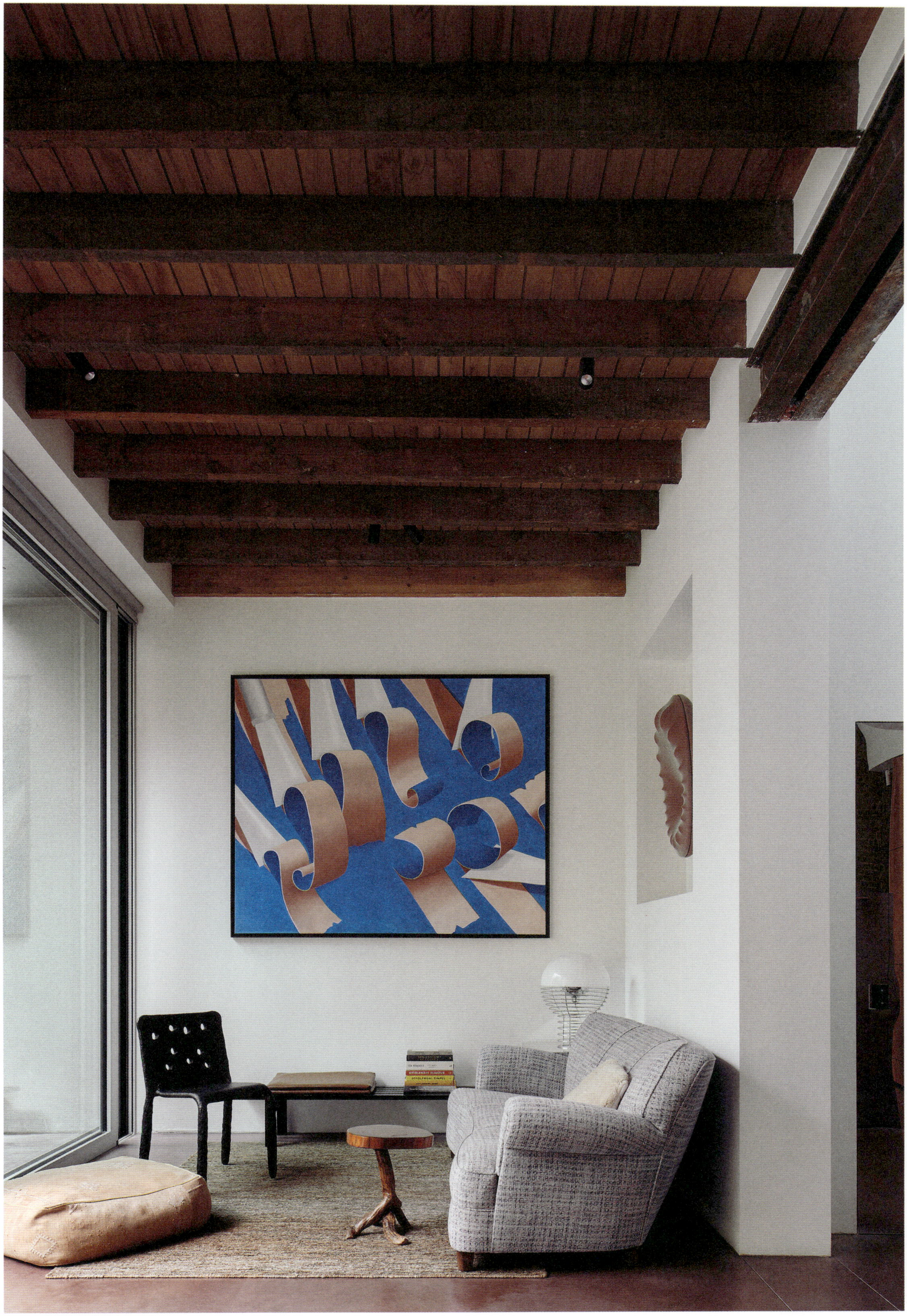

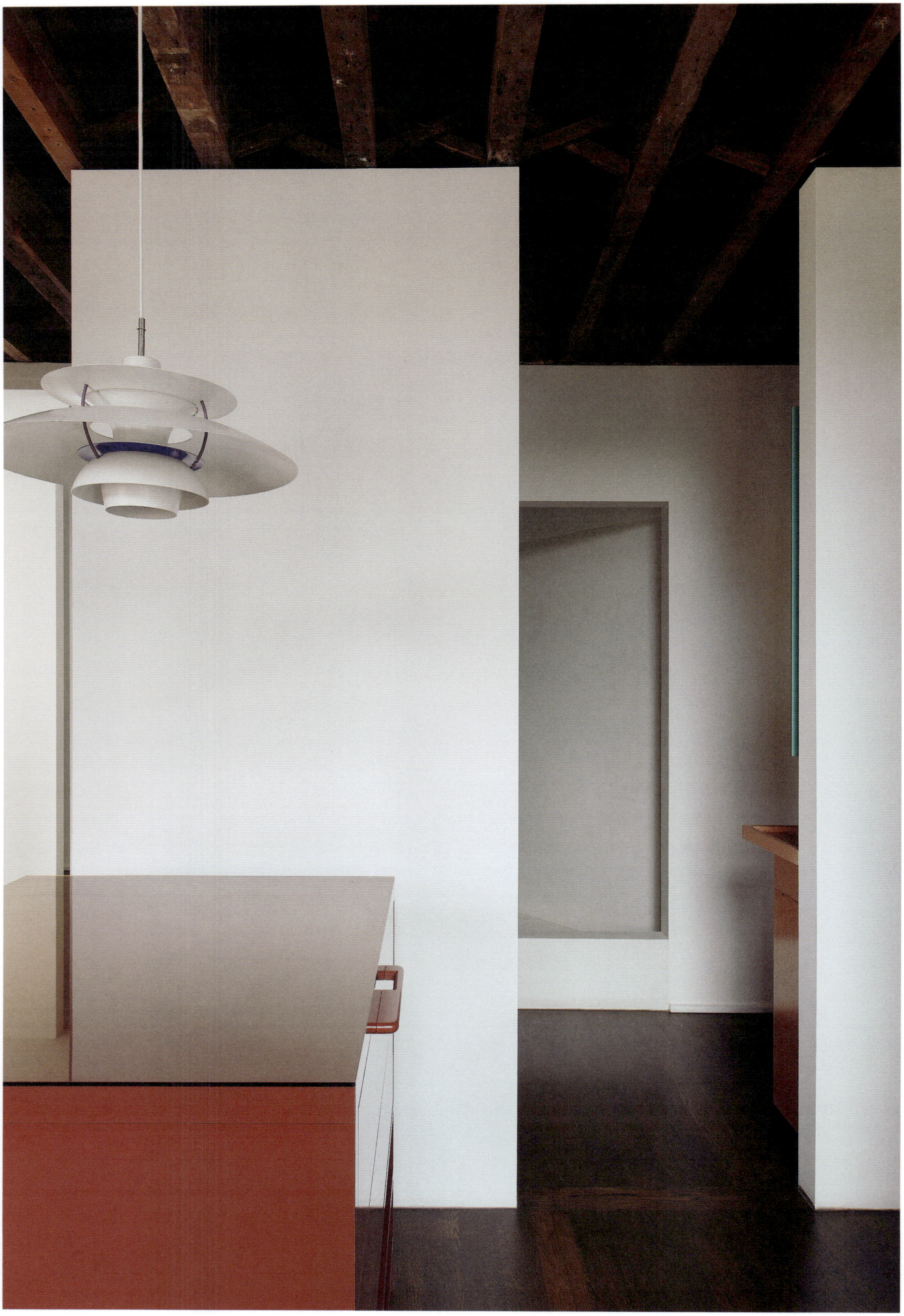

sam peeters

the architect's house

sam peeters

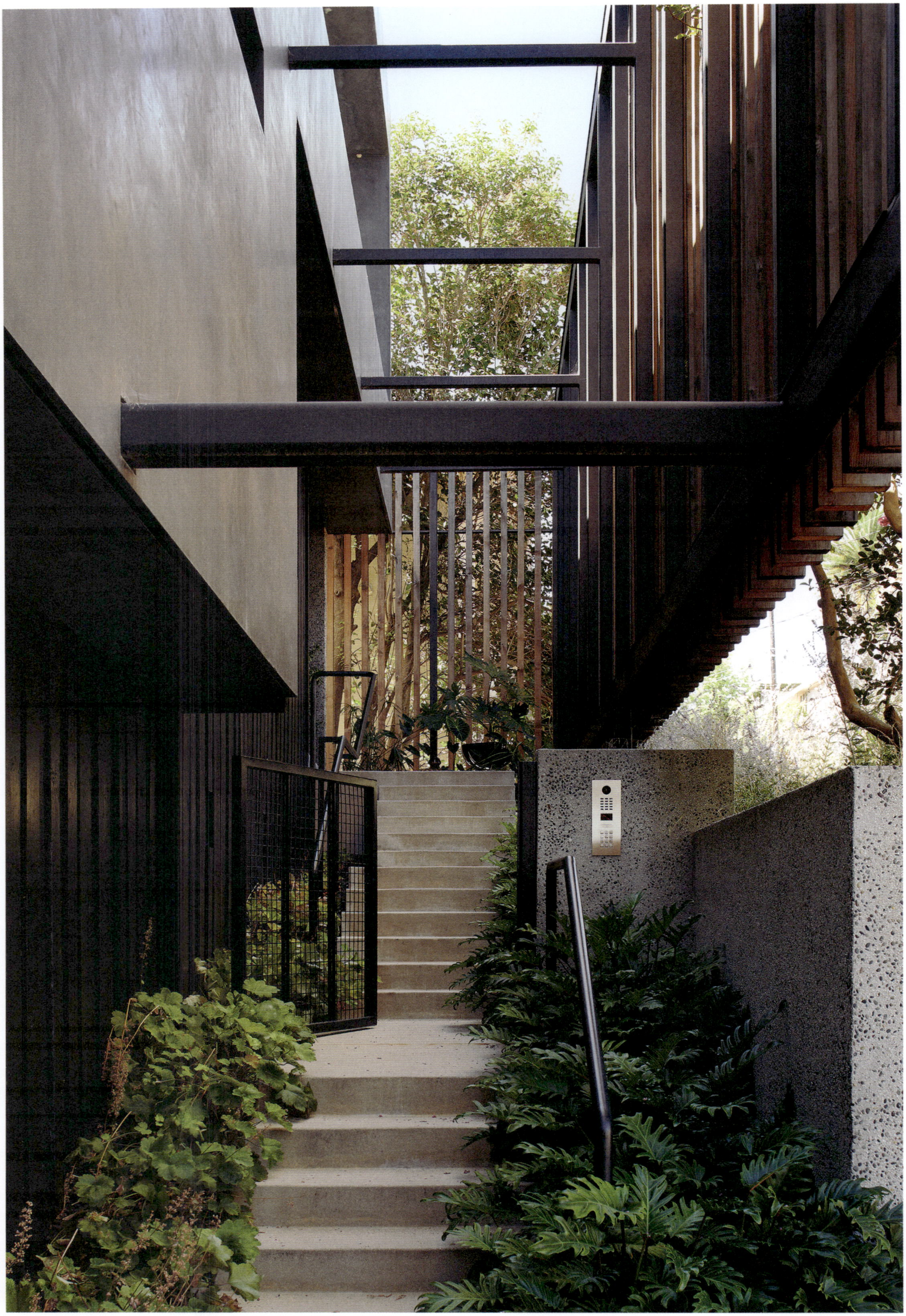

Peggy Hsu & Chris McCullough, Principals, Hsu McCullough

SHERMAN OAKS HOUSE, SAN FERNANDO VALLEY, LOS ANGELES COUNTY

Los Angeles benefits from some great hilly environments and Sherman Oaks in the San Fernando Valley is one of them. It was also the perfect choice for Peggy Hsu and Chris McCullough, principals of the architecture and interior design practice, Hsu McCullough, to create a home for themselves. 'We were looking for a hillside lot that was centrally located in Los Angeles County, in a neighbourhood that was less populated and afforded greater privacy,' says Chris.

While the house the couple designed appears entirely new, it includes a few remnants of an early 1960s ranch-style home that existed on the site. Like many other of the 1960s homes in the street, this one had been reworked in the 1990s by the former owner. 'The house was quite dated and "falling apart" so most of it was demolished,' says Peggy, who points to a remaining fireplace in the living area as one of the few elements that was retained, together with a number of established trees on the site (Hsu McCullough was also responsible for the landscape design).

The couple lived in the 1960s house for a couple of years before making any plans, wanting to see the sun's trajectory during the day. Apart from its condition, the house came with poor access to sunlight, was only single-storey and imbued with low ceiling heights that didn't address the ridge line on the property nor make the most of the views over the neighbourhood. 'We wanted to frame these views with a more pavilion-like feel, one that had a stronger connection to the garden,' says Chris who, with Peggy, was captivated by the unobstructed views of the city and mountains the site potentially offered.

These views certainly weren't a secret the day the property was auctioned; there was a bidding war among the crowd that attended. 'Everyone who inspected the place knew the property's potential,' says Chris. But to the couple's surprise, they were handed the keys on the day and started to think about what they could achieve. Some design features were inspired by other projects the practice was working on, but Peggy and

Chris wanted to explore the use of more raw and unfinished materials, and those that allowed for contrasting textures. A number of pilgrimages were taken to the homes of Luis Barragán in Mexico City. Barragán's use of black stone inspired the outdoor terraces, along with strategically placed plants that act as signposts in the home's passages. Barragán's use of colour, especially his way of creating golden hues, also influenced the palette for the living area, with a white oak-panelled ceiling and golden-painted walls that sit behind the bespoke shelves that display Chris's record collection. 'In our previous house, these records were kept hidden in a room. But here they add texture and another layer to the space,' says Chris. A collection of MiniDiscs has also been cleverly reworked by Chris into a portrait that's displayed on the wall of the dining area. Peggy also has a number of her own abstract paintings on display.

Designed for a couple and their dog, the brief to themselves was to have two separate studies, as well as spaces for a large collection of records and books. Chris and Peggy also wanted large walls to display their art and objects collected on their travels. The kitchen had to be integral to the living areas, which benefit from the views of the mountains. Featuring a simple dark palette of black-painted joinery, rich soapstone and charcoal-hued smooth stucco, the kitchen appears recessive. Pivotal to its design is the American black walnut island bench — a place for preparing food, eating, drinking, reading and, as Chris muses, 'all the words that end in "ings".' Other materials used by Hsu McCullough include western red cedar brise-soleil, which forms the facade/entry portico and reduces the harsh afternoon light to create a more dappled light within.

Being connected to the outdoors was also important, so there are two planted garden roofs, one located above the kitchen and one from the main bedroom. 'As well as being something beautiful to look at, the gardens attract birds, bees, butterflies and dragonflies. The plants also function in reducing the solar heat gain during the summer months,' says Peggy, and the water run-off in the rear yard, which lands in a basin, attracts local wildlife.

Floor-to-ceiling glass doors and large picture windows are a given for contemporary houses. But, according to Chris, 'these are expensive and require substantial steel structures.' To protect this house from the harsh light, there are deep eaves and a number of elongated skylights that allow for softer and less direct light. 'We also used quite a lot of brass, in areas like the bathroom walls to create a glow from the sunlight,' says Peggy.

Although the first floor is open plan, with the kitchen and living areas only loosely delineated, both areas function differently and have two distinct moods. The kitchen, for example, has an intimate feel, assisted by the lower ceiling height. In contrast, the living area features both a lighter palette and is endowed with plants, creating a continuous sightline to the densely planted garden. The home's planted trailing guardrail and open stair also strengthens the biophilic design. 'We love the part of the living area where it connects to the patio, and having coffee there in the morning,' says Chris, who enjoys simply gazing at the ridge in the distance.

One of the greatest challenges for Peggy and Chris was the design for the brise-soleil which features across the home's facade. 'We wanted it to appear to "float" off the facade as much as creating an exterior room or arrival point,' says Chris, who used the slope of the street to create retaining walls that also function as planters. 'It became even more challenging when we also wanted a water garden in the front with water plants and fish,' adds Chris, who studied this problem for months using 3D models to work out the most appropriate cladding solution. But the problems were solved and the couple continue to enjoy the efforts of their work: seeing how the light permeates the home and changes with the trajectory of the sun.

TIPS

It's wise to live in a property, even for a short time, before starting a major renovation.

Never renovate a house to please friends, parents, local real estate agents or people you think might later live here. Their opinions should not drive your design; instead, trust your architects and invest in creating a healthy environment filled with plants and light.

peggy hsu & chris mccullough

the architect's house

peggy hsu & chris mccullough

the architect's house

peggy hsu & chris mccullough

the architect's house

peggy hsu & chris mccullough

the architect's house

peggy hsu & chris mccullough

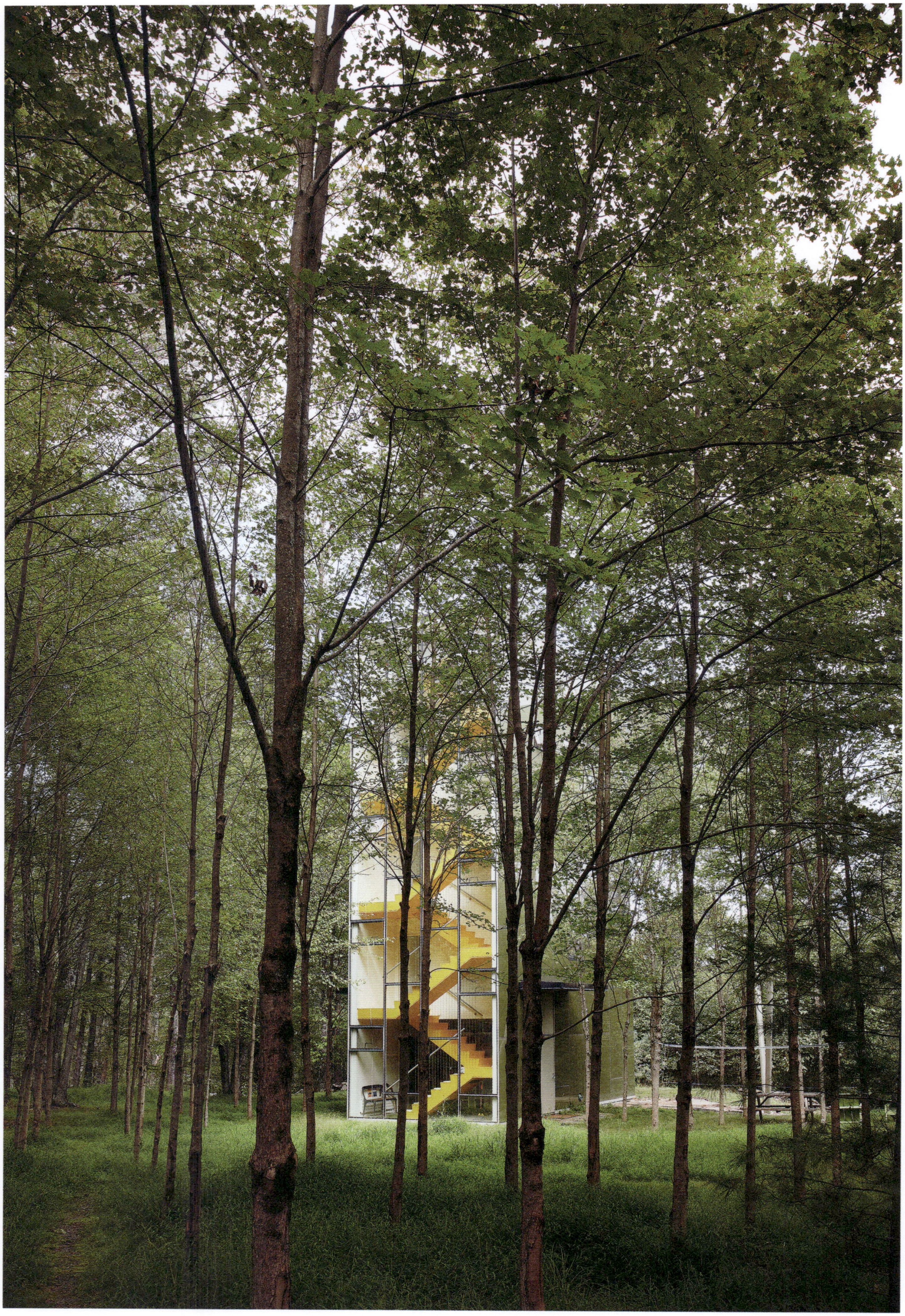

Thomas Gluck, Principal, GLUCK+
TOWER HOUSE, UPSTATE NEW YORK

Some houses remain timeless. They can't be dated, appearing as contemporary as the day they were completed. The Tower House, designed by architect Thomas Gluck for his family of four, was first unveiled in 2012. Located 160 km north of New York, in the Catskills, the Tower House, with its soaring height, is framed by established trees of equal stature. 'I refer to it as a treehouse for grown-ups,' says Thomas, whose father Peter Gluck, founder of the practice, purchased the 7-hectare site over 50 years ago. Part of the attraction was its location on top of a natural bluestone ridge.

The glazed tower, a two-hour drive from the city, is a sharp contrast to many weekenders found in the Catskills, which are often low-slung and anchored to the ground. In this instance, the 'anchor' is a stairwell that, with the adjacent bedrooms on each level, comprises 40 m². Often referred to as 'a stairway to the treetops', the bright yellow staircase adds a sense of playfulness to the very modern design. The stairway is not only a joyous feature of the house, it also functions as a thermal chimney, with the hatch at the top purging hot air during the warmer months of the year. And during the colder months, it acts as a heat bank. The reason for its unusual form was also driven by a wish not to impact the landscape, as well as to situate the main living areas at the top of the house to ensure both increased light and a broader perspective on the mountain ranges. And crowning the tower is a rooftop terrace, complete with a built-in barbecue framed by a thick grass carpet and a picnic table. 'It's certainly not the traditional backyard you find in the suburbs,' says Thomas.

Although each facade is glazed, only a portion is transparent with opaque glass strategically placed both for sun protection and for privacy. There are also dark green panels that moderate both conditions, while picking up on the canopies of the treetops.

'We wanted to capitalise on the natural topography with a vertical building that would also take advantage of the views of the Catskill Mountains,' says Thomas. Glass has always been an important material in the practice's work. 'The nature of glass's reflectivity is one of its least explored features. The opaque glass we used here reflects, but also camouflages,' he adds. And given the dramatic cantilever of the living area, perched on a small footprint, the project required the input of skilful engineers, with the three-storey V-shaped column supporting the top floor.

From the outset, it was important for Thomas to provide small yet efficient bedrooms. This not only brings the family together but encourages them – as well as guests – to explore the majestic surrounds rather than spending too much time inside. The bunk room, located on the first floor, was regularly used by the couple's children and continues to be used by them and their friends. And while there are two additional bedrooms above to cater for the fluctuating numbers of people that stay, along with bathrooms for each one, it's the expansive living areas on the top floor that draws everyone together. 'The focus is more on the immediate view of the trees and the forest canopy,' says Thomas, who painted the ceilings, walls and floors completely white to disassociate the floor plan from the other surfaces. 'There's a sense of "floating" in the trees.'

Unlike many weekenders, in which the kitchen forms part of the open-plan living area, the kitchen in the Tower House is partially concealed behind the dining area – with sliding doors in cavity walls allowing the living areas to be closed down when not in use, thereby saving on heating.

To complement the clean and modernist aesthetic in the home, Thomas opted for classic contemporary furniture – a Knoll sofa and chairs such as the Womb Chair by Eero Saarinen, the latter in a vibrant orange that adds a splash of colour to the interior. 'Most of the art we've displayed on the walls is found objects,' says Thomas, pointing out a twisted branch found in the woods.

While many homes, particularly weekenders, feature kitchen and living areas on the top level of a house to maximise both views and light, it's unusual to see a home like this with the bedrooms located in the 'branch' of a structure. 'It's certainly not a traditional arrangement, and many have commented over the years that it was a crazy idea. But everyone who stays here reacts so strongly to the experience,' says Thomas.

At the moment, Thomas and his family are more than able to mount and descend the stairs. However, Thomas has the future in mind, allowing for the addition of an elevator when he or his family can't manage the stairs. 'I see this elevator as taking the form of a freestanding tower connected with small landings at each level.'

For Thomas, people often look at fairly obvious solutions to how they want to live and how a house is supposed to look. 'These preconceived ideas limit the opportunities to live and design differently,' says Thomas, who also recognised the importance of sustainability when the house was designed. This house, for example, was designed to have no heat in 80 per cent of the place when it's unoccupied. The living room, the stairs and the bedrooms come without water piping and are left unheated throughout winter. Only the core, which measures 4.3 x 4.3 m, is heated, with heavy insulation for the walls. In the summer, the stair provides the cooling strategy, with the hot air released through the roof hatch.

TIP

Design a house that responds to the way you want to live, rather than simply following the usual path of emulating what others do.

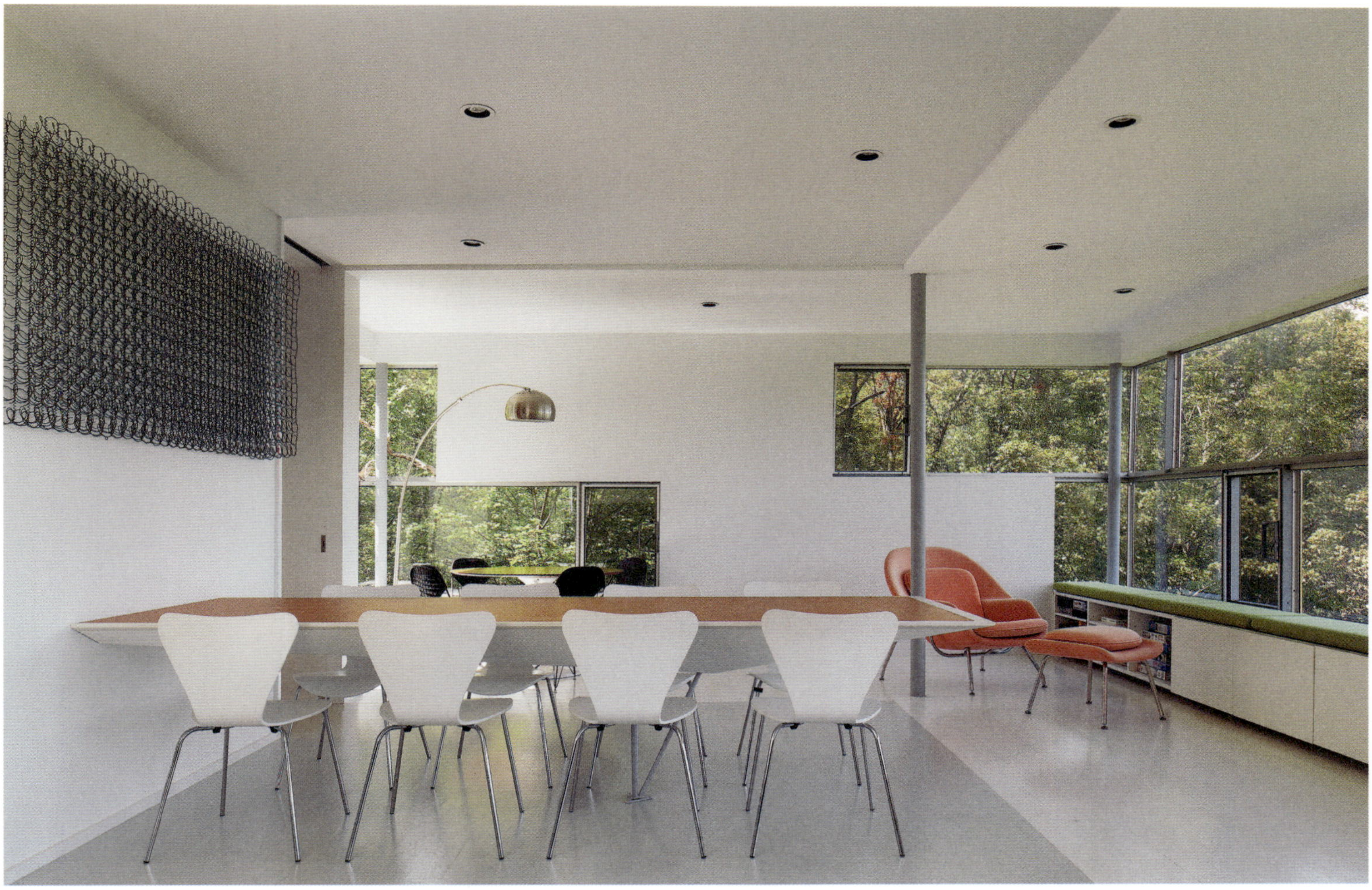

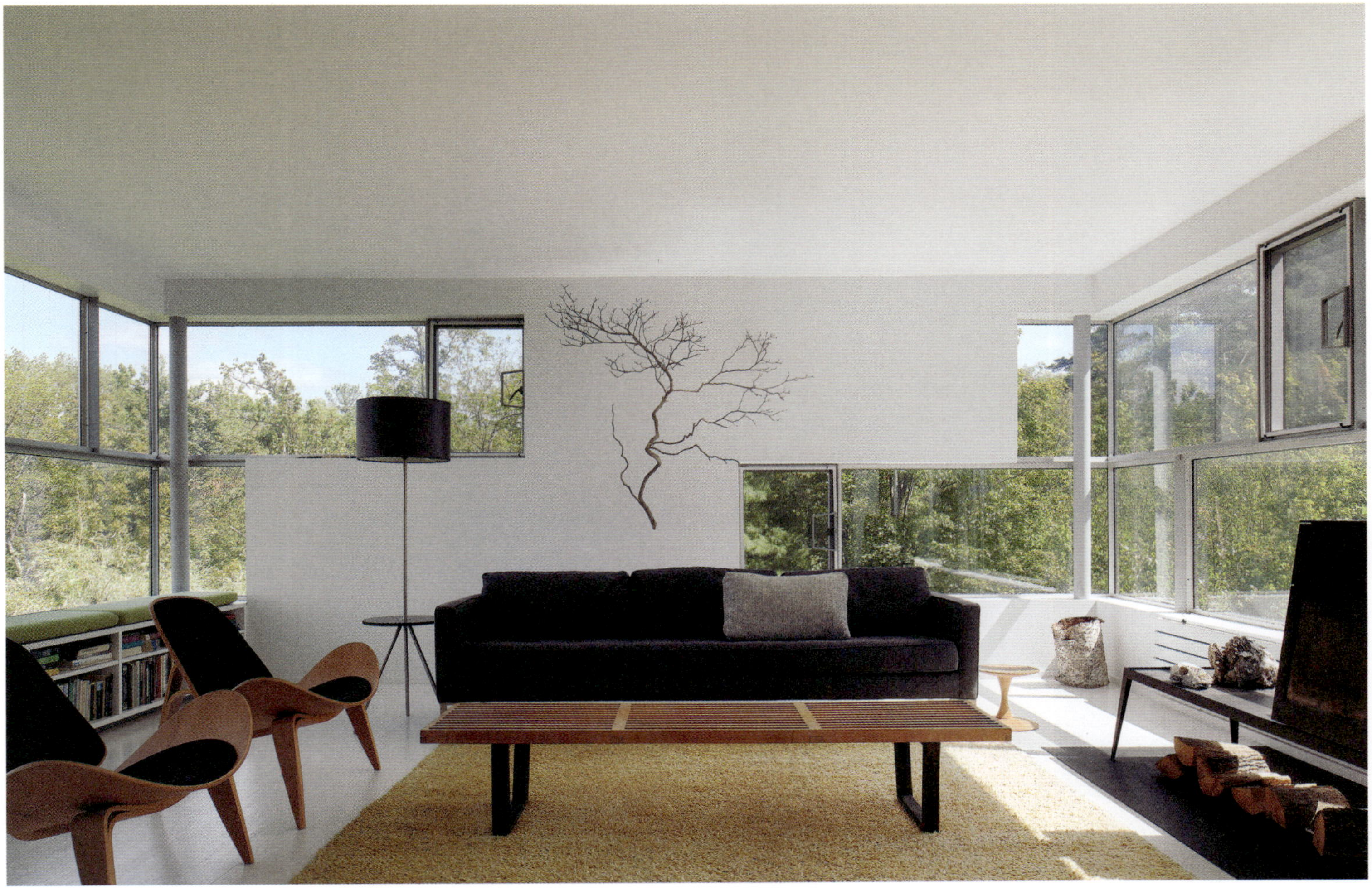

the architect's house

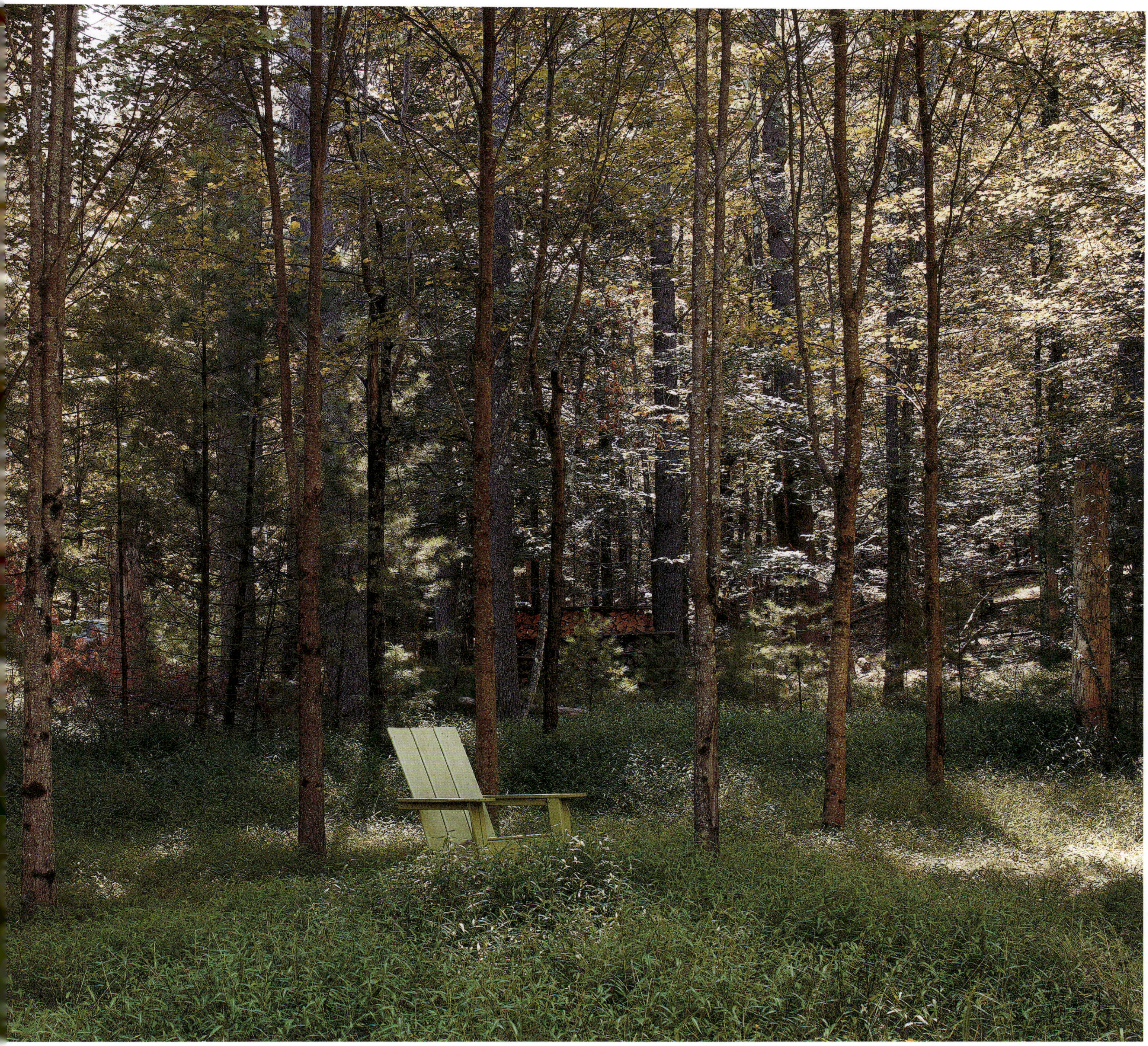

the architect's house

thomas gluck

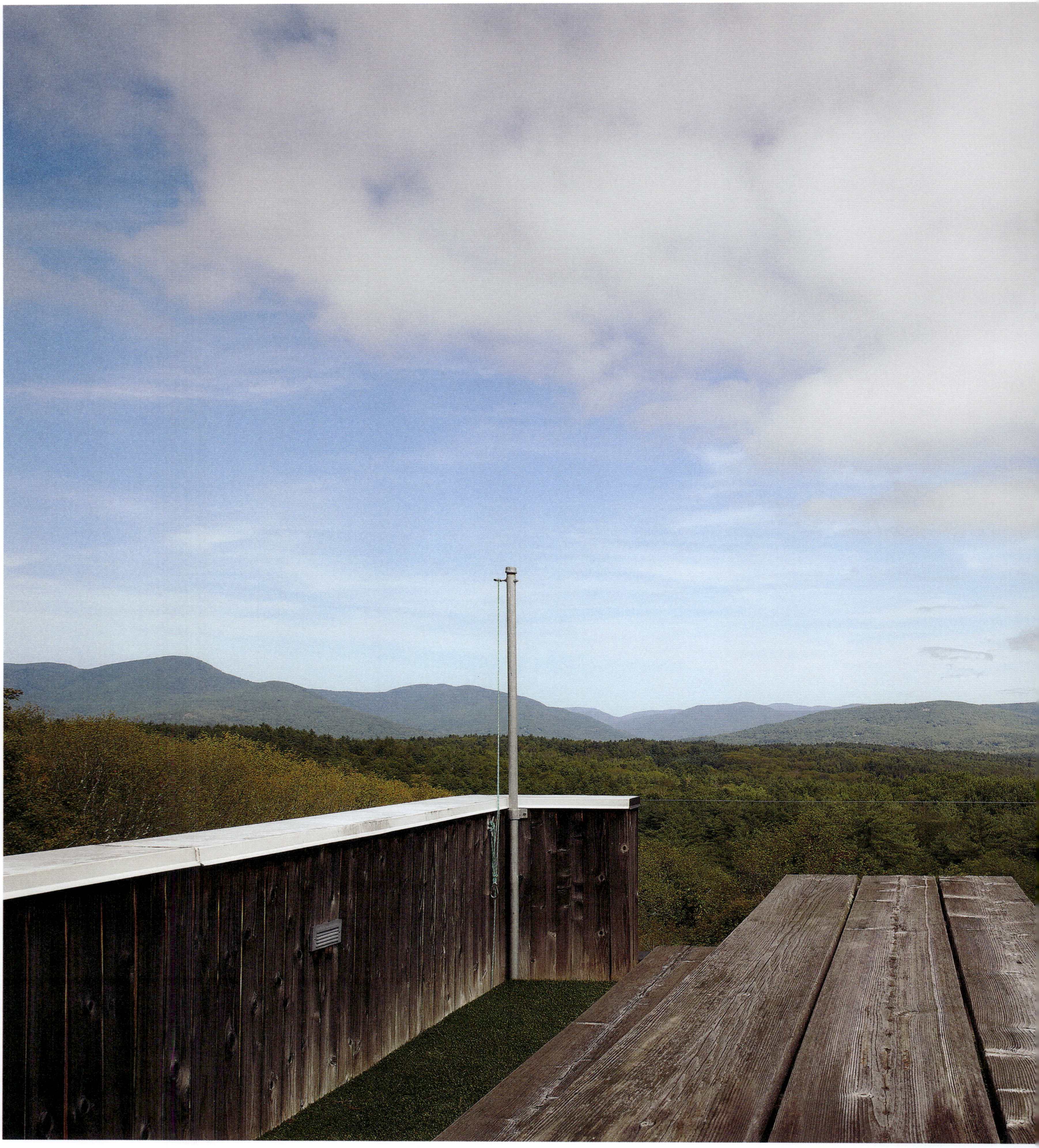

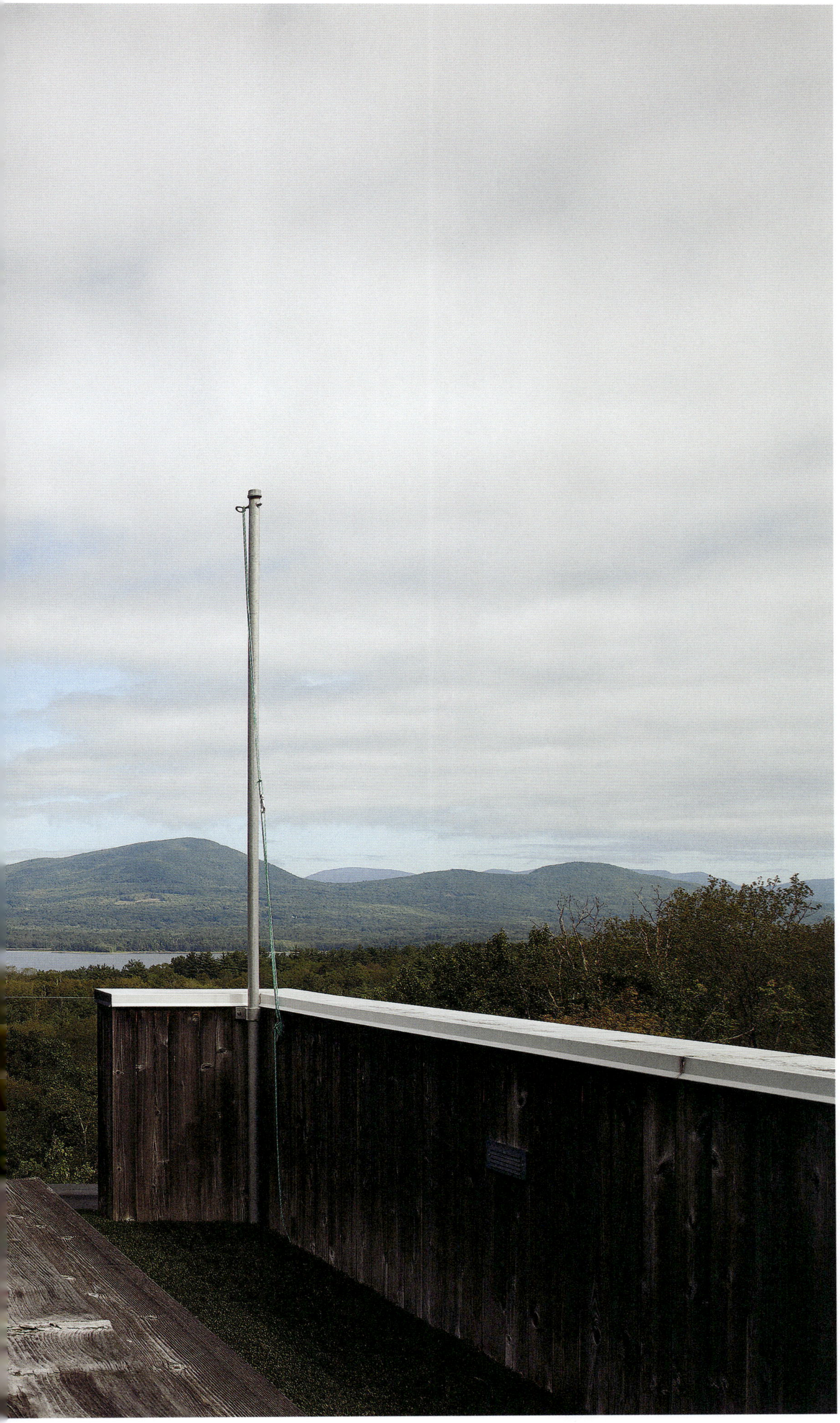

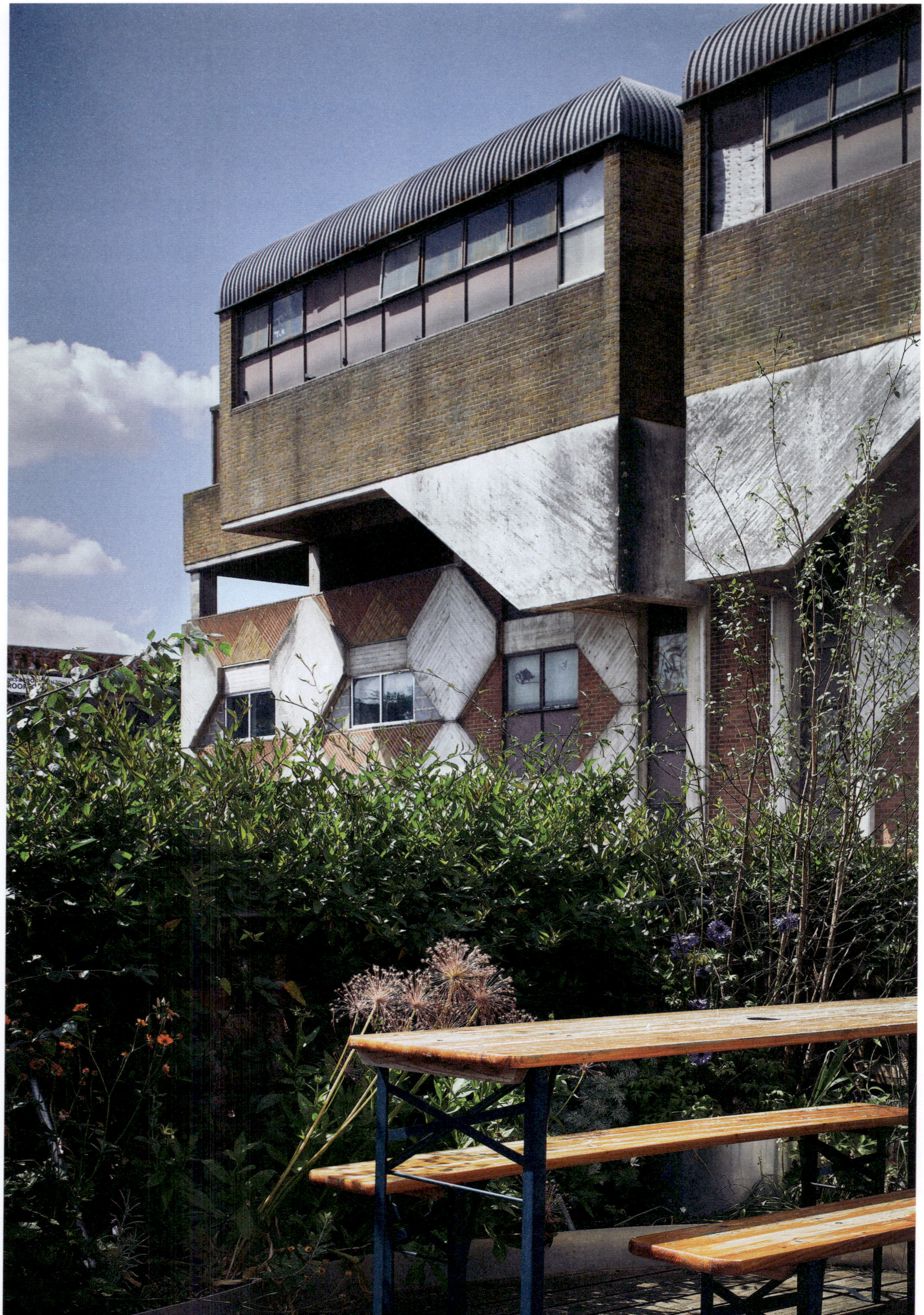

Percy Weston,
Co-Director, Surman Weston
PECKHAM HOUSE, LONDON

There was only one other party bidding for this curvaceous-edged corner block of land in Peckham when it came on to the market. Although vacant land so close to the city's centre is rare, the size of the plot (approximately 100 m^2), and the gas main located in the middle of the site, reduced its appeal. And while it's only a 10-minute train ride to London Bridge, the immediate surrounds, according to the architect Percy Weston, are 'somewhat chaotic', pointing out the seven-storey 1960s Brutalist car park directly opposite. The brick viaduct and the neighbouring 1970s brick terraces are also an acquired taste.

Working with Surman Weston's co-director, Tom Surman, who collaborated closely with Percy on designing and building the house, the starting point for the design was the gritty context. 'We needed to be able to reconcile all the different elements that surrounded the block,' says Percy, who explains the site's existence – a residual plot that was simply left over after the neighbouring 1970s brick terraces were completed. 'It was fairly unused land, adopted by the neighbour's pets as a toilet,' he adds.

While the Peckham house is on a relatively modest site, Percy was able to create a three-level home with small pocket-sized gardens at the front and back designed by Lidia D'Agostino, together with a rooftop terrace that benefits from views of the Shard and the city skyline. Featuring a hit-and-miss 'skin' of red bricks that references the load-bearing handmade stock bricks of the Victorian terrace and the machined brick in-fill panels of the car park, the house's bricks conceal the triple-glazed windows. However, the glazed greenhouse on the terrace peaks above the brick parapet and offers additional illumination to the street at night.

Designed for Percy, his artist partner Rhian and their four-year-old son Ellis, the move to the house was perfectly timed. The family was living in an apartment in nearby Deptford and required more space. 'That [apartment] was too small and we were keen to have a garden – not that we actually expected to have one so close to the city centre,' says Percy.

Designed over three levels, the floor plan comprises the living area at the front of the house, which benefits from a picture window to the garden, as well as attracting the afternoon light. The living area leads to a slightly lower-level dining and kitchen area (due to the gentle fall of the site), the latter discreetly placed to one side to ensure any clutter isn't visible. And picking up the cue from the shape of the plot, there's a curvaceous set of doors with a hint of Art Nouveau that leads from the dining area to the back garden. As with the Art Nouveau style, there's a sense of craft in Percy and Tom's design, which includes the exposed timber rafters made from English larch (sourced from Devon) and carefully placed brickwork. The change in level between the living area and the dining/kitchen area also created a change in the height of the ceilings, with the slightly lower ceiling in the lounge (2.7 m at its highest point) providing a sense of intimacy.

When it came to the kitchen and dining area, Percy selected terrazzo for the floors and a moisture-resistant MDF for the joinery, painted in an olive green. Offcuts from the English larch ceiling joists were used to make an end-grain timber floor in the living room.

Although the house is relatively modest in scale, it feels considerably more spacious due to the amount of storage. There's generous storage in the kitchen, as well in the front garden for bikes and other items not regularly used. And to ensure the family and guests don't need to climb the stairs for the bathroom, there's also a toilet concealed next to the stairs. The staircase is made of spruce pine and the cobalt-blue handrail is steel.

In spite of the size constraints, Percy and Tom were able to include two double bedrooms on the first floor, as well as a single. And rather than giving every bedroom an en suite, there's a shared bathroom. Although the ground level is where the family spends most of their time, it's the glasshouse on the roof terrace that is a focus, particularly for entertaining friends. Accessed via a sliding hatch at the top of the stairs, the glasshouse becomes another room. Although it's only 4.2 x 2.4 m in area, the off-the-shelf structure allows the outdoors to be used beyond the summer months. 'In winter, it's at least 5 to 10 degrees warmer than outside, which means you can still have breakfast here during the cooler months,' says Percy, who also designed the hatch that provides a source for releasing heat (the Venturi effect) during the summer months. Framed by garden beds, the terrace also benefits from a verdant outlook.

While the house is now well lived in, Percy remembers the difficulty in building during the Covid-19 pandemic. 'It did take a considerable amount of effort, with timing and with materials, as well as being a slight distraction for other staff in our office. And of course, there wasn't a 100 per cent certainty that we could actually build a house on the site, given that it was a plot without planning permission when purchased, complete with a gas main through the middle (the council assisted with its removal). But although building the house themselves, while obviously using contractors such as electricians and plumbers as well, was strenuous, there was the ability to make changes during the build. 'There were opportunities to change certain details,' he adds.

The house is certainly not 'precious' but it is filled with an eclectic assortment of furniture, objects and art. You definitely wouldn't say that the furniture is high design, but they're pieces he and Rhian have collected over the years. Some of the art is by Rhian, as well as by Percy's late mother, Nicolette Ismay, who was also an artist. What was residual land is now a family home that just feels relaxed and a place to enjoy. 'We're certainly not keen to fill it with designer furniture, designed within an "inch of its life". It's a place to use,' adds Percy.

TIPS

When you're thinking about which architect to use, you need to have a connection with that person, share similar values and importantly, know how you want to live.

It's important to get the planning right from the outset. And when you're working with smaller spaces, make sure there are still moments of spatial generosity.

Don't underestimate the cost of building. Be realistic with the timing and your budget.

percy weston

the architect's house

percy weston

the architect's house

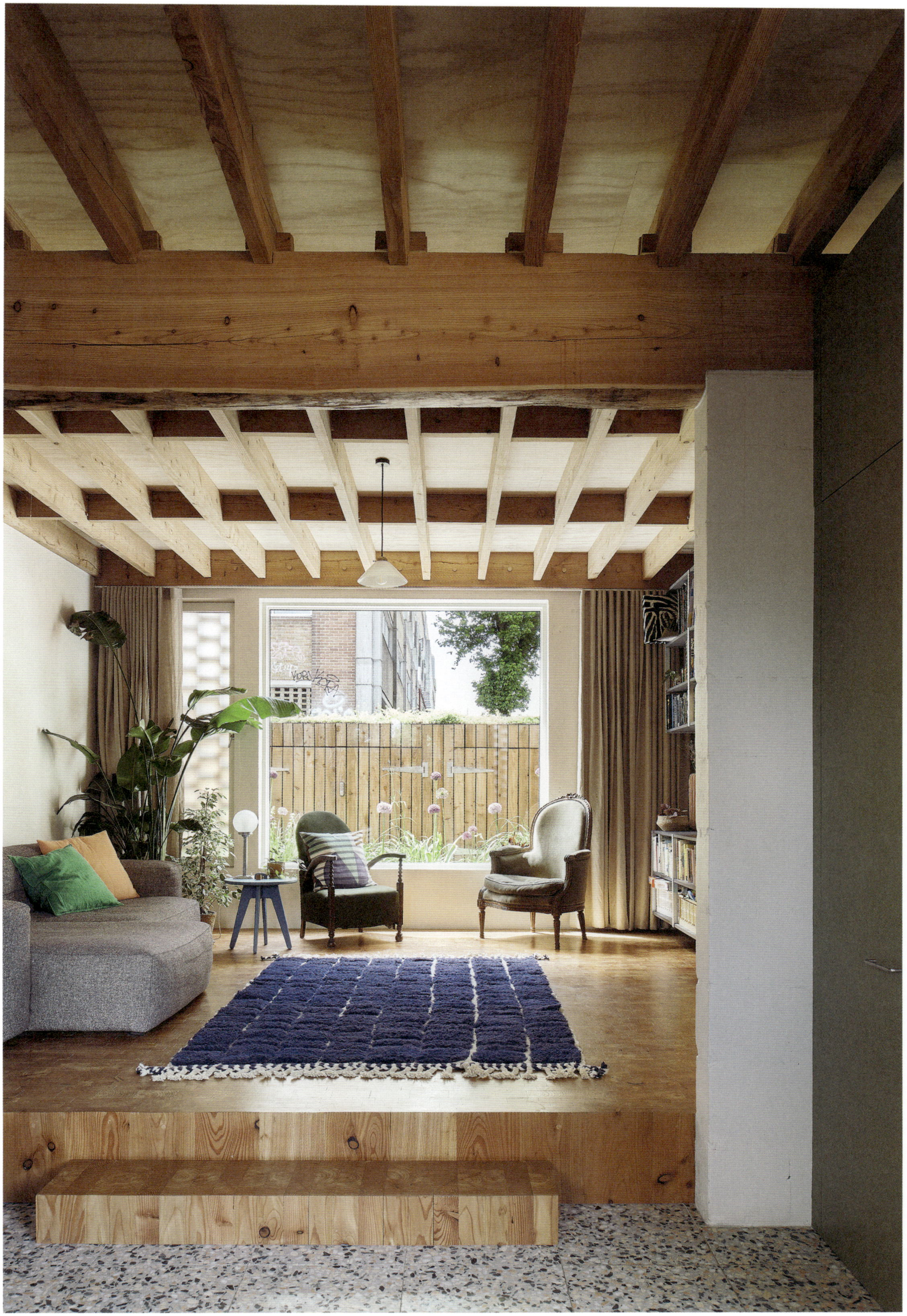

the architect's house

percy weston

the architect's house

percy weston

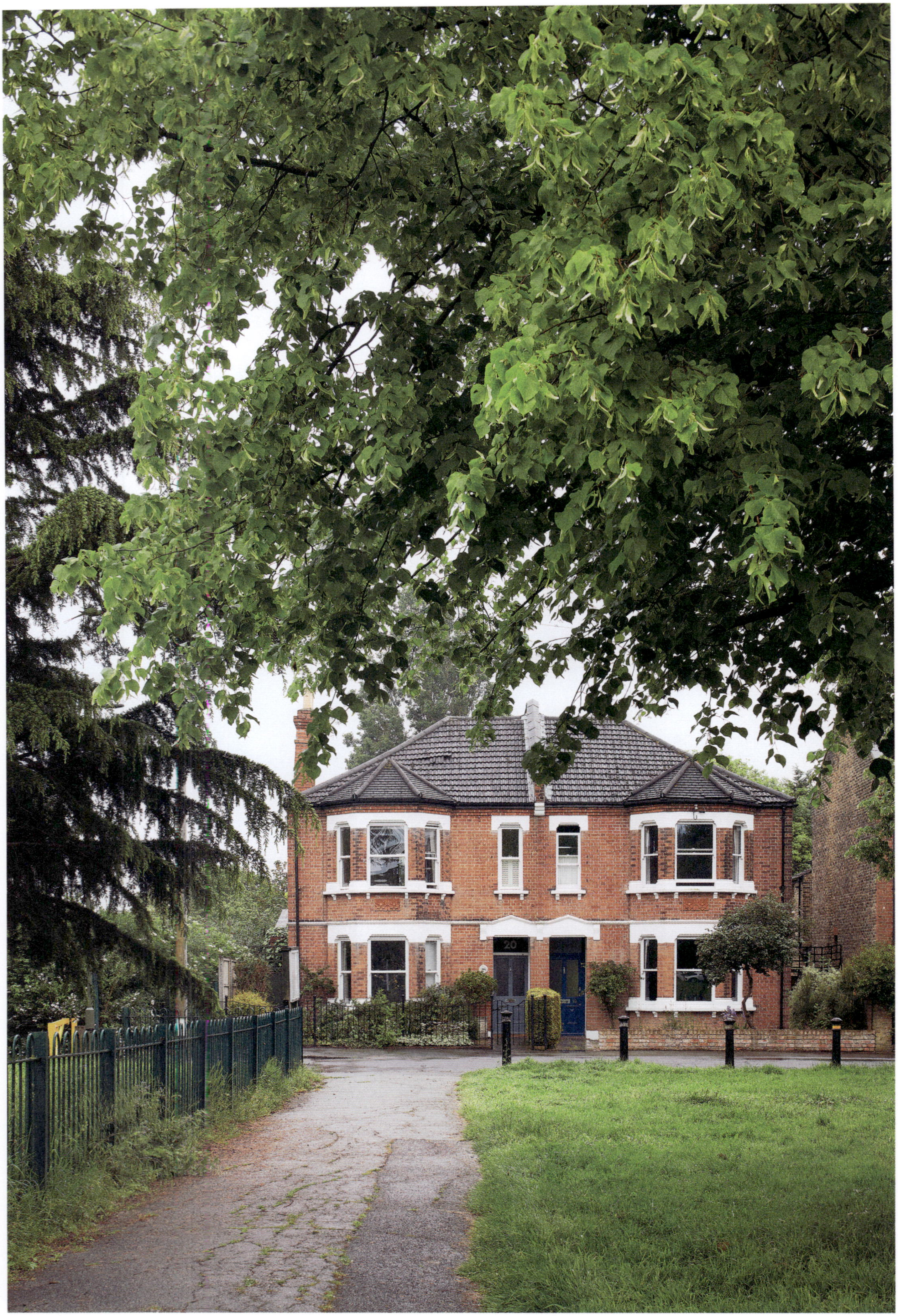
20

Mat Barnes, Director, CAN

SOUTH-EAST LONDON HOUSE, LONDON

Street appearances can be deceptive. This is certainly the case with this home located in Sydenham, in South London. The Edwardian semi-detached, with its traditional bay windows, conceals a vibrant contemporary home for a couple with three children and two cats. A tad Memphis and evocative of the deconstructivism popular in the early 1980s, it's a playful and joyous abode. 'Originally, my wife Laura and I were looking for a mid-20th-century home that would give us more space and a blank canvas to work with,' says architect Mat Barnes, director of CAN. 'Older properties tend to attract higher values in London, so it also made sense to focus on homes from the more recent past,' he adds.

However, the search for a new home led to a period home, circa 1905, that was far from a blank canvas ready to tweak and more of a crumbling pile. 'We heard about this house through Laura's best friend's parents, who live next door. It had been empty for six years and inherited from the original owners by their great niece, who was living in Poland and not interested in living in London,' says Mat, who was pleased it hadn't come on to the market. The price allowed the couple to think they could realise the home's potential.

While the 1950s home the couple left behind was serviceable, it was too small for their three children, Aurie, Sidney and Ivor. The run-down Edwardian house is larger in size and it came with more bedrooms and a back garden. A park directly opposite also afforded the couple greater outdoor space on their doorstep. The new location is also well connected to the centre of London via a number of transport links and is also just a 15-minute walk to Crystal Palace and its recreation grounds.

Mat and Laura's had been in the same family since the 1960s – the period that was initially their focus for a new abode. On first inspection, the house seemed fairly derelict

mat barnes

with no hot water taps no heating and windows that weren't properly sealed. The roof was also leaking. Even though it was less than ideal, the couple decided to live in it while their planning application to renovate and extend was being processed. 'It was never going to be a complete demolition, as the existing structure was solid and it would have been far more costly in terms of our budget and the carbon required to demolish and rebuild,' says Mat.

Given it was Mat and Laura's house and not designed for a client, Mat started on site as soon as planning permission was received, making decisions on the interior finishes and materials as the build progressed. The usual process with clients is to create a scheme before any building work commences.

One of the first moves was to open up the rabbit warren of rooms on the ground floor, which were extremely small. However, the front room, with its bay window, was retained and painted in a deep midnight blue. Complete with the original fireplace and decorative plaster wall sconces, this enclosed living room, inspired by the Sir John Soane Museum house in London, is the perfect retreat at the end of the day when young children have gone to bed. However, past the living room and entry, with its original turned timber staircase, the house takes on a strong contemporary aesthetic.

A change in level delineates the kitchen and dining area, with the first few stairs clad in tiles spelling out the phrase 'waste not want not' – a phrase that Mat's grandmother often cited – and there's also a small step down to the informal living area, which is framed on either side by deconstructed brick walls and bright red steel beams that traverse the ceilings. 'The house was quite plain in character, void of most of its period details; this really allowed us to go quite wild with the interiors.' Mat referenced a number of buildings and places to produce the design, including the cobalt blue trusses at the iconic Hopkins House in Hampstead Heath, designed by Michael and Patty Hopkins, and the stage set of mountains at Disneyland, which informed the form of the parapet on the rear extension. Made from foamed aluminium, there's a certain fragility to the mountainous silhouette. 'The Matterhorn Bobsleds ride at Disneyland, with its surrealistic skeletal frame, was at the forefront of my mind during construction,' says Mat. Like Disneyland's Matterhorn, Mat was keen to emphasise its fakeness and also distort its scale – a necessity given the width of the Edwardian semi-detached house.

Once the Matterhorn parapet was in place, the themes of the landscape developed: the finish for the dining table was conceived as a lake, and a cave-like treatment was given to the concrete walls. Mat disparagingly refers to the contemporary addition as an 'antithesis' to the rest of the house: 'worthless architectural plaster elements arranged on the walls, riffing on the arrangement of objects at the Soane's Museum.' However, unlike the Soane house – also seen as one of the first modernist homes – with its 'floating' dome in the dining room, this house features a number of sustainable materials, such as the unusual recycled chopping boards and milk bottle tops used for the kitchen joinery. 'We reused much of the waste material from the original house for the renovation,' says Mat, who reused the offcuts from the kitchen cabinetry as facings for the new concrete lintels above the windows on the existing house.

Art is also integral to the house. The arrows, by artist Liam Fallon, are displayed on the kitchen wall connecting the open-plan spaces. Other works by Jeremy Deller, one titled 'I Blame the Internet' and another 'Thank God for Immigrants', shows the family's concern both for technology and broader society.

For Mat, whose practice includes a fair dose of residential work, the challenge for his own house was to keep the budget in check while pushing the design and the materials used. Although the children each have their own bedroom, the family tends to gravitate to the kitchen and informal living areas that connect to the back garden. And even though renovating a house normally comes with creating a new garden, the previous owners had gone to some length to develop one, with a number of mature trees, including fruit trees.

TIPS

I would try and make a lot of the interior design decisions on site. Materials, textures and colours look very different in different lights and there's nothing like seeing them in situ to help you make the decision.

Allow your house to be as unique as you and your tastes. Many people go for the latest contemporary style instead of allowing themselves to design a house that truly captures their taste and personality.

As with most architects who design their own home, there are always a few things on the wish list that didn't eventuate. Mat would love to have included a green roof behind the mountain and there are plans to create more colour, texture and interest in the four bedrooms (including the main bedroom) upstairs. 'But these things can be done in a more leisurely manner. There's no rush,' adds Mat.

the architect's house

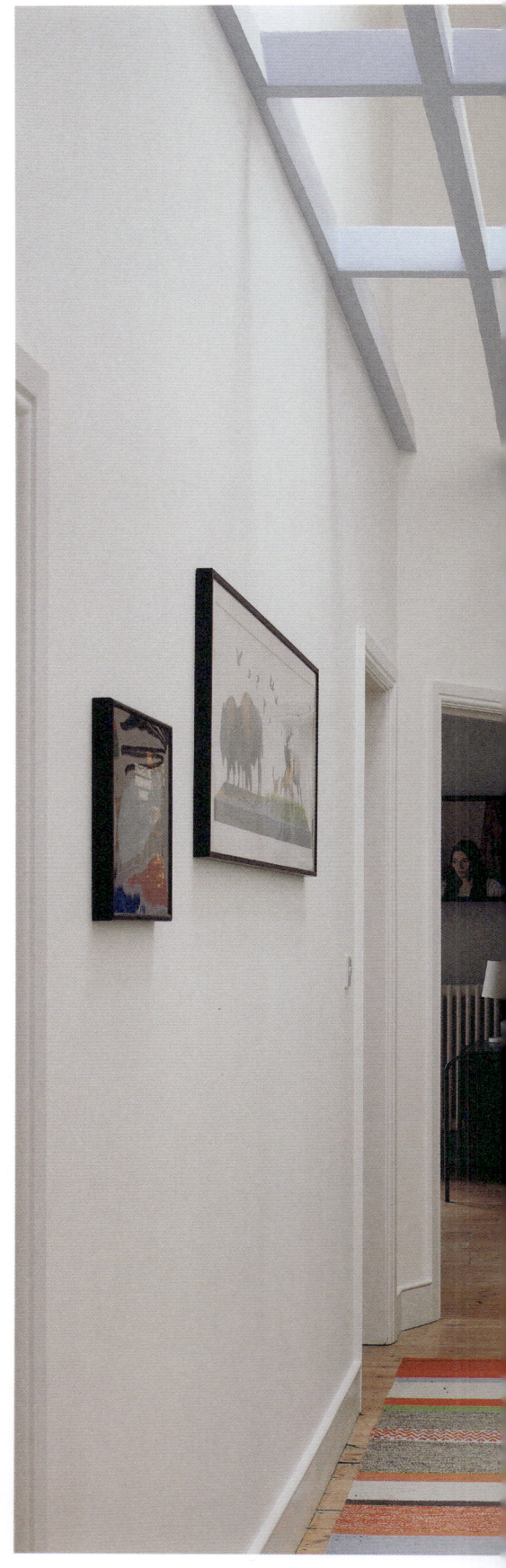

mat barnes 121

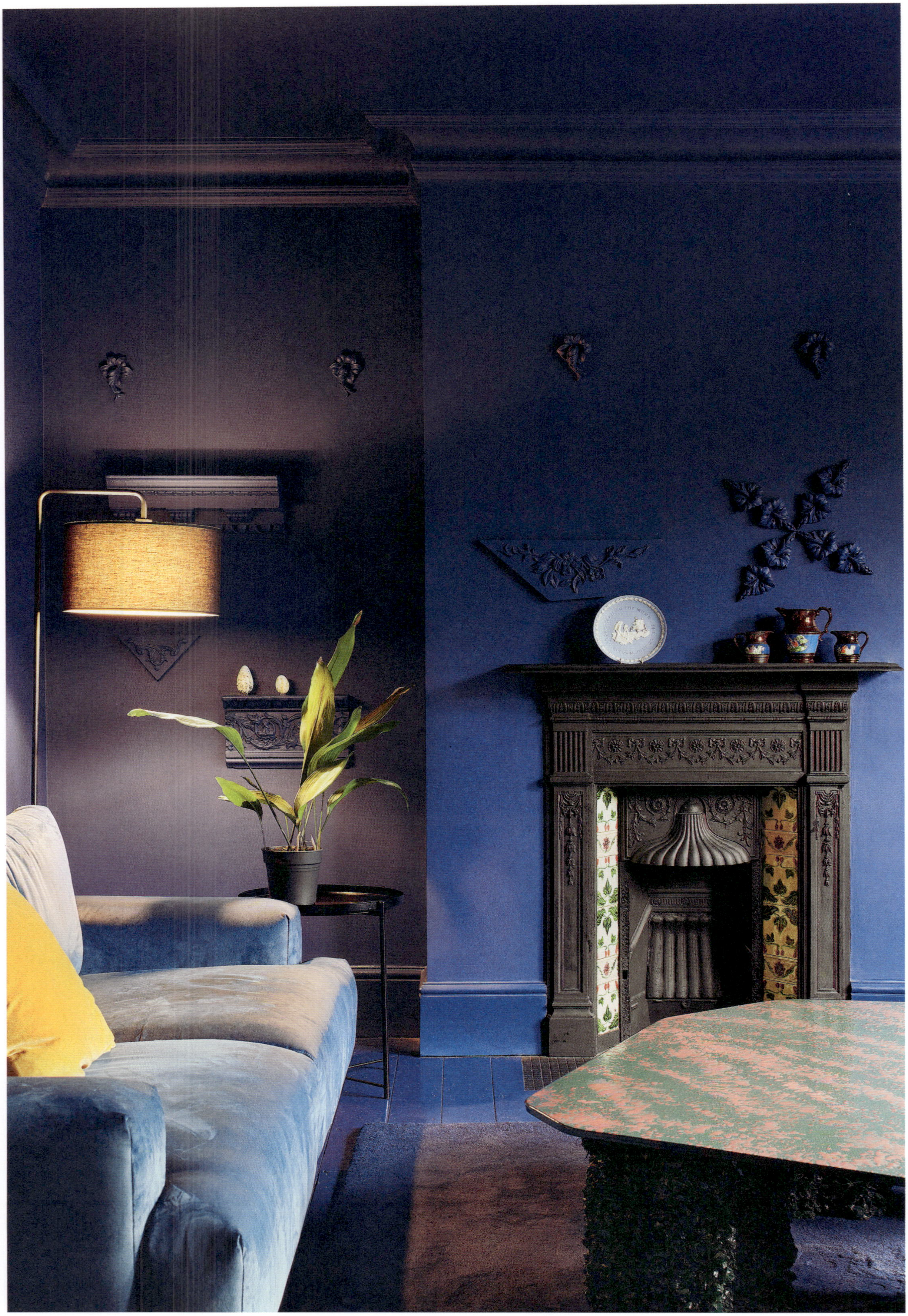

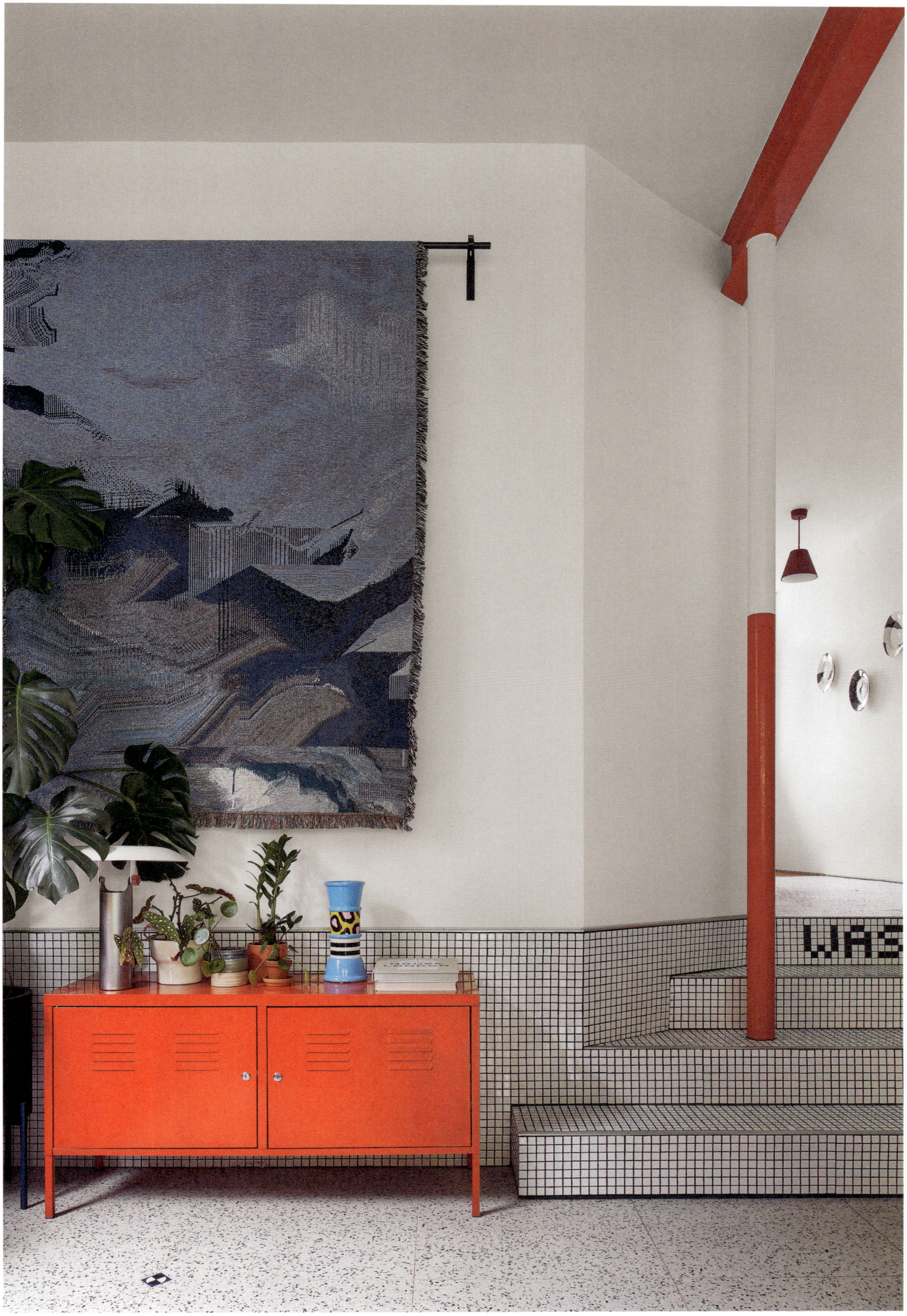
WAS

the architect's house

mat barnes

the architect's house

mat barnes

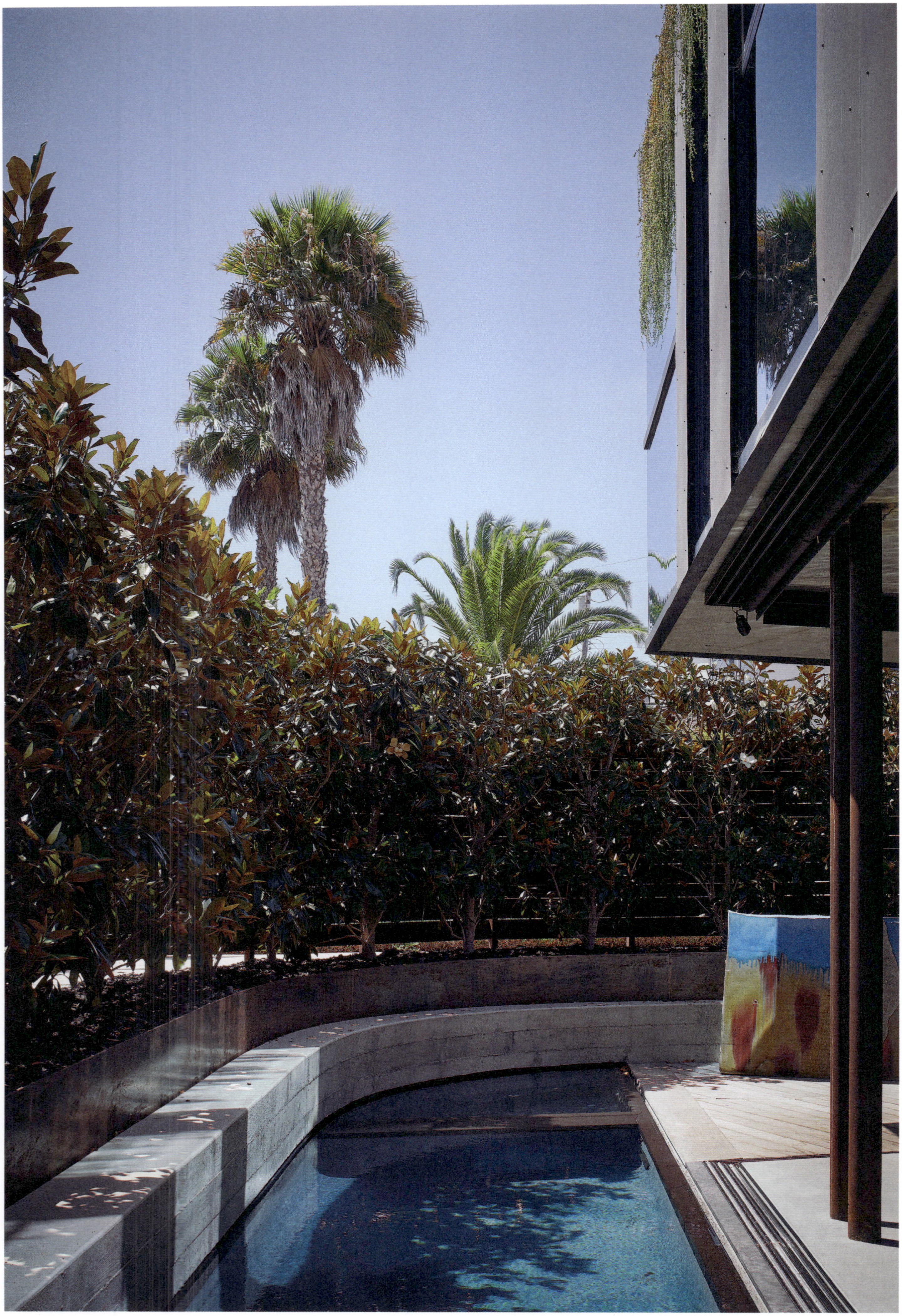

Matthew Royce, Director, M Royce Architecture
VENICE BEACH HOUSE, LOS ANGELES

Venice Beach in Los Angeles is popular with both locals and tourists. Known for its surf culture and bohemian spirit, this hip neighbourhood is dotted with cafés, restaurants and bars. It's also home to architect Matthew Royce, director of M Royce Architecture, and his wife, Farnaz Azmoodeh. A landmark home on its trianglar-shaped site, it's also an attraction for architectural buffs.

Matthew had previously rented various apartments around Los Angeles and the opportunity to build his own home from scratch was 'the dream of any ambitious architect'. For Matthew, Venice Beach was always on his wish list. 'It's one of the most walkable and charming neighbourhoods in Los Angeles. It's only a 20-minute walk to my office and I'm continually bumping into friends and neighbours, which is unusual given that the city is so car-centric.' And while cars pass by the house, there are still signs of the historic streetcar line that once circled the site from the early- to mid-20th century.

Formerly, the site was a fairly rudimentary single-storey house which was demolished to make way for this four-level home with a separate guest house (the couple regularly have friends and family to stay). Constructed in board-formed concrete, glass and raw copper, its inspiration came from a number of architects, including Peter Zumthor, Tadao Ando, Le Corbusier and Louis Kahn. The concrete creates a solid base for the home, providing an anchor to the site, with the structural steel allowing for a sense of lightness on the floor plates located above. The copper panels used for the facade, which will patina in time (turning to shades of brown and green), create privacy where needed. 'The way these architects were able to use natural materials and concrete in such a strong and tectonic way has always been a huge influence on my work,' says Matthew.

Designed over four levels, the triangular-home features a guest bedroom suite/multi-functional space at basement level; it's the perfect place to escape to when the peak of summer comes around. Directly above is a kitchen, dining and living area, a tad lower than ground level to create the effect of a sunken lounge, and above is the main bedroom suite with a generous en suite and a walk-in dressing area. At the top of the 'pile' is another bedroom, together with an en suite that leads to a triangular-shaped terrace. Approximately 280 m² in area, with a separate guest house of 140 m² and likened to driftwood due to its unusual timber construction, the property is a generous spread in one of the city's most coveted neighbourhoods.

Rather than creating traditional rooms designed for different purposes, the Venice Beach house was conceived as a series of distinct vertical levels with very few doors. The basement, for example, has large sliding glass doors that open to the views of the sky, with a waterfall creating passive cooling on warmer summer days. There's also a sense of intimacy in the kitchen/living area, allowing for privacy in what is a particularly prominent corner. The adjacent swimming pool also provides for thermal control, with moisture from the water filtering to the indoor spaces. And on the upper levels, the sleeping quarters, as well as being spaces to relax in, create a meditative atmosphere.

With its many sculptural pieces of furniture, objects and art, the house has a gallery-like feel. 'A number of the works are from Iran, where my wife comes from,' says Matthew, pointing out a number of hanging sculptures by Ruth Asawa, an American artist of Japanese heritage who was well known for her woven metal pieces. These complement the architecture, their light and shadows forming patterns on the home's many concrete surfaces, as does the stunning array of colourful concrete and ceramic sculptures by South Korean artist, Lee Hun Chung. Matthew and Farnaz also appreciate furniture and design by some of the most illustrious creatives from the 20th century. Beside the kitchen bench is a sculptural, almost origami-shaped steel armchair designed by Bruce Gray (1993); and in the main bedroom, there's a customised geometric rug (1926) by textile designer Anni Albers who was affiliated with the Bauhaus school in Germany. There's also an armchair designed by Josef Hoffmann at the start of the 20th century. Each piece has been thoughtfully placed to give it sufficient 'breathing space' to be fully circled and appreciated, not dissimilar to sculpture.

While it was relatively easy to curate the furniture and art, Matthew's biggest challenges were designing around the tight triangular shape of the property and constructing a basement – the latter was a huge engineering problem that needed to be solved, made more difficult with the site's location on a prominent corner that also required a strong traffic management plan. 'These issues were difficult but they resulted in the uniqueness of the design concept,' he says.

The opportunity for an architect to design their own house also comes with the ability to experiment, with some ideas able to be put forward to future clients. The swimming pool, for example, is level with the interior floor – achieved through a precisely engineered hidden stainless-steel structure that allows for the pool's infinity edge. And to fit the legally mandated two covered car-parking spots in the basement, Matthew used a mechanical lift system with one spot situated above the other. There are also solar glass vacuum tubes located on the roof that provide hot water to a storage tank, which is then directed to the kitchen and bathrooms before arriving at the swimming pool for heating. This ability to experiment can also be seen with the over-scaled aircraft hangar door that was designed for the living area of the guest house.

Although there are numerous spaces to which the couple tend to gravitate, Matthew singles out the curved bathroom located on the top level. 'It's reminiscent of a space you might see in a gallery. The small skylight at the core creates a Pantheon-like feel. It's extremely quiet and private and the natural light is sublime at different times of day,' says Matthew, who is also mindful of the home's changes in mood depending on the time of the day, the season and the weather. 'Each level offers different views, temperatures, art and light. On extremely hot days, there's nothing more pleasurable than reading a book in the basement,' adds Matthew, pointing out the Hollywood Hills from the rooftop terrace.

TIPS

It's as essential to work with nature, the site and the views as it is to take into account the quality of the light and also the climate. Often people want to impose their own vision on the land and ignore the qualities of that specific place.

It's important to choose materials with a specific design strategy in mind, rather than just being driven by taste. Many homeowners tell me they like wood or the colour blue for example, but my question is always why? Every design choice should strengthen and enhance the narrative.

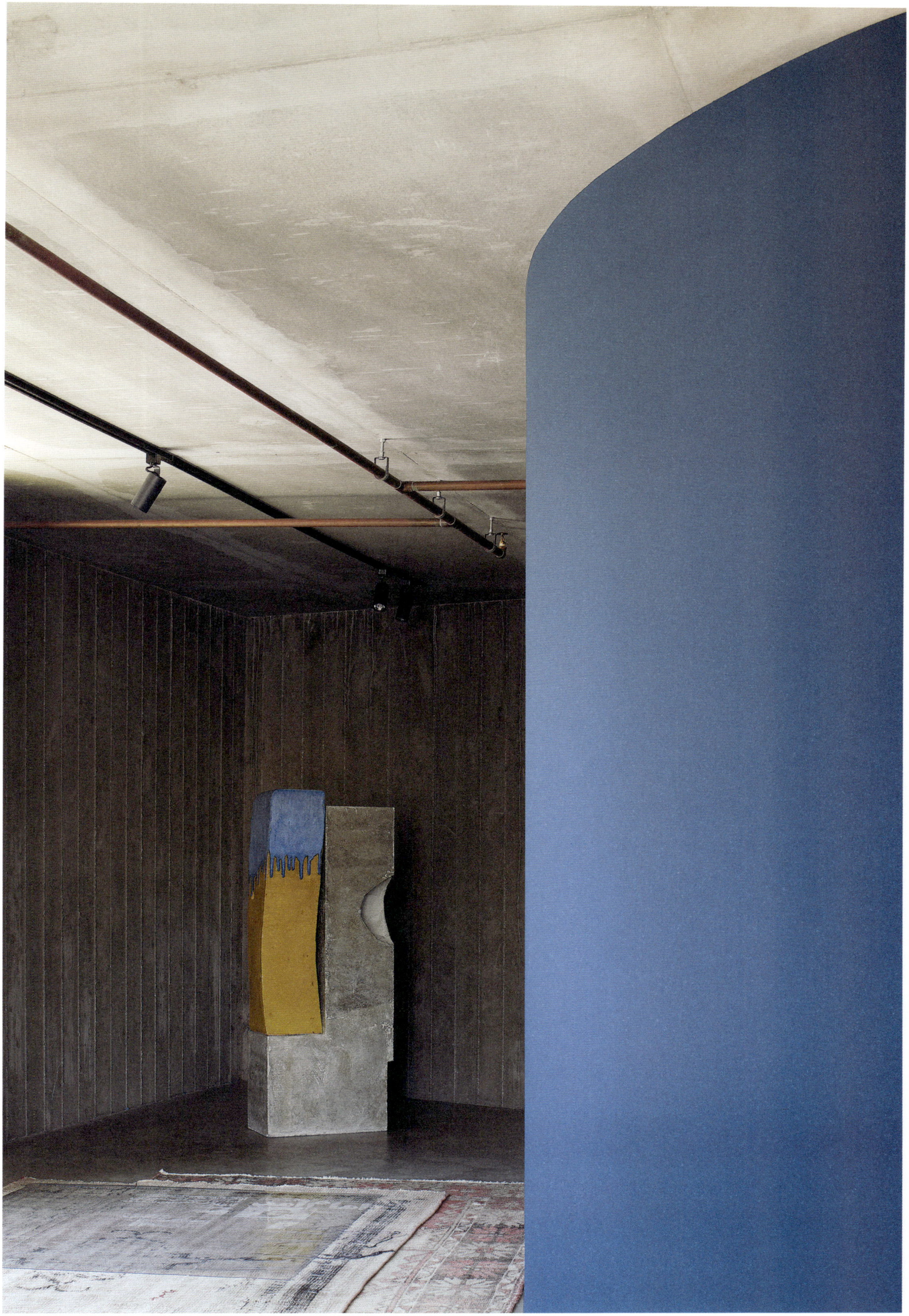

the architect's house

matthew royce

the architect's house

matthew royce

136 the architect's house

matthew royce

the architect's house

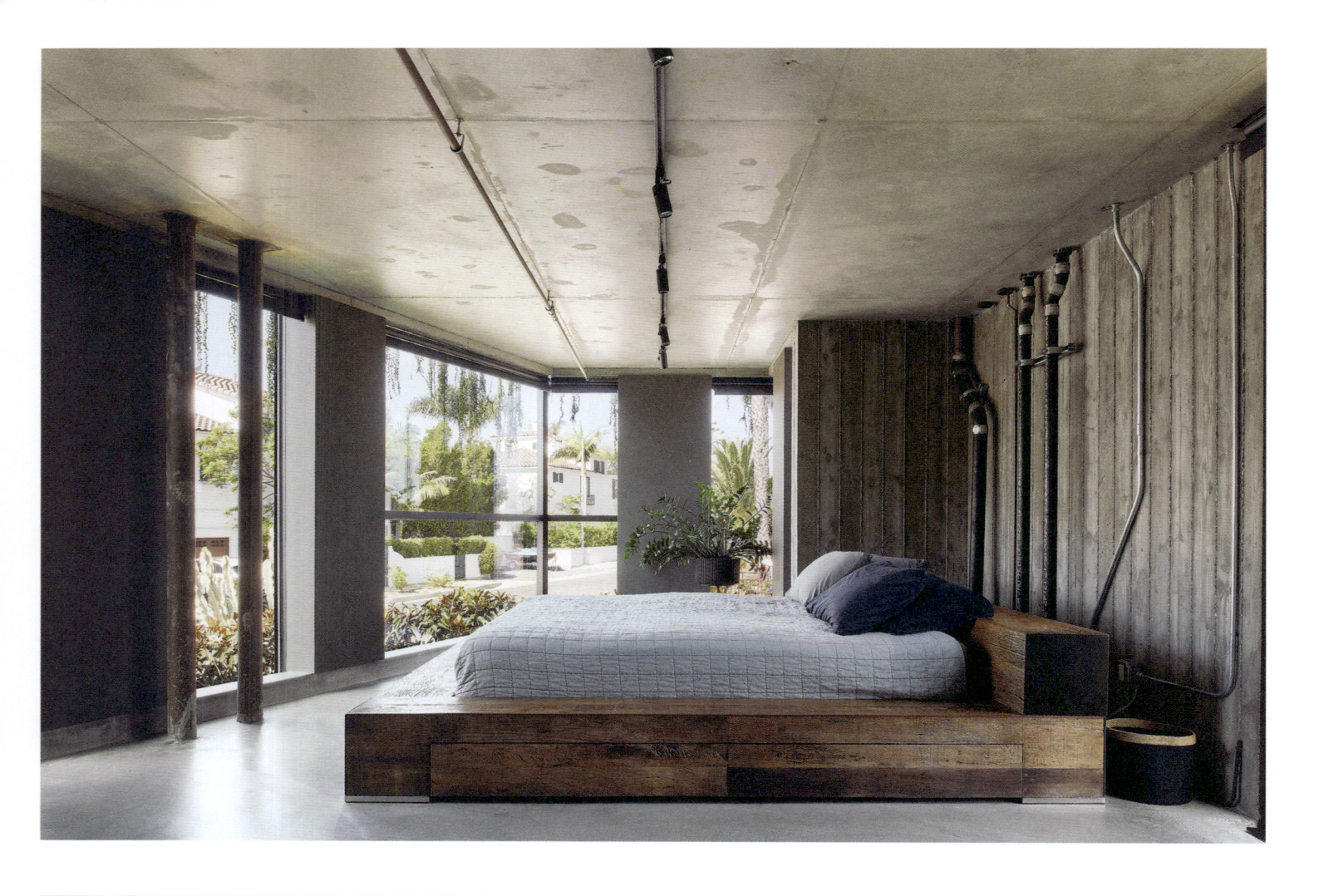

matthew royce

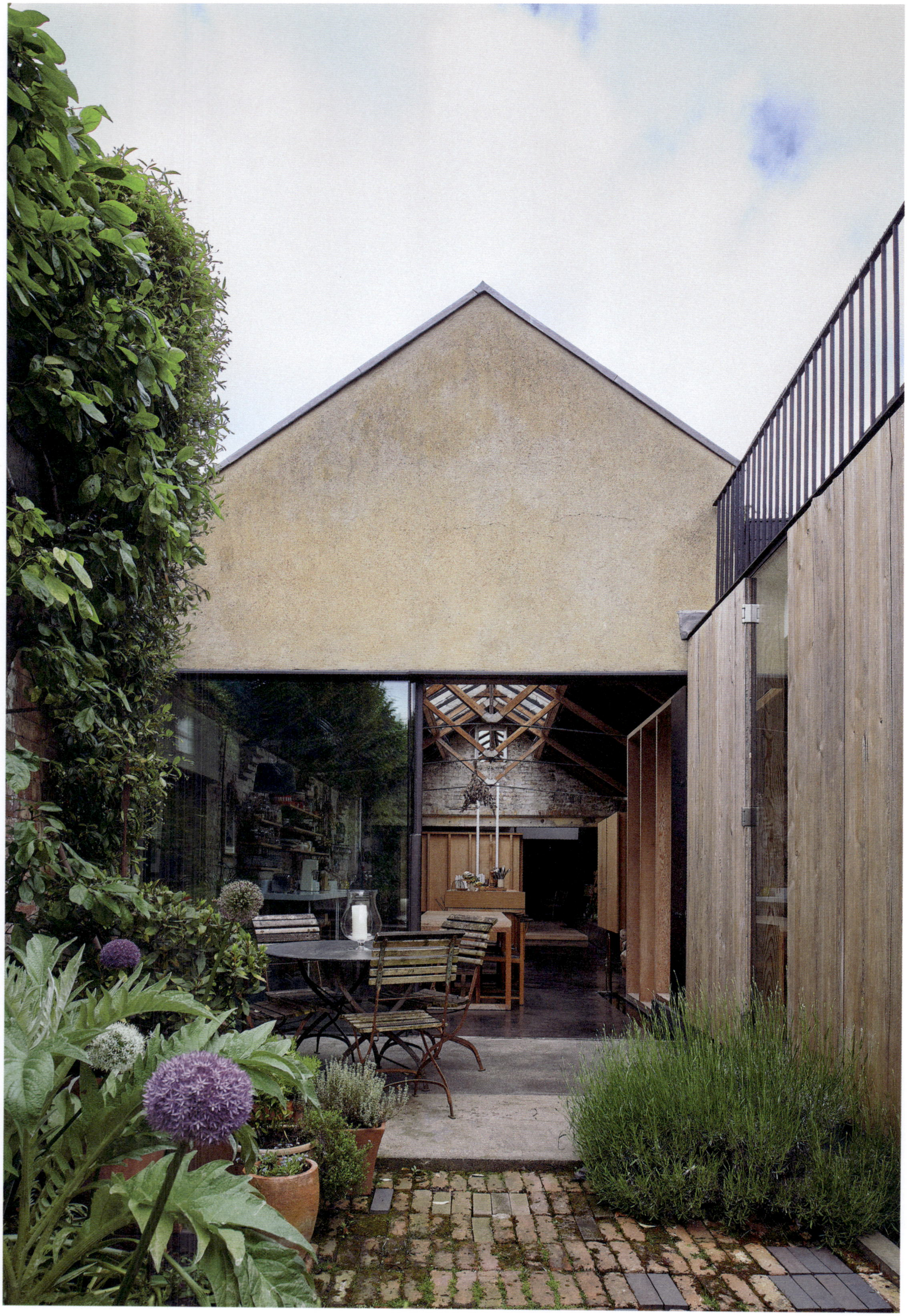

Jonathan Tuckey, Director, Tuckey Design Studio

COLLAGE HOUSE, QUEEN'S PARK, LONDON

For a house that's over 20 years old, there's something quite timeless about this warehouse conversion. The home's rustic aesthetic has become a strong design direction in the last five years, with the movement towards recycling and revealing, rather than concealing, a building's history. But owner Jonathan Tuckey, director of Tuckey Design Studio, certainly wasn't looking into his crystal ball at the time. It was the opportunity of taking an old building and creating a new lease of life for it – while creating a home in the process – that drew him to it. 'At the time, we were searching for a building that was unloved, and one where we could see its potential. But we were also looking for a non-residential building which we could have some fun with and adapt into a truly unique and bespoke home,' says Jonathan.

One of the reasons for searching for a non-residential building was financial: more space could be available for the budget. It might also provide a blank canvas, allowing for a 'collage' – hence the name – to express the family's values and the way they wanted to live; for it to be a place to grow with them over time. Part of the appeal of this 19th century warehouse (circa 1870) was also its anonymity at street level. It is set behind an unassuming entranceway that allowed Jonathan to create an element of surprise once past the threshold.

This area of London also becomes more animated behind some of its historic facades thanks to a combination of residential and commercial activities, from organ making, fashion design and second-hand furniture dealing to recording studios and garages. Jonathan's home backs on to a primary school, from which the sound of children increases during the lunchtime period. A large canteen-style door in the rear fence can be closed for complete privacy or left open to see and hear the children at play. 'There are always ebbs and flows of intense noise during playtime, and then silence,' he says.

Originally built as a commercial laundry that cleaned sheets and clothing for some of the city's well-heeled, there are numerous reminders of its former status. Later, the building was transformed into a metal workshop that fabricated stainless steel. During this stage of the building's evolution, the entire site was roofed over to become an entirely enclosed space. When Jonathan purchased the property, he simply cleared it out and used it as workshops, studios and storage until a plan to convert it into a home was realised with the appropriate planning permission. He converted part of the space into an office to allow him to be onsite during the design and build phases. At that time, he also hosted an exhibition, as well as a party or two, to see how people could use the space.

Given it was a commercial rather than a residential building, there was no insulation and it had no rooms nor any outdoor space. There were no windows and no visible entrance. While many now would see the opportunities, 20 years ago, few, if any, would have been brave enough to take on such a project. 'We didn't see the task as riddled with problems, rather as an opportunity to devise an internal configuration with a domestic focus,' says Jonathan, who wanted to express his own aesthetic as much as adapting and reusing existing materials.

While he didn't have a distinct vision from the outset of what the building would look like as a house, Jonathan was drawn to the courtyard-style houses found in southern Europe and North Africa – with a procession of spaces centred around an external living room. Jonathan was also drawn to a sparse palette of materials, as used by Sigrud Lewerentz, a leading Scandinavian architect from the 20th century, known for employing materials such as beech plywood, Douglas fir, brick and copper pipework. 'I was also thinking about the Katsura Imperial Villa in Japan, as well as the rooftops in the film *Mary Poppins*,' adds Jonathan.

The house not only has fluid and interconnected spaces, but also separate rooms, such as bedrooms and bathrooms. At ground level are the living area, the open-plan kitchen and dining area and, to one side, overlooking the courtyard garden, two bedrooms with a shared bathroom for the children. Later, a 'teenager' roof terrace was added to allow them to entertain their friends. And more recently, as the children started their university years and moved out, this space has morphed into one bedroom and two studies.

The kitchen and living areas feature exposed brick walls that act as a backdrop for art, memorabilia and showcasing some of the building's 'scars' or history. 'These original materials were elemental in the design, having a wonderful patina,' says Jonathan, who enjoys pointing out the various markings. To complement the past, Tuckey Design Studio sourced a new version of the original brick. These new bricks were made by Blockeys, with a beech plywood used for the interior and exterior along with black pigmented concrete. 'In time, both the new and old materials have been inexorably bound together,' he adds. Other materials, such as the vitreous enamelled steel which was used for the kitchen counter and also for the entrance, was produced by enamellers located on the Isle of Wight who make all of the London Underground signage. Two new chimneys were also added, memories of something that could have been but never was.

While there were structural issues to address, there were also challenges with the site itself: landlocked and hemmed in on all sides by neighbouring terraces, the primary school directly behind and a number of walls that were completely void of any windows. But on the plus side, the building's pitched roof, with its central skylight and timber trusses, remains an important feature of the home. And on what was previously an enclosed property there's now a garden with a reflective pool that's the focus of the living areas. 'I love the fact that all the rooms are orientated towards the garden, whether it's the kitchen or most of the bedrooms – particularly in summer,' says Jonathan, whose focus in winter is on listening to music, reading and spending time around the kitchen bench. 'Even towards nightfall, the light and atmosphere feel quite special.'

TIPS

People forget that what architects do is not the foreground but the backdrop.

A house is for living in, for evolving in; it's a place to accommodate the objects and clutter of day-to-day life.

the architect's house

jonathan tuckey

the architect's house

jonathan tuckey

the architect's house

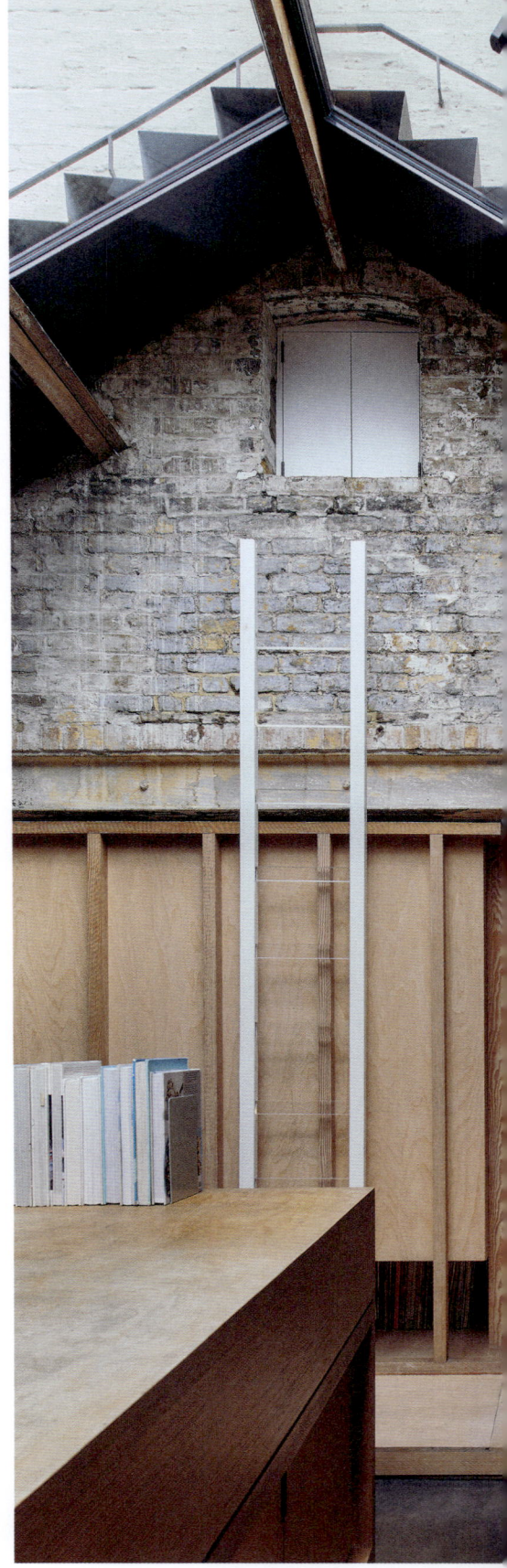

jonathan tuckey

the architect's house

jonathan tuckey

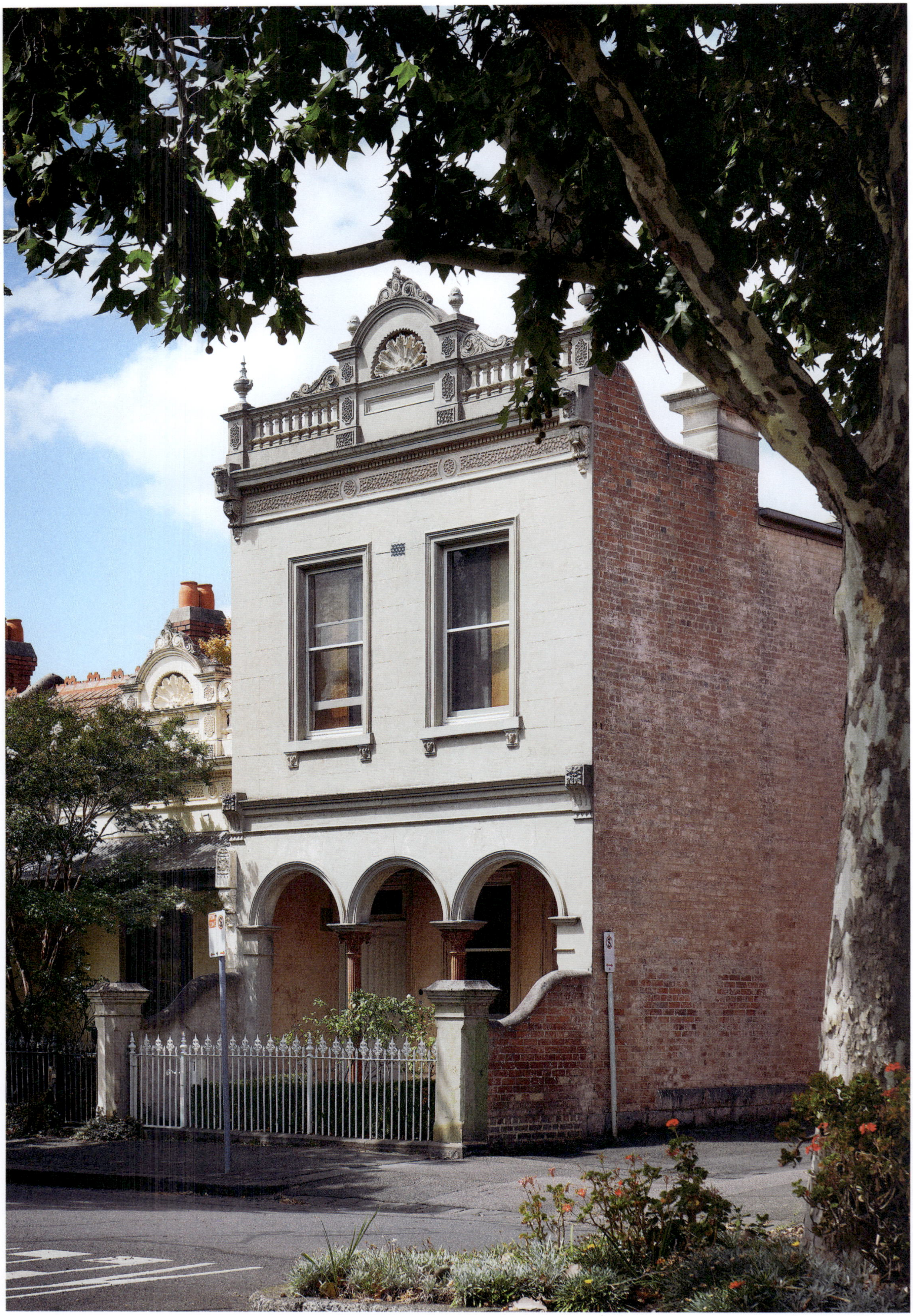

Robert Simeoni, Director, Robert Simeoni Architects

CARLTON NORTH, MELBOURNE

'Sombre Italianate' is how architect Robert Simeoni describes his late-Victorian house (circa 1888) on a heritage-listed street in the inner-city Melbourne suburb Carlton North. Artisans have restored the decorative and slightly weathered facade, its distinctive arched columns now displaying a rich patina. 'The process of restoring the house was a very honest one. We wanted to ensure that the house was not only restored, but the sense of the spirit of the house remained,' says Robert, who lives in the house with his wife Sharon and their son Roby.

Robert first stumbled on the house a few years ago. While the heritage-listed street was an attraction, finding a house virtually in its original condition is rare, particularly as most period homes in the neighbourhood have been 'renovated'. 'The house had only been lightly touched in the 1950s,' says Robert, pointing out the square opening connecting the formal living and dining areas at the front of the house. 'The process began by carefully observing the layers that had occurred over time, removing some, until each retention or removal resulted in a soft balance between holding on to the history of a place and beginning a new chapter.'

The pleasure of restoring the house included discovering a note from the previous owner in one of the door jambs saying, 'This frame was replaced by G. Watson 30-6-56. Original frame dated 6-3-88.' Each action unveiled the hands that had once been there. Fifty years disappeared in the lifting of carpet, 100 years passed in the lifting of a floorboard.

Rather than a brazen entrance, there's a sense of discovery, a certain mystique behind a double layer of shuttered windows and sheer curtains. Even the side glass panels, framing the front door, have been discreetly designed with slim Victorian-style apertures. Similarly, instead of the garage dominating the property, access is via a side lane, with the corrugated iron door blending with the corrugated fence. A series of scaffolding poles, wrapped with rope, makes reference to Robert's Italian cultural past, still legible and meaningful.

But this is where the story changes. Instead of adding a large open-plan kitchen and informal living and dining area to the house – the normal approach worldwide – Robert placed the new stainless-steel kitchen in exactly the same spot as the original. And instead of the pokey cupboards and old-fashioned pot-belly stove that previously existed, there are now sleek steel cupboards and splashbacks. Simple and functional linoleum covers the kitchen floor, new laundry and a guest toilet. 'I wanted to keep to the home's original floor plan. I felt it was complete as soon as I first walked in,' says Robert. He puts himself into the shoes of a previous resident, imagining what it might have been like for someone sitting in the kitchen and reading the newspaper in 1914 when the First World War was announced. 'There's a sense of history and layers that run through this place.'

The outside toilet is part of that history and is still in its original position, complete with its rough timber posts. But instead of braving the cold, as would have been the case for the former owners, guests access the toilet from the laundry, beautifully fitted with new joinery. Even a brick vent in the structure has been poetically updated with a steel and glass cross-shaped window.

The same thoughtful approach can be seen in the upstairs, comprising two bedrooms, including the main bedroom and a separate dressing room, the latter accessed from a passage instead of from the main bedroom, which is the usual approach. This dressing room features an unusual timber screen that serves as the wardrobe. Inspired by architects Walter Burley Griffin and Marion Mahony's Newman College, where Robert visited friends while studying architecture at the University of Melbourne, this raw Victorian ash unit is one of the few contemporary insertions in the home. A similar concertina-shaped wardrobe appears in the main bedroom.

One of the greatest departures from contemporary living is the singular back door that leads to the elongated eastern-facing garden (the length of the property is 50 m). 'Having a glimpse of the garden is so much more exciting than putting everything out there at once. This door almost beckons you to take the next step,' says Robert, who further orchestrated this view and light by including shutters on the door to moderate both. The garden, as with the house, remains fairly original, with a number of the trees and shrubs along the path self-sewn. 'I prefer the idea of a garden that's left to develop its own direction, instead of being overly curated,' says Robert.

It wasn't the wrestling over whether or not to open the rooms to the garden that was Robert's concern; from the outset it was getting the sort of finish and detail he was searching for. 'It's the type of detail that in the end is almost not seen.' A similar concern was also present with his selection of materials – he wanted to ensure that each interaction became a layer upon the existing, resting above it lightly enough to feel like it could be removed if the house needed it so. And while the past is beautifully captured in this house, so is the fine Italian touch. A black painted canvas by artist Susan Norrie reveals a script from the 1960 Italian film *L'Avventura* by Michelangelo Antonioni. 'It's one of my favourite films, but this painting has a certain quietness and reflectivity about it,' says Robert. In the dining area, there are fabric swatches from a blanket brought from Italy by Robert's father. Concealed behind operable wall panels, only the family is mindful of their existence.

TIPS

You need to search for the essence of a house, which lies below what is apparent.

When you're renovating a home, think about how the spaces feel rather than looking at them simply in terms of their size.

Smaller and more curated views can often be more rewarding than the larger gestures.

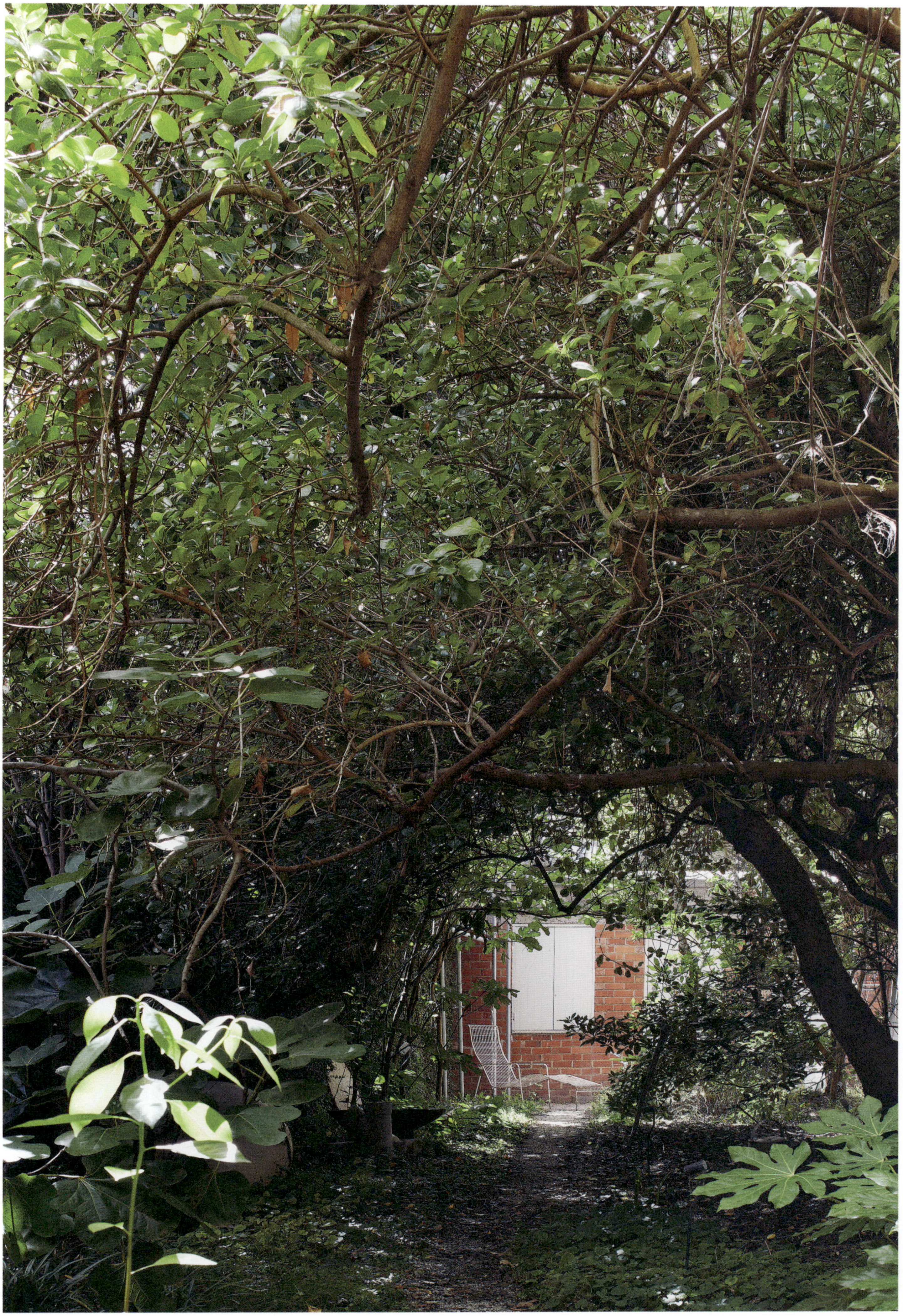

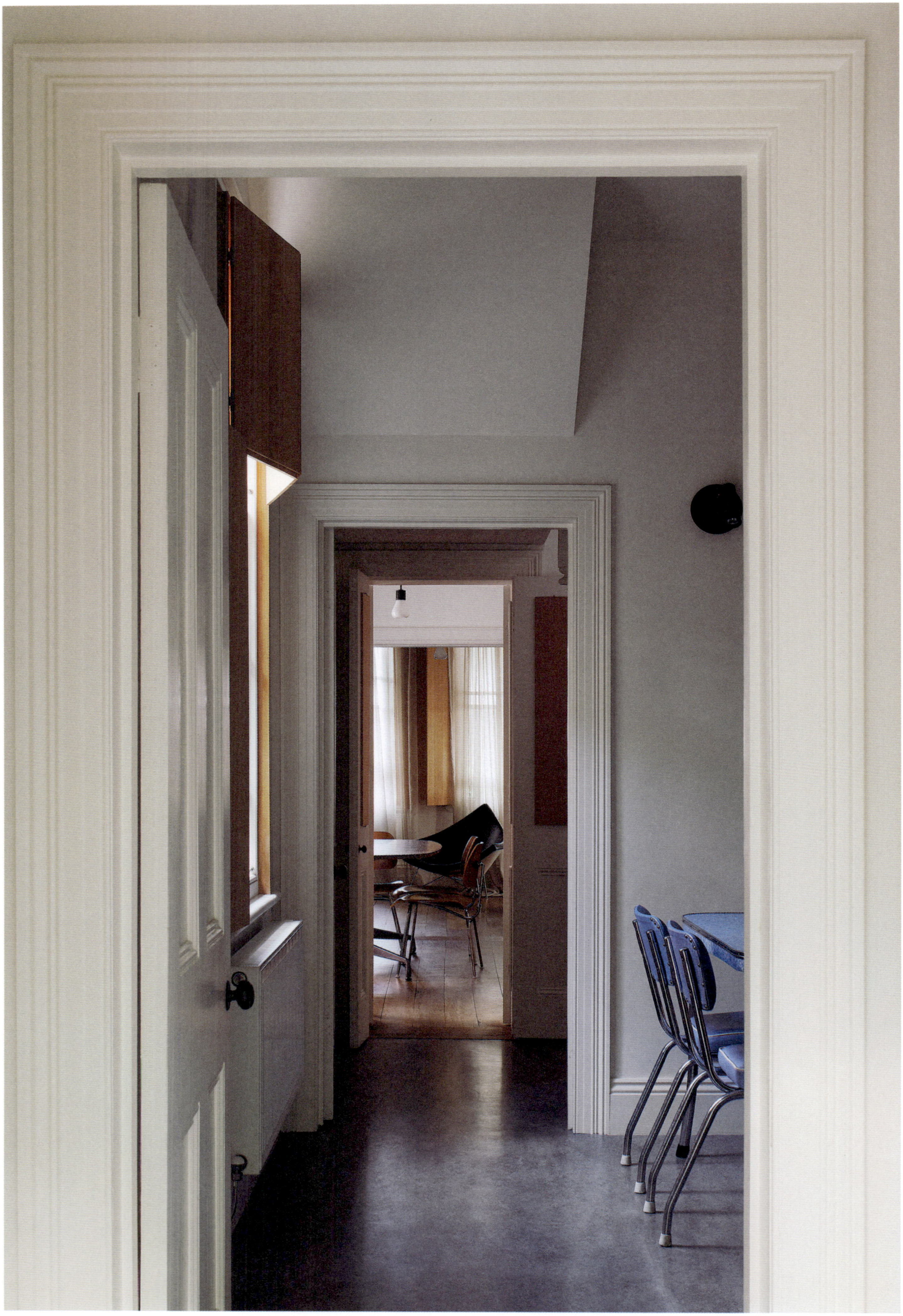

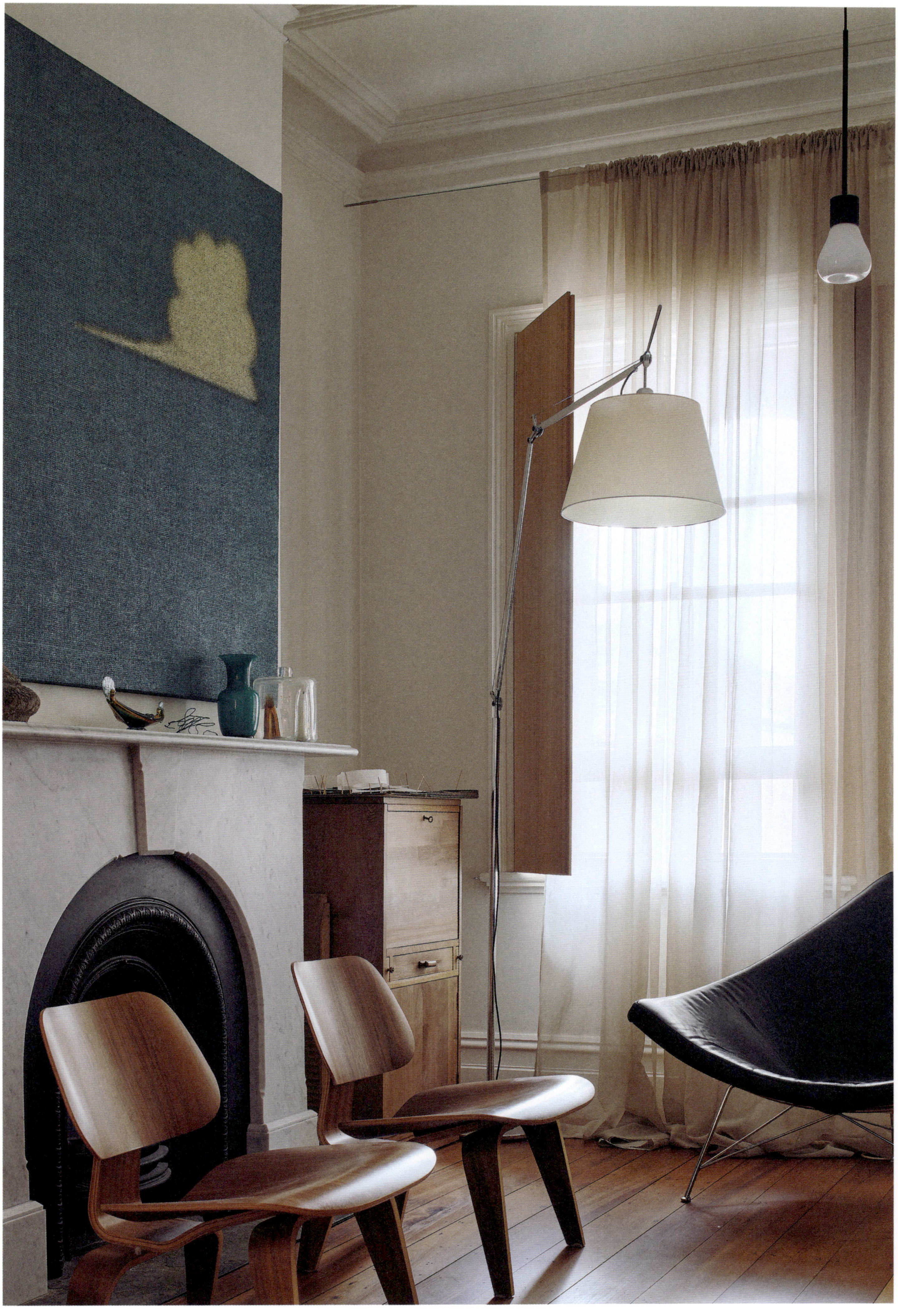

the architect's house

robert simeoni

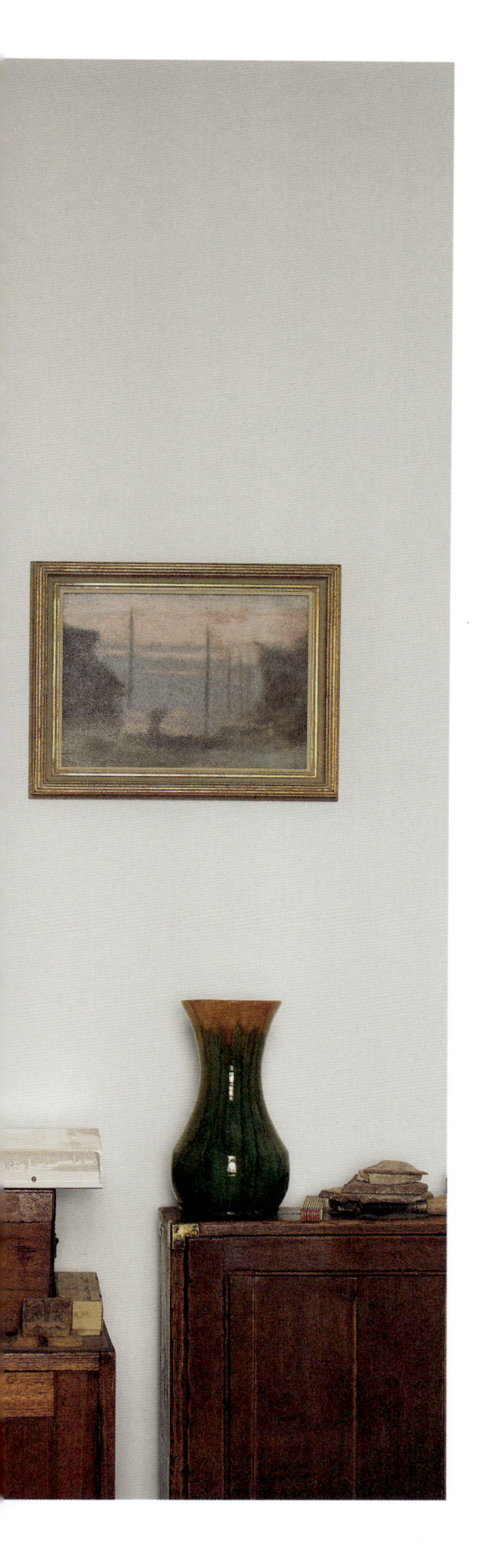

the architect's house

robert simeoni

the architect's house

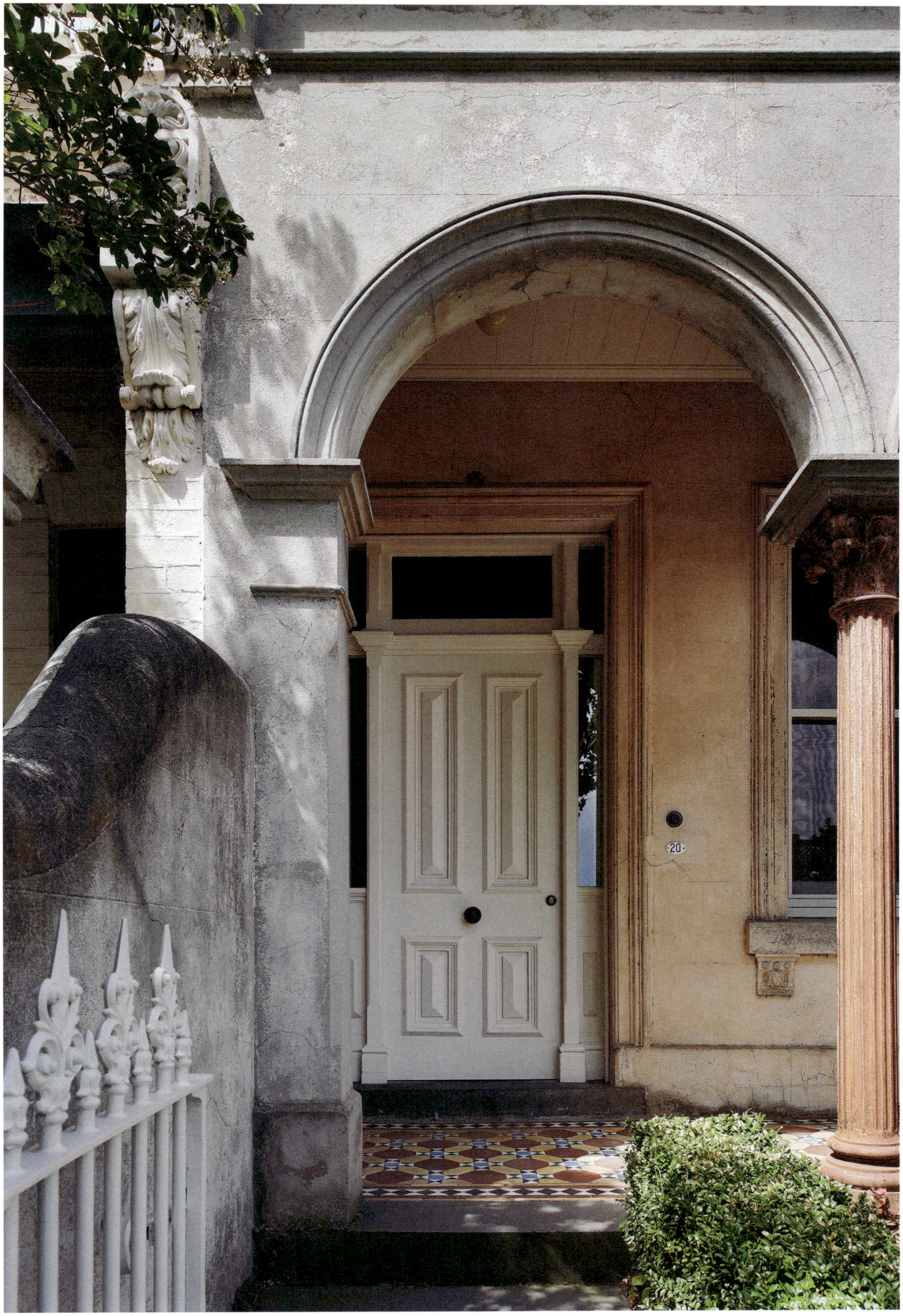
20

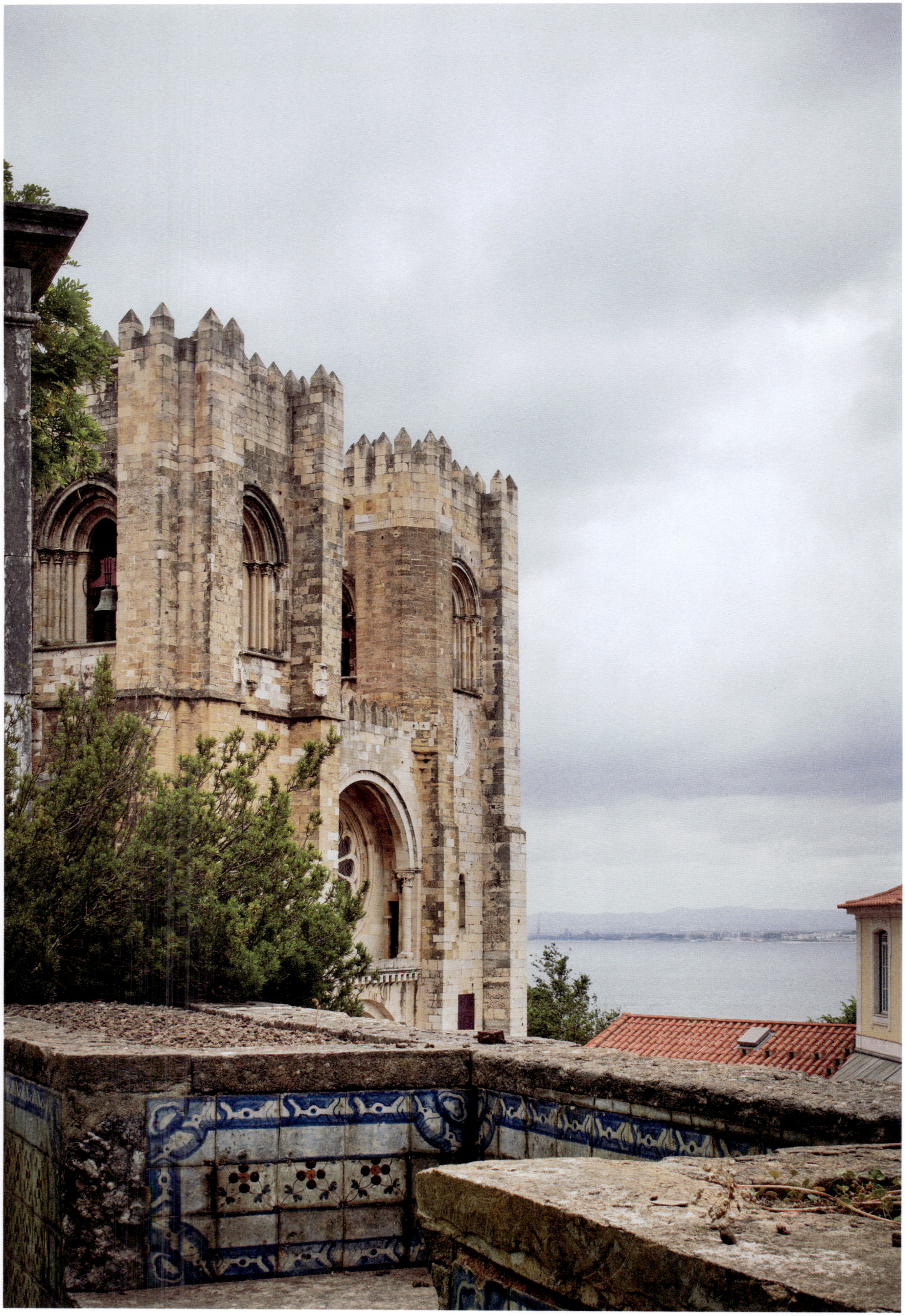

Manuel Aires Mateus, Architect, Manuel Aires Mateus

LISBON HOUSE, LISBON

This 18th century townhouse (thought to be built after 1755) is the home of Manuel Aires Mateus and his wife Sophia, who is also an architect. Wedged between a medieval castle and an old Romanesque cathedral, the house, according to Manuel, 'allowed a certain freedom of appropriation.' The decision to move to this new house in 2006 coincided with the birth of the couple's first child.

While Manuel and Sophia didn't have a specific location in mind at that time, in the early noughties, their neighbourhood was relatively inexpensive. A number of architects, artists and friends had already moved into the area, attracted by its affordability as well as the surrounding old buildings, many dating to the 18th century. It also benefited from being close to the centre of Lisbon.

The building, like many in the area, is referred to as 'Pombaline' in style, named after Sebastião José de Carvalho e Melo, the first marquis of Pombal, who was instrumental in reconstructing Lisbon after the great earthquake of 1755. Manuel and Sophia's level in the building was initially its service area. 'Sophia and I didn't see the project in terms of constraints but rather as allowing us the opportunity to be flexible with the spaces, responding to the way we wanted to live and the experiences we wanted to achieve,' says Manuel, who was also attracted to the views of the river.

Given the number of unknown factors in purchasing an historic building, there wasn't a preconceived idea of what the design should be; it was more a matter of slowly discovering what was there and then changing things as discoveries were made. However, there were certain elements that were always going to be integral to the design, including the Lisbon stone floors (known as Lioz) together with repurposing the same stone that was buried in the garden. 'Discovering all this Lioz allowed us to reuse it for practically everything – in certain walls and in areas such as the treads for the stairs,' says Manuel, pointing out the existing conical-shaped openings between the dining and the living area, now also framed in this stone. 'There were a number of logical decisions that were made as new things were discovered,' he adds.

One of the biggest discoveries in the process was the cistern. The garden came with a well that, following an archaeologist's advice, had to be emptied. 'I think they knew what would be discovered before we had even emptied the cistern. It's a very special place that would form part of our renovation, although it's a space that has no functional purpose,' says Manuel. Manuel started building a hole behind a reinforced arch to connect the cistern from inside the house, with the result that the digging caused many things to collapse, with the exception of a huge foundation arch that revealed an existing tunnel. 'These surprises continued the more we excavated, which also meant that we needed to find solutions.'

While the couple has been living here for almost 20 years, the house is far from static. Over this time there have been a few minor renovations, perhaps the most notable being the kitchen. Initially designed with children in mind (the couple's first-born son was three years old when the place was completed and the second has been raised here), the kitchen has increasingly become more of a living room, becoming more central to the family. It now contains more furniture and artwork, including a number of objects displayed on the kitchen bench. The dining room, designed for entertaining, is now more of a library/home office and is also, in Manuel's words, 'denser', with his children often studying there.

The Lisbon house is certainly not a traditional home, with clearly defined rooms that have a singular function, but what makes this property so special, apart from the element of surprise, is the continual presence of stone. A Roman pedestal and a Gothic capital were discovered in the renovation, some of which the couple were unable to date. 'We're in the centre of the ancient Roman city,' says Manuel, who sees the use of stone, both ancient and new, as a common 'thread' in the design. While some original openings were retained, others linking the living areas form part of the renovation. The new crisp brick-rendered wing comprises the bedrooms, with the children's bedrooms located on the lower level and the upstairs given over to the main bedroom suite.

Unlike homes designed for clients, where there's a fixed scheme set in place, for Manuel's own home continual changes were being made – every week. 'Clients need a greater degree of predictability,' says Manuel, who nevertheless enjoyed the building process and also the serenity the house still offers after so many years. Some things, such as the bathroom, were more recently updated, which included the installation of a stone bath which was designed by their studio.

For Manuel and Sophia, 'houses should be designed for life', though 'this project was complex and expansive.' The garden is certainly designed for the long term. Originally a French-style design, it was considered far too complicated for the couple's more relaxed way of living. Hence the fountain, for example, was dismantled and reassembled at the entrance to the building, with the house and garden treated in a more holistic manner.

TIP

You need to understand what 'designing for life' means. It requires a different approach for every person, whether they live on their own, with a partner or have a family with children, and is about thinking in terms of an experience, which is the most important condition when designing a house.

manuel aires mateus

the architect's house

manuel aires mateus

the architect's house

manuel aires mateus

the architect's house

manuel aires mateus

the architect's house

manuel aires mateus

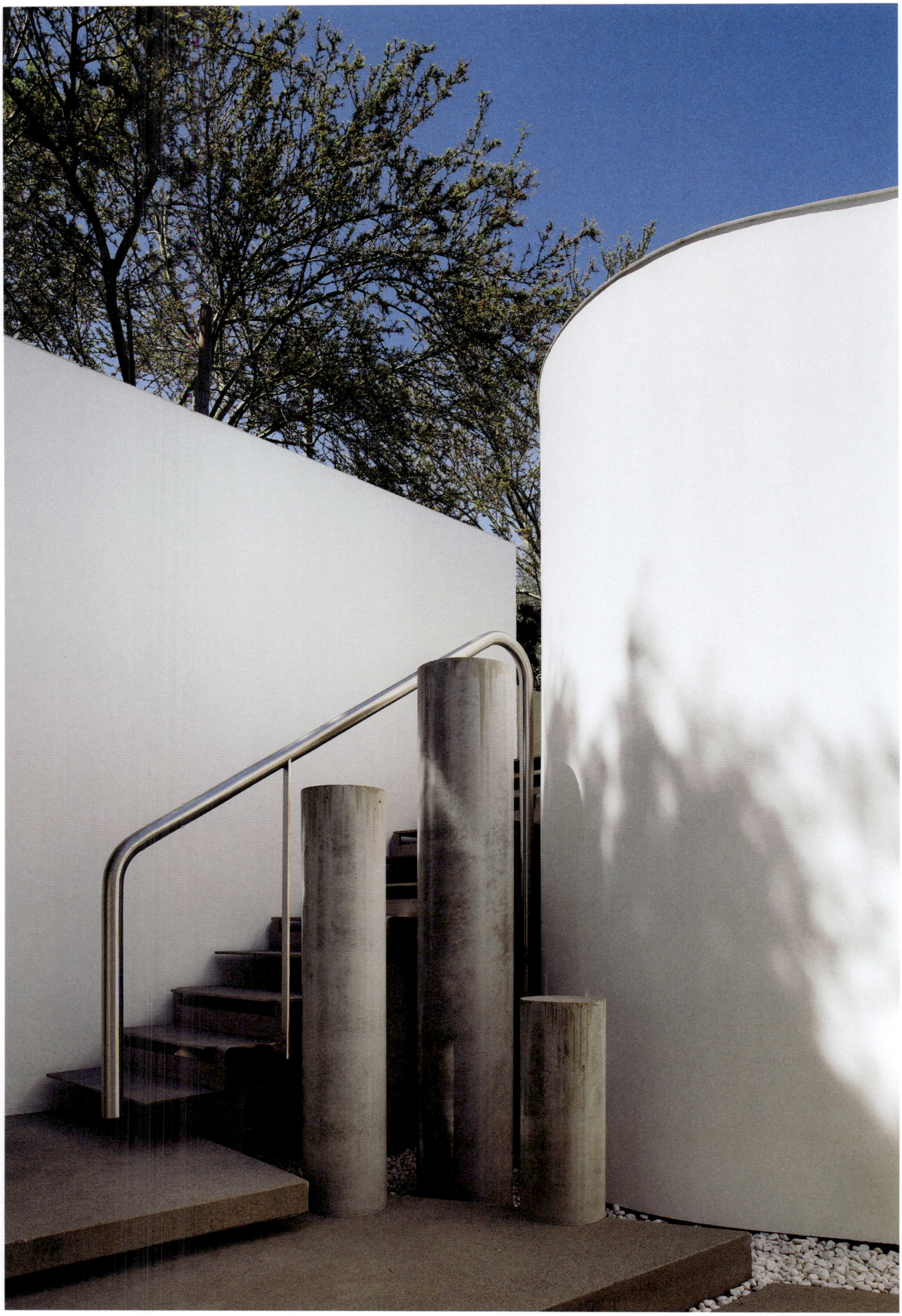

John Friedman & Alice Kimm, Co-founders, John Friedman Alice Kimm Architects

JARZM HOUSE, SILVER LAKE, LOS ANGELES

Inspired by the work of John Lautner and Richard Neutra, who made their mark in Los Angeles, this contemporary three-level house in the Los Angeles neighbourhood of Silver Lake pushes design boundaries as well as navigating the site's 20 m fall. John Friedman and his wife Alice Kimm also credit the influence of architects Rudolph Schindler and Paul Rudolph as spearheading their design to create a unique home for themselves and their three children, Rae, Zoey and Milo, and their two cats, Stella and Jasper.

The opportunity to create a new home arose when the couple came across a rare vacant plot of land in a neighbourhood they'd always loved, offering views of the Silver Lake Reservoir and the Dodger Stadium. The site, while extremely steep, benefited from having two street frontages, with access to the home from the highest point. 'The cultural "vibe" was also inspiring. Walt Disney's studio at Silver Lake, as well as other television and film studios, are in nearby Hollywood and Burbank,' says John Friedman, who also appreciated the site's location near Downtown LA, where the JFAK office is located.

John and Alice rented a house in the area while designing plans for the new house and, while not exactly sure what type of house would eventuate, it was always going to be orientated to the reservoir and the views of the San Bernardino Mountains, which are covered in snow during the winter months.

While the couple drew inspiration from Lautner, Neutra, Schindler and Rudolph, at the forefront of their minds was the work of Mexican architect Luis Barragán and Portuguese architect Álvaro Siza. 'We were interested in creating "experience" as the key generator in our work, with moments of detail, recognition, joy, surprise and even provocation,' says Alice, who, like John, sees a house as a 'stage for living'. But this house was also designed to accommodate the family's needs.

At the top level, reached via concrete stairs, is the open-plan kitchen, dining and living areas, as well as two of the children's bedrooms, a bathroom and a toilet. One of the most noticeable features of the kitchen/dining area is the large yellow crane that straddles the ceiling and cantilevers beyond the glass balustrade and sliding glass doors. It was designed to manoeuvre the heavy dining table to poolside three levels below. At the central level, there's the main bedroom suite and en suite, two separate walk-in dressing areas and two rooms used as home offices. There's also the third child's bedroom. And at ground level is a large multifunctional space set up as a rumpus room for the children. Piercing the three levels is an open-treaded staircase, with a powder-coated aluminium display case used for books, objects and artefacts. There's also a separate studio and garage accessed from the lower side of the street, with the studio rendered in vibrant pink, a nod to the palette of Luis Barragán. The house was planned so that it could become four independent dwellings, with each floor having its own separate entrance, bathroom and kitchenette. 'We intentionally eschewed a double-height living space in favour of more, and varied, gathering spaces,' says John.

The home's interior has predominantly white walls, extensive glazing to allow for generous views of the neighbourhood and a substantial amount of garden, both within the property and through borrowed sightlines from neighbours' green spaces. The bank of white-painted aluminium shelves that cut across the home's three levels, adds texture as well as creating a partial 'veil' over some of the rooms. The home's white walls also create the perfect backdrop for the couple's collection of art and photography, including a photo of a movie warehouse by Benny Chan, as well as an aerial photo of Los Angeles, also taken by Chan. Other works are by Gregory Crewdson and Lee Olvera and there is a photograph by Catherine Opie in the main bedroom.

The mirrored dining table was designed by John and fabricated by Chris Berkson of Berksonfab with two gas struts that allow the legs of the table to be lifted so it can easily move above the glass balustrade when it's being lifted down to the terrace. The coffee table in the living area, with its magenta glass top and aluminium base, also references the bookshelves.

While John and Alice could have increased the breadth of their views by placing the house further up the hill, they took the option of a lower elevation, thereby preserving the views of their neighbours so that they could also benefit from an outlook of the reservoir. This decision also provided the opportunity to create a sense of mystery from the street and allows for a more intriguing entry sequence. The choice to place programmable coloured LED lights in a cove above the central stair atrium also gives the interiors a painterly feel and produces different moods at night – with the lights emanating from the house and providing a beacon for those either in the neighbourhood or passing through.

Although the crane was conceived to allow the dining table to be lowered poolside, when the large sliding doors are left open, it feels akin to being outside. 'We don't use the crane very much but we both feel that it adds a bit of humour to the architecture,' says John, who also enjoys applying a whimsical touch to some of his projects, be they residential or commercial. 'But we are still enjoying sending over the turkey from the island bench to the dining table on days such as Thanksgiving,' he adds.

TIPS

Natural light is extremely important and ideally every room should receive natural light from two different directions.

Find spaces you like and measure them so that you know roughly how large you want rooms to be – spaces can be deceptive.

Have a frank conversation about construction costs up front, without trying to sugar-coat them. Costs are high at the moment and, even for architects, it's hard to get your head around what can be achieved within a given budget. You need to be realistic.

john friedman & alice kimm

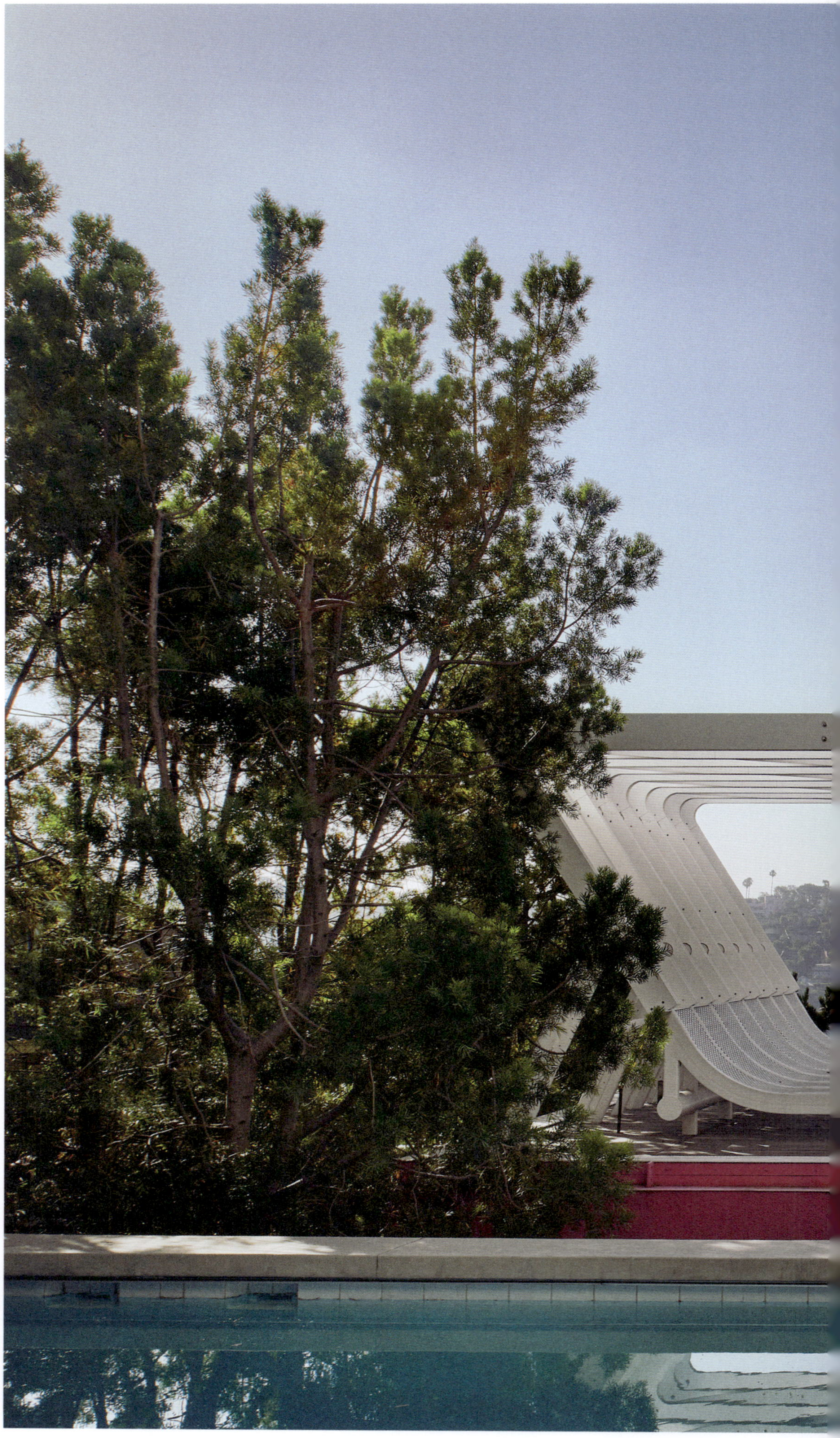

john friedman & alice kimm

the architect's house

john friedman & alice kimm

the architect's house

john friedman & alice kimm

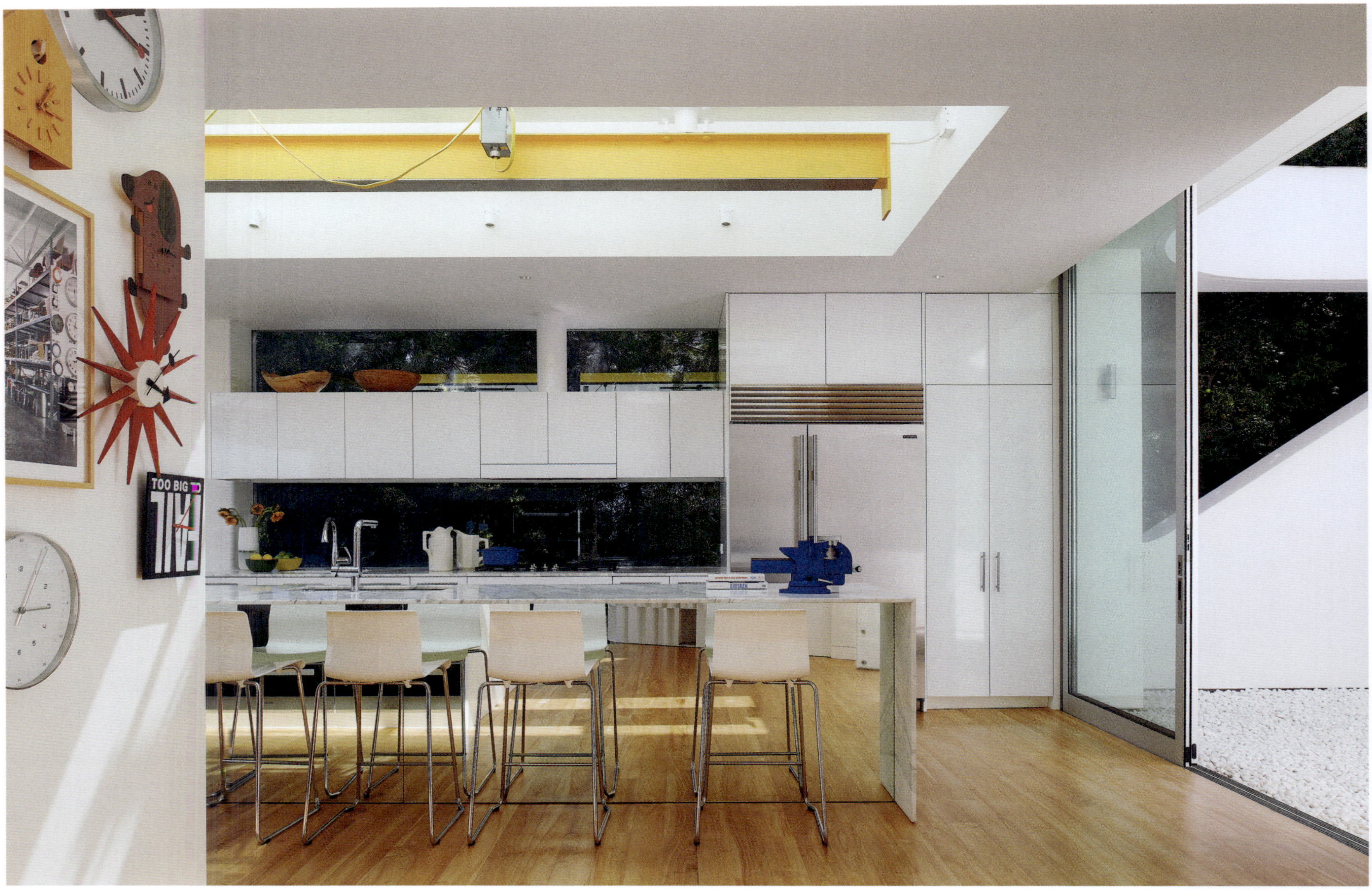
TOO BIG
FAIL

john friedman & alice kimm

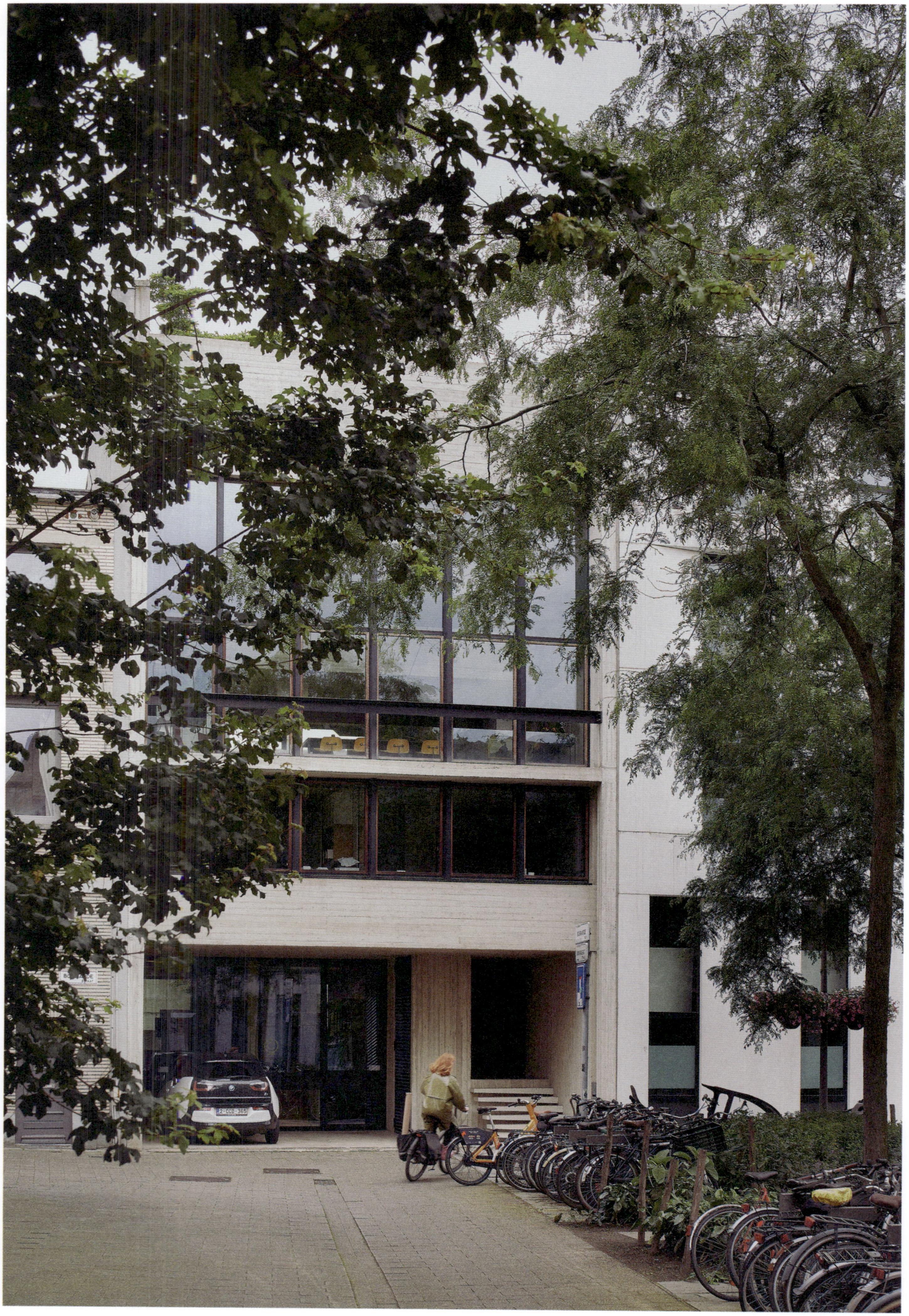

Ilze Quaeyhaegens & Gert Cuypers, Architects, cuypers & Q Architects

ANTWERP HOME AND OFFICE, ANTWERP

When Ilze Quaeyhaegens and Gert Cuypers purchased their plot of land in 1992, located in Sint-Andries in the centre of Antwerp, it was fairly dodgy. The square directly in front of the couple's front door was used by the police as a car park and their site only consisted of a rudimentary shed-like building used as a photographic studio. 'The area is referred to as "the parish of misery", a socially deprived medieval enclave,' says Ilze. While the locale now benefits from its own square, there's now also a youth hostel designed by architect Vincent Van Duysen to ensure there's still a mixture of social groups.

For many years, cuypers & Q Architects ran its practice from what had been the photographic studio, where, as Ilze recalls, 'comfort was spartan'. On the positive side, the area is right in the middle of the city and easily accessible by public transport and within both walking and cycling distance of all urban amenities. 'We love the neighbourhood. Everyone speaks to each other and there's a mix of cultures and ages. It's a place that regularly attracts tourists who come to the city centre, particularly on Saturdays,' says Ilze.

Ilze and Gert brainstormed a number of possible alternatives for the site, starting on this project after 2012 when planning permission was given. The idea for the home/office was for a stacked building, an urban plinth with a practice that spans three floors and has a patio/terrace. Above the office space is a four-level house with terraces and balconies, including a rooftop garden that offers expansive views over the Antwerp skyline. Rather than feeling like a townhouse, it feels more akin to a detached house in the suburbs with its own private garden.

The bedrooms create a buffer between the practice and the living areas of the home, the latter providing an open duplex-style arrangement. There's also a secluded double-height garden room that doubles as a music room; it connects to the roof garden and is accessible only via an external staircase or lift.

People often see the influence of Le Corbusier in the home/office. However, in formal terms, the couple sees the design as more in keeping with the architectural language of Belgian architect Juliaan Lampens, known for his Brutalist designs, while the building's exposed concrete is reminiscent of Brazilian architecture from the 1960s and 1970s. The building was conceived as a 'massive and rough carcass' according to Ilze, with exposed concrete combined with generous glazing and fixed items of furniture loosely delineating many of the spaces. 'The mass provides a sufficient amount of thermal inertia and also comfort,' says Gert, whose material selection was ash wood and white laminate in areas such as the kitchen. And in the office, only cabinets have been added, sandwiched between the floor and the ceiling and capable of being completely removed.

In the house itself, there are only a few spaces that are fully enclosed, including both of the children's bedrooms, with raised bed niches in both rooms allowing for additional space. The bedroom level features relatively low ceilings and low horizontal windows, creating a sense of intimacy. The kitchen, located directly above, also has a relatively low ceiling but feels more generous, flanked by double-height spaces either side, the dining room and the covered terrace. It's these contrasts that animate the living areas. 'You never feel enclosed because of the diagonal views through the building, and because the space is filled with light all year round,' says Ilze.

The wood-printed concrete walls and ceilings in the house also add warmth and texture. The floors and stairs are made from concrete, the latter being sanded and then polished to create a terrazzo effect. Other materials included black-lacquered steel for some windows, as well as Afrormosia, a resistant wood used in its natural state.

Both the kitchen and bathrooms are designed as 'boxes' that are placed within the concrete shell and conceived as items of furniture. The rooms designed for the children are inspired by furniture, made from high-pressure laminate and easily removed, allowing for the spaces to be completely reconfigured in the future. The couple deliberately played with the scale of spaces next to each other – low spaces versus high ceilings, small spaces versus larger areas.

Ilze and Gert also leaned towards using a mixture of older and newer pieces of furniture. The Danish sofas, for example, came from Ilze's family, as did pieces such as the Harry Bertoia Diamond chairs. Other items, such as the Eames chairs, were found in vintage stores. The home and office are also filled with plants, including a ginkgo biloba found on their patio. There is also an over-scaled planter on the roof of the office that provides tomatoes and herbs, and on the roof terrace there's a magnolia as well as a fig tree, together with grape vines. Ilze and Gert had assistance from landscape architect Jan Van Minnebruggen from the Netherlands practice BoschSlabbers; he has a deep understanding of plant selection and creating green rooftop gardens. Art also adds another layer to the home: a few works by Belgian sculptor Panamarenko are displayed on the dining room wall. There's also a multi-panelled work by Roeland Tweelinckx which was purchased long before the house/office was built. And there's a collection of 'stuff', including books, souvenirs, cards and pictures that give the home its warmth and personality. As Gert is also a musician, there is a collection of his guitars.

Ilze and Gert still recall the height limitations that faced them at the time. 'We were prevented from going even a few centimetres higher,' says Ilze. And being in the middle of the city also created some challenges in terms of the building process. 'When I look back, it was an achievement just to erect the concrete walls,' adds Ilze.

TIPS

Avoid building in the wrong location and be mindful of the orientation.

We believe it's important to understand seasonal change as well as to follow the trajectory of the sun on a daily basis. We can absorb the early morning sun and also the evening warmth in the kitchen while preparing meals.

Think differently to others; fixed ideas about how a house should look can prevent you from being innovative.

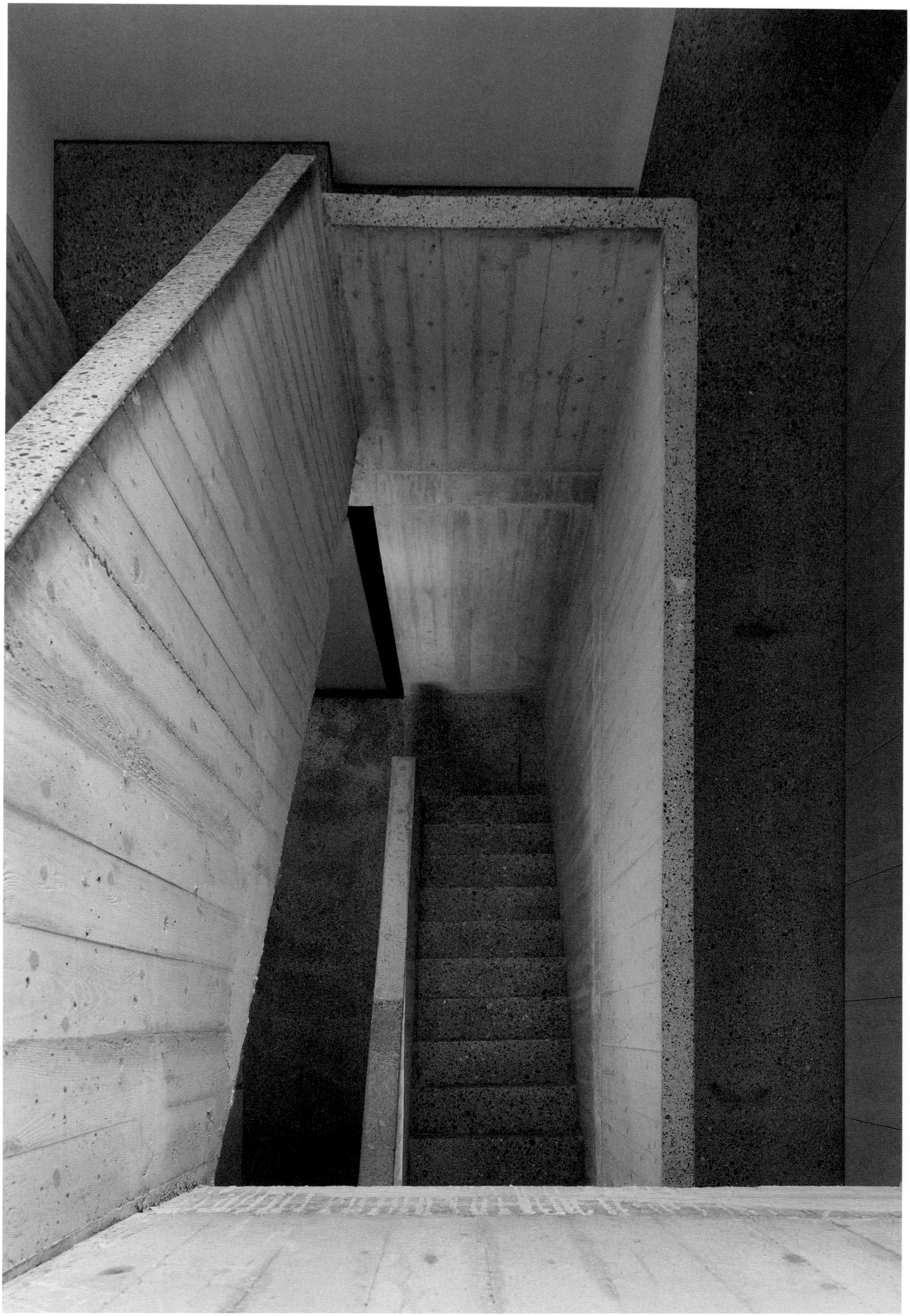

the architect's house

ilze quaeyhaegens & gert cuypers

the architect's house

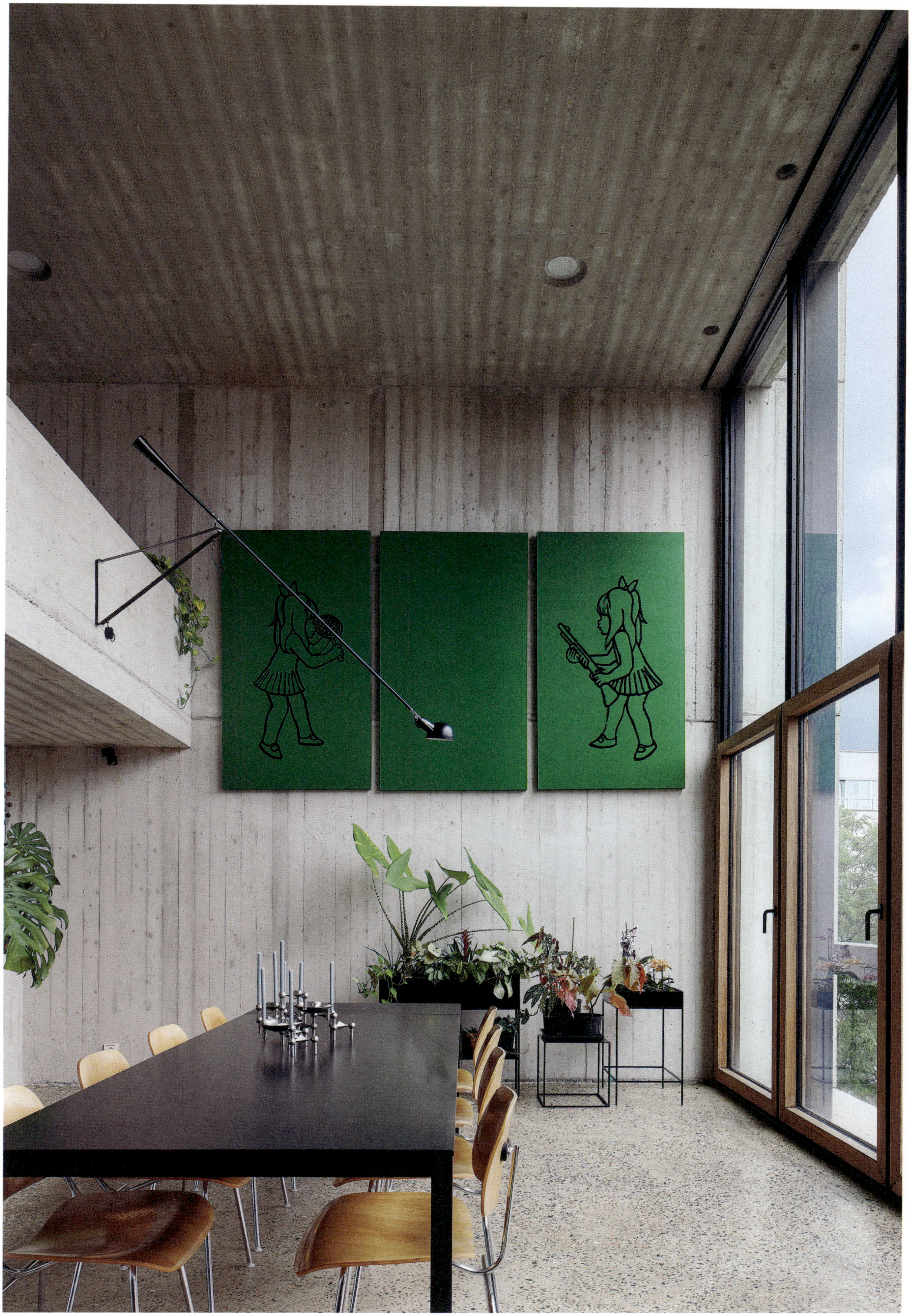

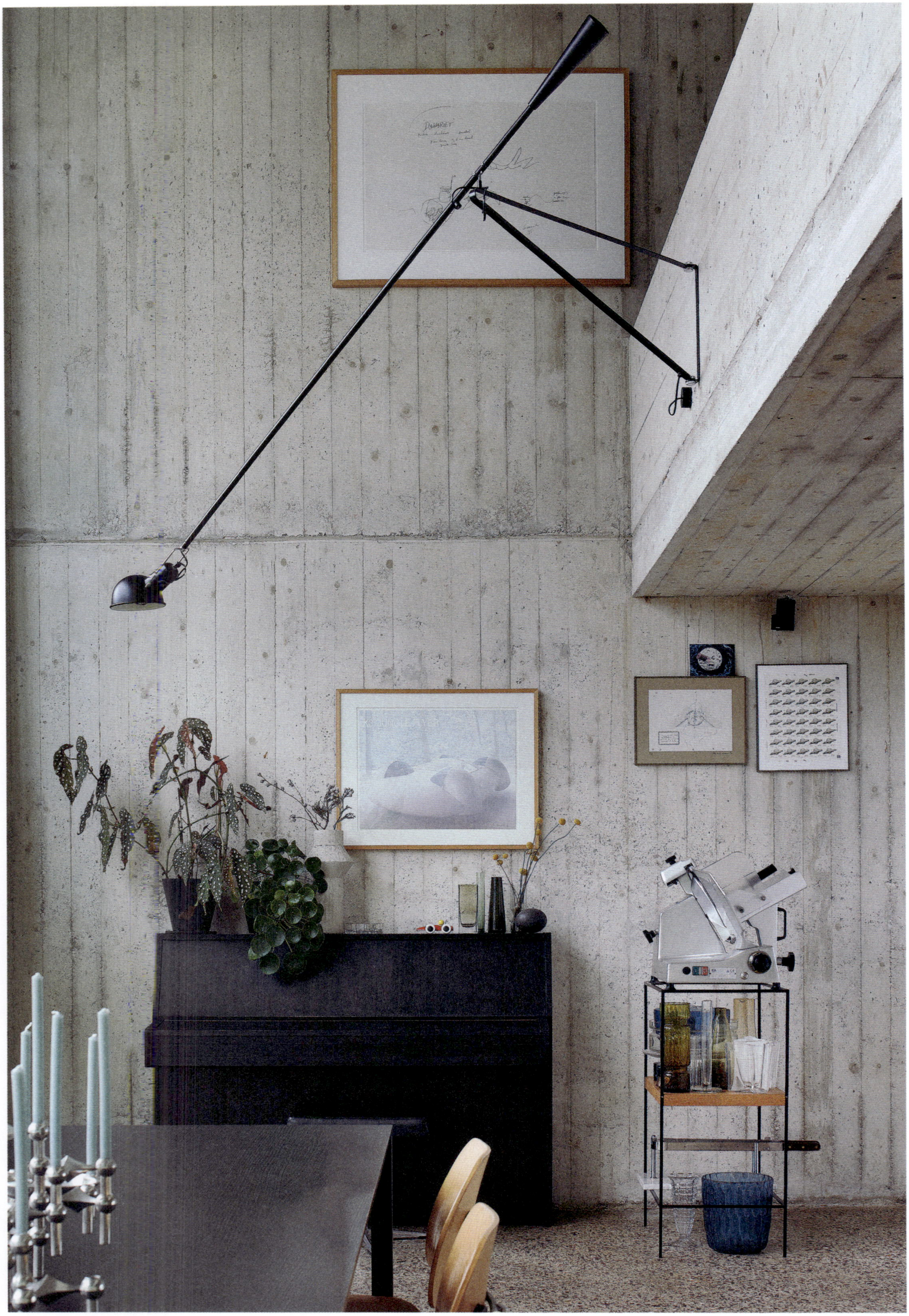

ilze quaeyhaegens & gert cuypers

the architect's house

ilze quaeyhaegens & gert cuypers

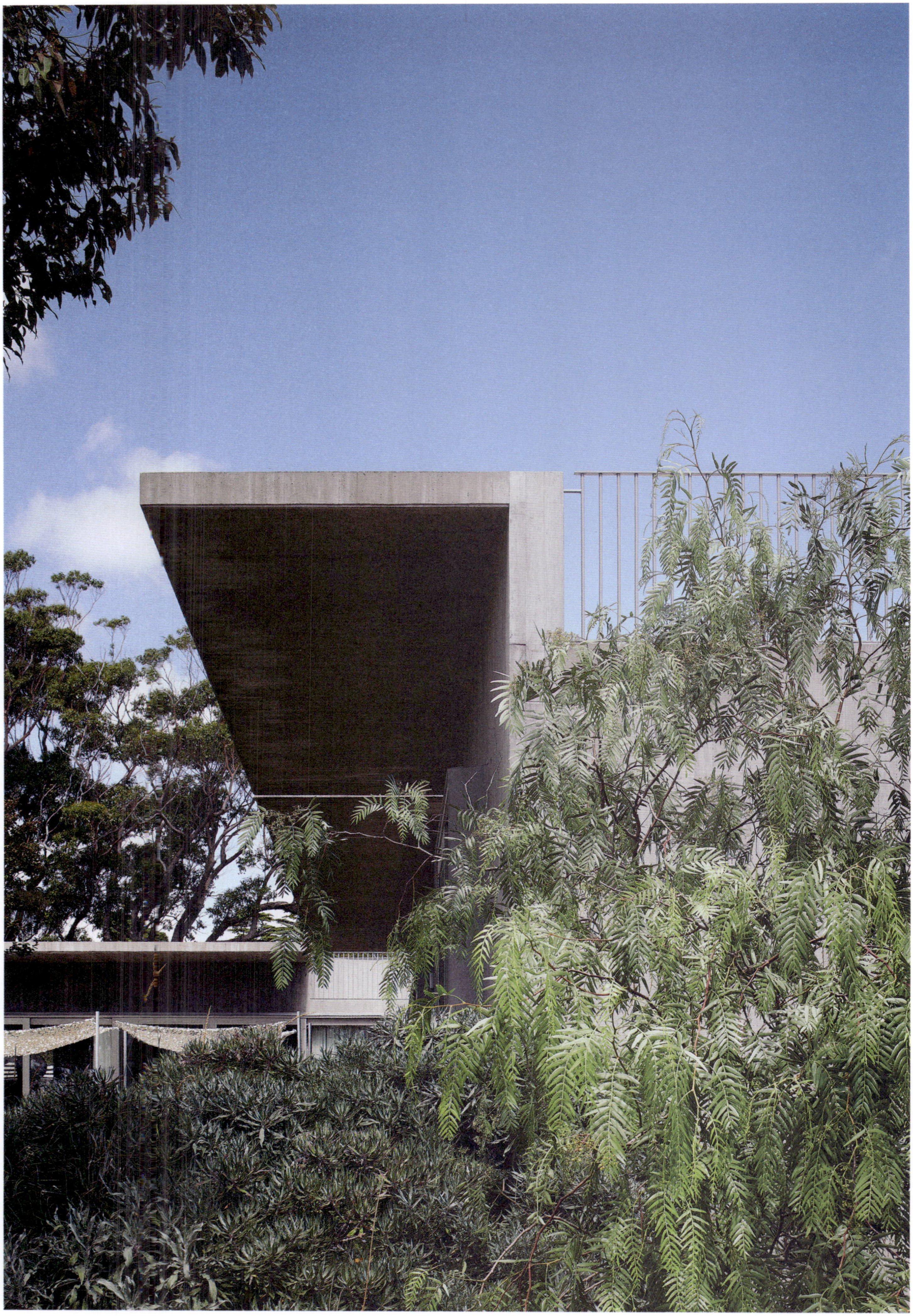

Jeff Provan, Manuel Aires Mateus, Neometro and MA+Co

THE MORI HOUSE, MORNINGTON PENINSULA, VICTORIA

Mori is Japanese for a forest, but the Mori House is certainly not situated in dense vegetation. Rather, it can be found at Mount Martha, on Victoria's Mornington Peninsula, framed by gnarled coastal tea trees. It was this unique landscape that partially inspired Portuguese-based architect Manuel Aires Mateus, working in collaboration with Neometro's design director Jeff Provan and local architects MA+Co, to create a new beach house. 'These tea trees felt quite ancient to me, yet at the same time quite fragile,' says Manuel, who was impressed with the property's outlook over Port Phillip Bay.

Designed for Jeff Provan and his wife Mariko, it was fortuitous the couple walked into Aires Mateus's office in Lisbon seeking a new house Down Under that would provide them, their extended family and friends, with 'a place to sleep, a place to eat, areas to relax and a place to swim' (hence the swimming pool), with Jeff and Mariko having a specific aspiration for every space.' This approach is often cited by Manuel to his students at the Accademia di Architettura in Mendrisio in Switzerland. 'Mariko and I had experienced a number of buildings designed by Manuel, including the Hotel Santa Clara in Lisbon and a beach house at Comporta, which has a sand floor in the kitchen,' says Jeff, who had read a quote about Manuel's practice as 'creating ruins of the future'. These different experiences proved to the couple that they could expect a similar approach for their own home – a highly bespoke design that would go well beyond just their pragmatic requirements.

With the couple's aspirations for each space, the design slowly 'morphed' into five buildings – two self-contained bungalows, a studio, and a garage/storage area that is independent of the main house, which comprises a living area, kitchen and dining area (with the pantry leading to a courtyard), as well as a main bedroom suite and a separate bunk room for the children. 'We wanted the spaces to feel relaxed; places you want to take your shoes off and enjoy the feel of the floors,' says Jeff, pointing out the concrete ceilings and floors throughout the house. To add texture, a number of the in-situ concrete walls are board-printed. Where concrete isn't used, there's a strong dose of Douglas fir.

Given that Neometro, an architecturally focused development company, has a tendency to build its apartments, townhouses and many of its homes in concrete, it seemed an obvious choice to use concrete for the Mori House. So, rather than many of the lightweight beach houses found along the peninsula, the separate concrete pavilions linked by courtyards are firmly anchored on the site. As with Manuel's instinctive feeling that the landscape was 'ancient', he also drew inspiration from the crucifix, not in terms of religion but in the tradition of early settlers making a cross with a stick in the dirt to mark the spot for a new home. With strategically placed slithers in the concrete ceilings, a crucifix is formed, casting rays of light into the interior; their intensity depends on the time of day.

There's also a dedicated *tatami* room that forms part of the main house, featuring traditional *shoji* screens. Mariko's sourcing and careful placement of timber benches and rocks found in the courtyards also links back to her Japanese heritage. And while Manuel's initial design didn't include a roof terrace, Jeff and Mariko were keen to take advantage of the unimpeded views of the bay. But rather than simply a rudimentary steel staircase tucked to one side for access, there are two, one of which takes on a strong sculptural form and makes a statement upon arrival. 'Having the two staircases creates a sense of movement with the garden extending to the roof terrace,' says Manuel, whose staircase has an Escher-like feel to it, albeit considerably more chunky than ethereal.

While Manuel was hand-drawing many of his ideas in his Lisbon office, he was also regularly having Zoom calls both with the Provans and MA+Co as the design progressed. 'We were working with CAD and interpreting many of the hand sketches, but also ensuring these responded to the local context, well before Manuel first visited the site,' says architect Karen Alcock, director of MA+Co. 'In line with Manuel's instincts, we understood that Jeff and Mariko wanted a place that captures the way they live, a place they could chill out in rather than making an architectural statement just for the sake of it,' says Karen. While the home can easily accommodate large paintings and sculpture, the furnishings, fittings and objects are relatively simple given it's a beach house. Large paper lanterns are suspended over the kitchen table and there is a Noguchi pendant-style light in the entrance. The couple also opted for a number of mid-century designs, such as Hans Wegner's 'Wishbone' chairs and the 'Butterfly' chairs for the outdoor terrace. And although the house is relatively large for Jeff and Mariko when they are there on their own, it certainly feels an appropriate size when their children and grandchildren come to stay.

For Jeff and Mariko, the idea from the outset was to have a house that had 'longevity', or in Jeff's words, a 'forever house'. Like an ancient ruin, the Mori House will be an important focus for them and their extended family for generations to come. For those travelling along the coastal road, the home's concrete structure will also form a rich patina in time, like the ebb and flow of the sea on the rock walls nearby.

TIPS

Think of a house as a place to sleep, a place to eat and areas to relax, and have a specific aspiration for each space.

jeff provan, manuel aires mateus

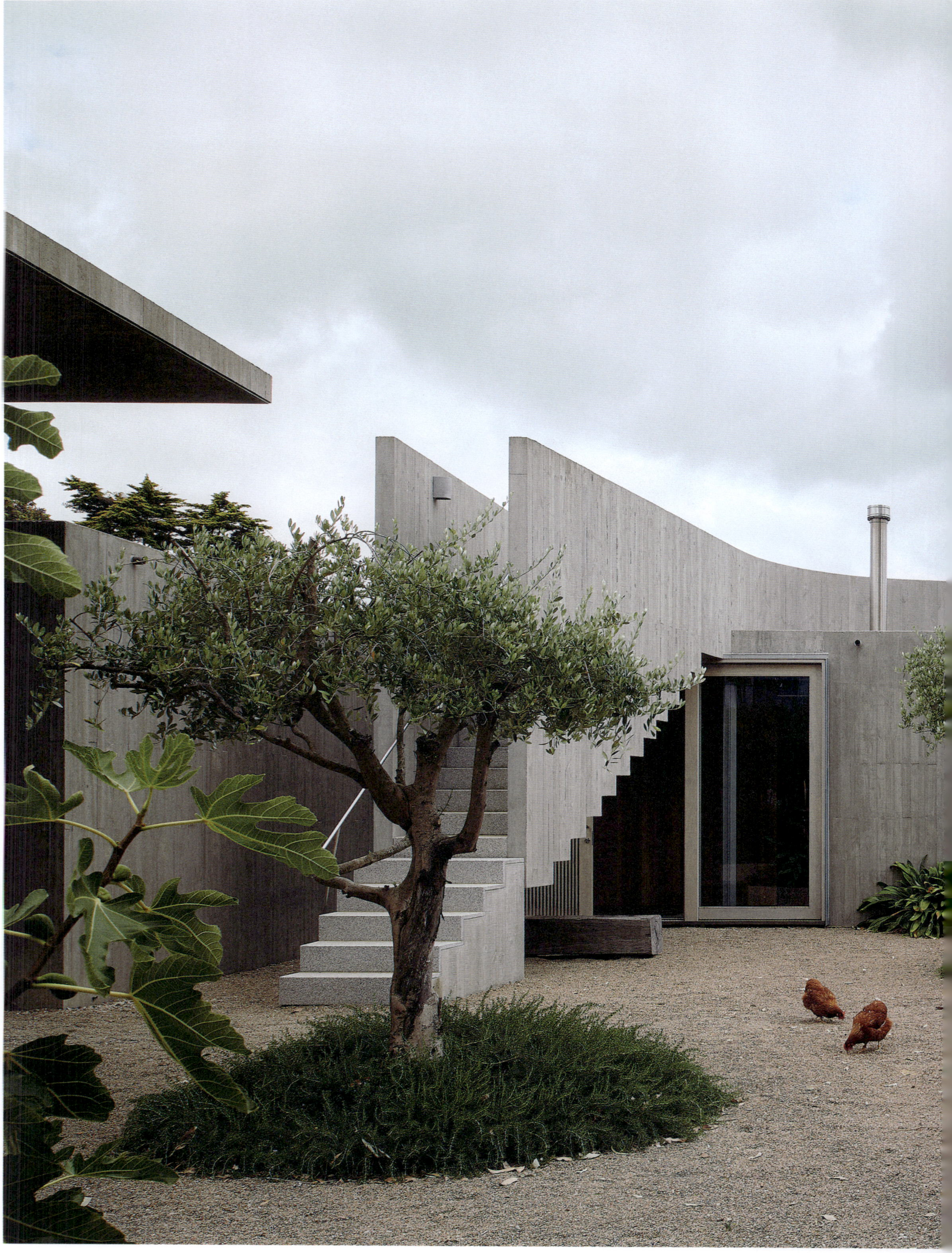

jeff provan, manuel aires mateus

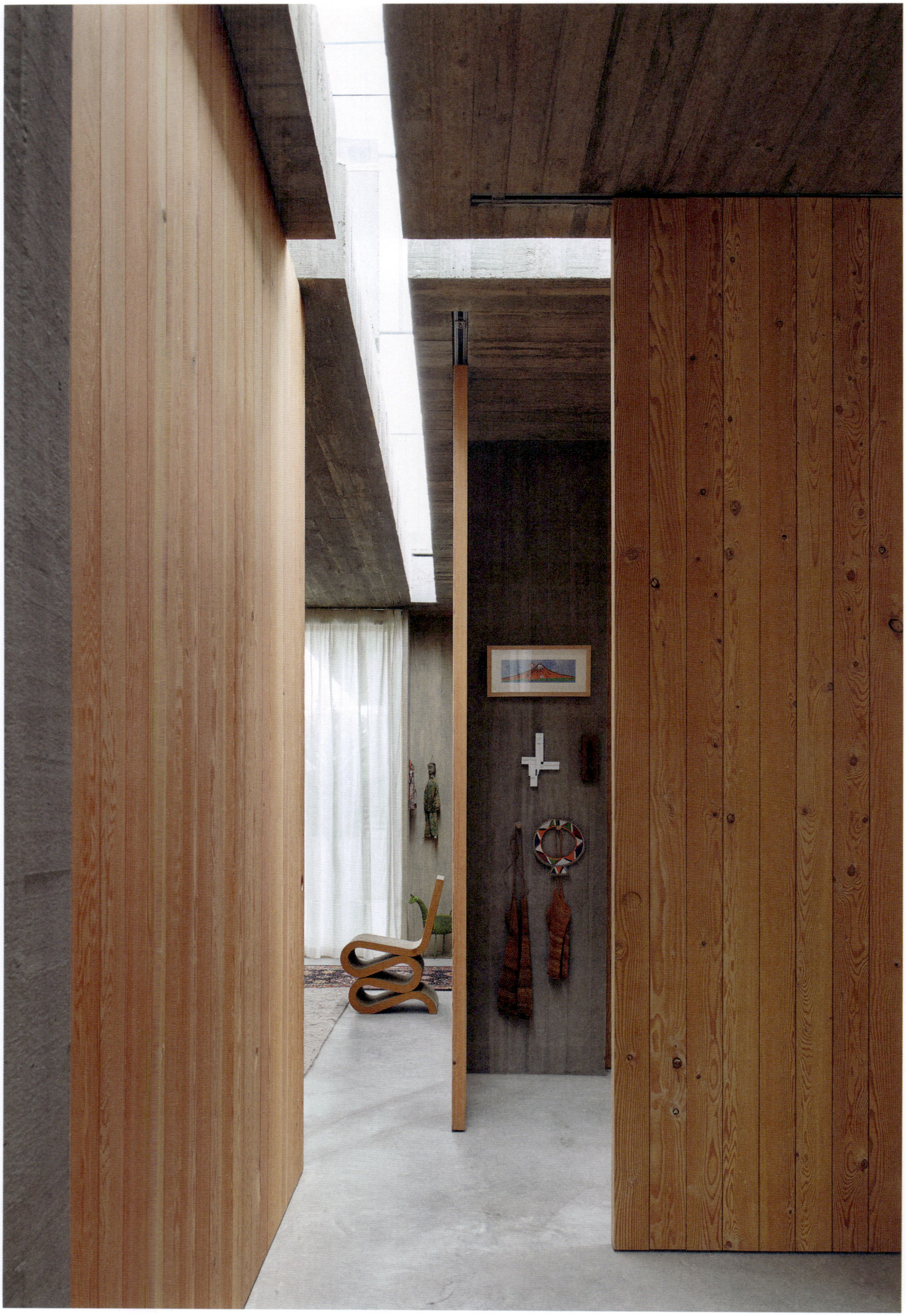

jeff provan, manuel aires mateus

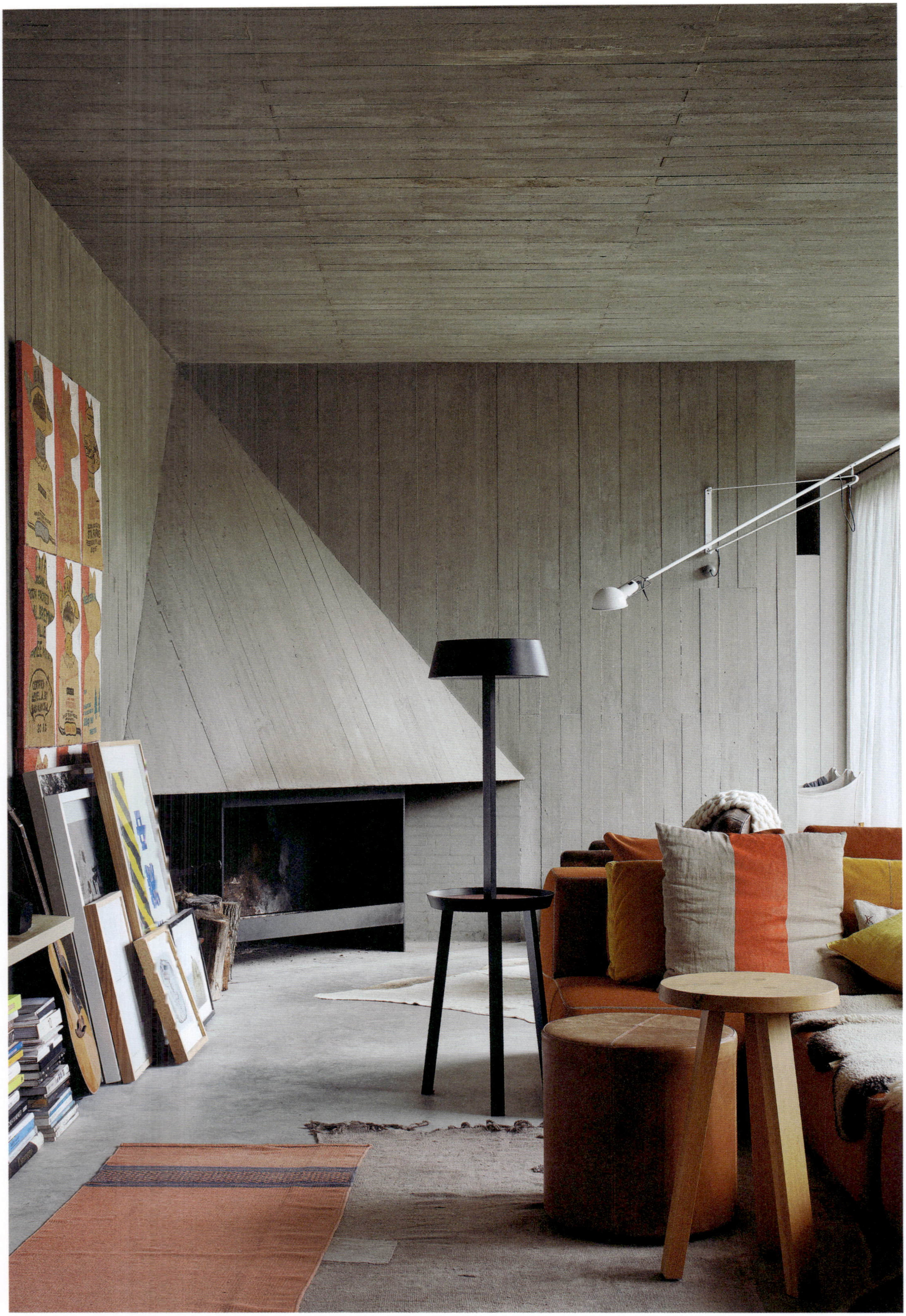

jeff provan, manuel aires mateus

the architect's house

jeff provan, manuel aires mateus

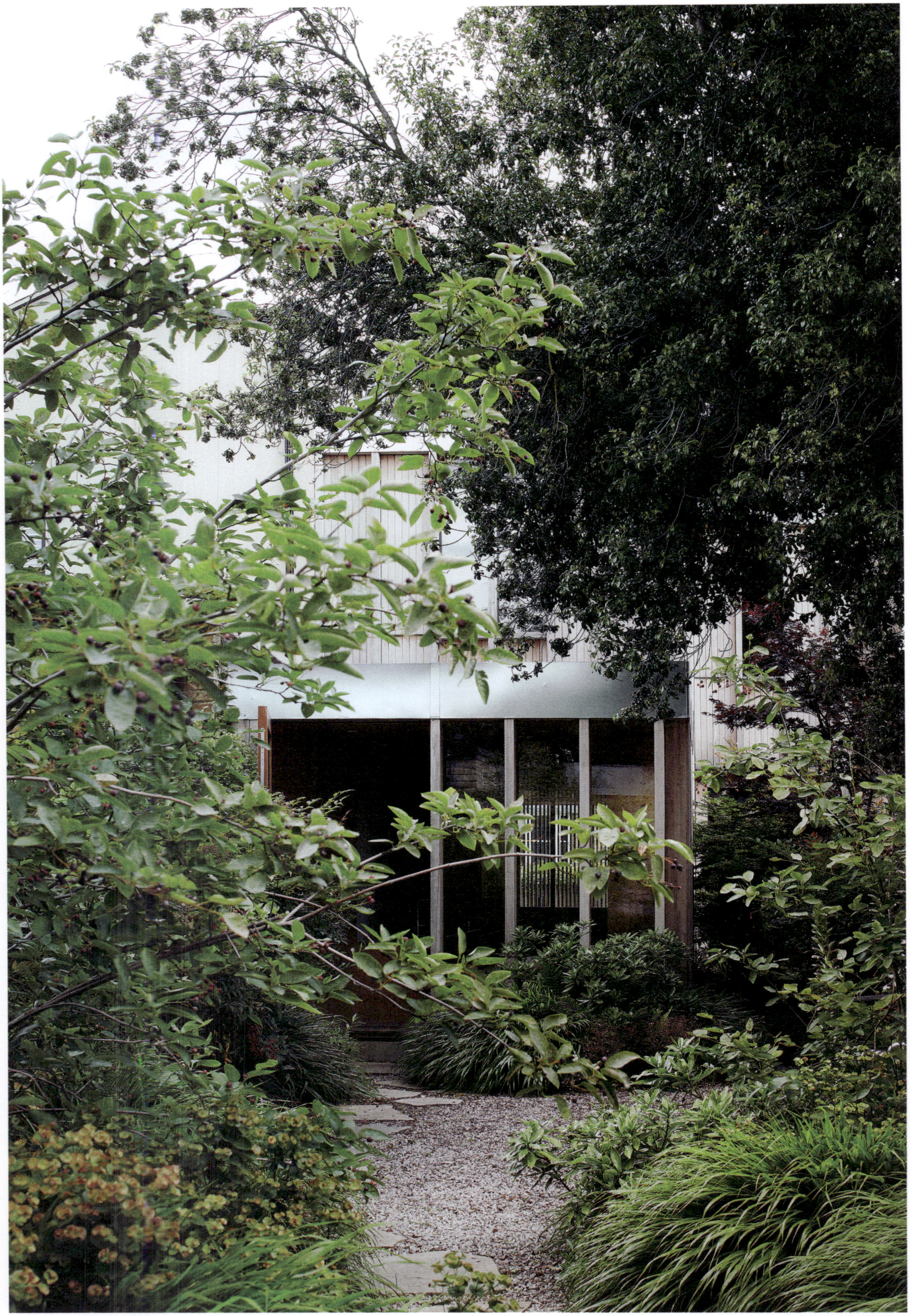

Zach Fluker & Liz Tatarintseva, Architects, ao-ft

SPRUCE HOUSE, WALTHAMSTOW, LONDON

Finding a suitable site to build on is extremely challenging, irrespective of one's budget. Many face heritage restrictions as well as other constraints, whether it takes the form of a protected tree or simply neighbours not wanting any new developments. This was certainly the case for Zach Fluker and his partner, Liz Tatarintseva, who were recently joined by their daughter, 11-month-old Zoe. 'When we were looking, you could sense from certain neighbours that even a new house, let alone apartments, would certainly not be welcomed,' says Liz, who managed to find both a suitable block and neighbours open to having a new house next to them in Walthamstow, a 30-minute ride on the Underground to the centre of London.

Although the neighbours were agreeable, the couple still had to navigate the local council's heritage guidelines, given the location is within a Conservation Area. Originally developed in the Victorian era as a group of shops dating from the early 1880s, the street evolved over time and has slowly become predominantly residential. In spite of its narrow width of approximately 5 m, this site was once home to two shops, a toy maker/seller and a cobbler. 'Given these restrictions, we couldn't expose a third level to the street,' says Liz, pointing to the slate roof that is only two storeys from ground level.

When the cobbler and toy dealer moved on, the plot was built on in the 1960s, with a simple two-storey house that had undergone a number of renovations. 'There was nothing there that was worth retaining, given it had virtually no connection to the garden or to the street,' says Zach, who excavated the site about half a metre to allow the new house and studio to feel immersed in the garden.

While the London house loosely follows the floor plan of an original Victorian terrace, being long and narrow, the choice of materials and the open-plan spaces are decades away from the bricks and mortar of the past. ao-ft made the decision from the outset to build with cross-laminated timber (CLT) both for its strength and its aesthetic. So, from the front elevation with its CLT vertical battens, to the home's interior walls and ceilings and through to the detached office, there's an elegant simplicity of 'less is more'. The built-in joinery is made from spruce and the floors are polished concrete. The only departure is the customised powder-coated and perforated steel staircase that pierces the three levels, creating a more industrial feel against the extensive timber-lined interior. And on the upper two levels, there's a fine concrete screed – or what's referred to as 'micro-cement' – that allows for a more seamless design.

At ground level, a couple of steps down from the street, one gets the immediate sense of how important joinery is to a home with modest dimensions. The built-in storage in the front portion of the house, framing the lounge, conceals things such as the television screen. Behind one of the cupboards is also a guest bathroom and at arm's length from the kitchen's steel countertop is a pantry. And while the furniture is minimal, purposefully so given the arrival of Zoe, there are additional built-in benches, one in the lounge and the other in the dining area, which were deliberately conceived as part of the construction and used to underpin the house. Rather than build wall-to-wall, ao-ft made the decision to create a vista from the living area through to the studio by means of retaining a side garden.

'We're a small practice so we can afford to work from home. Having a 15-metre-long path between the house and our studio, which is located at the back of the garden, also allows us enough separation between home and work,' says Zach. Alfie, the dog, also enjoys the opportunity to have a considerably larger garden. 'Our former home was a small cottage in Hackney, with very little room to move, inside or out,' Zach adds.

The concealed timber-batten door at the entrance acts as a privacy screen, also allowing for cross ventilation during the warmer months of the year. 'We also keep the front door open to strengthen the connection to the street,' says Liz – the couple opted for a low front fence to allow for engagement with neighbours. 'When we're in our studio, you can see right through to the street,' she adds. Timber shutters on the ground floor, when left opened, further strengthen the connection to the street, as well as animate the facade. These shutters, together with the wraparound glazing at ground level, are also a subtle nod to the Victorian shopfront that once existed here.

On the first floor is Zoe's bedroom, also lined wall-to-wall with CLT and built-in joinery, and a second bedroom and shared bathroom that includes a laundry. And on the top floor is the main bedroom and bathroom, stepped back from the first floor to allow the bedroom to recede in the streetscape.

Although the house is considerably larger than the cottage Zach and Liz left behind, it's still fairly modest in size and in the materials selected. Approximately 115 m^2 in area, with the studio being an additional 14 m^2, the house feels significantly larger than the traditional Victorian terrace with its typical shotgun corridor down one side. 'I think having so much glazing, as well as including an operable skylight above the stairs, makes the place feel lighter and more spacious,' says Liz.

Given the couple's admiration for CLT, the walls have been left completely free of art, with the detail beautifully expressed in the form of timber joints and thoughtfully crafted built-in units. The same approach was taken with the bathrooms, only here there's the addition of terrazzo. 'We love sitting on the concrete bench in the lounge and just watching the way the garden continually changes. It's become quite dense over a few months rather than years,' says Zach. While some architects working from home may prefer clients not enter the main house but come directly to a separate studio, here there's great pride in taking potential clients through the living areas and then the back door and to admire the garden designed by Meeuwsen Muldoon. 'It gives people quite a strong idea at this point where we are coming from; they see the ideas and values that resonate – at least with us,' adds Zach.

TIPS

Think about where light is needed most in a house and also about cross ventilation.

You don't have to build boundary to boundary even if it might be permitted. Not having our side garden would have greatly compromised this design.

zach fluker & liz tatarintseva

the architect's house

zach fluker & liz tatarintseza

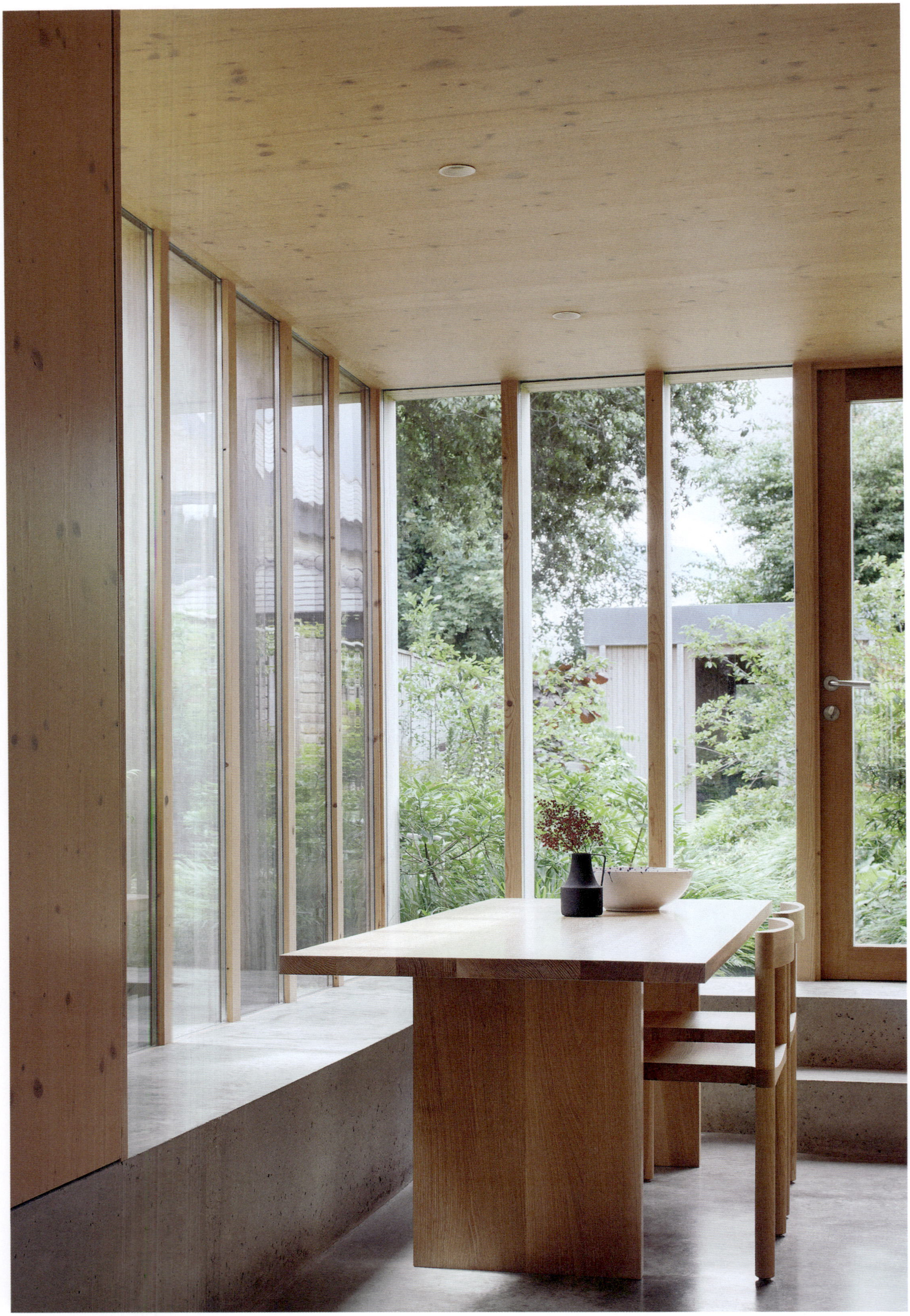

zach fluker & liz tatarintseva

the architect's house

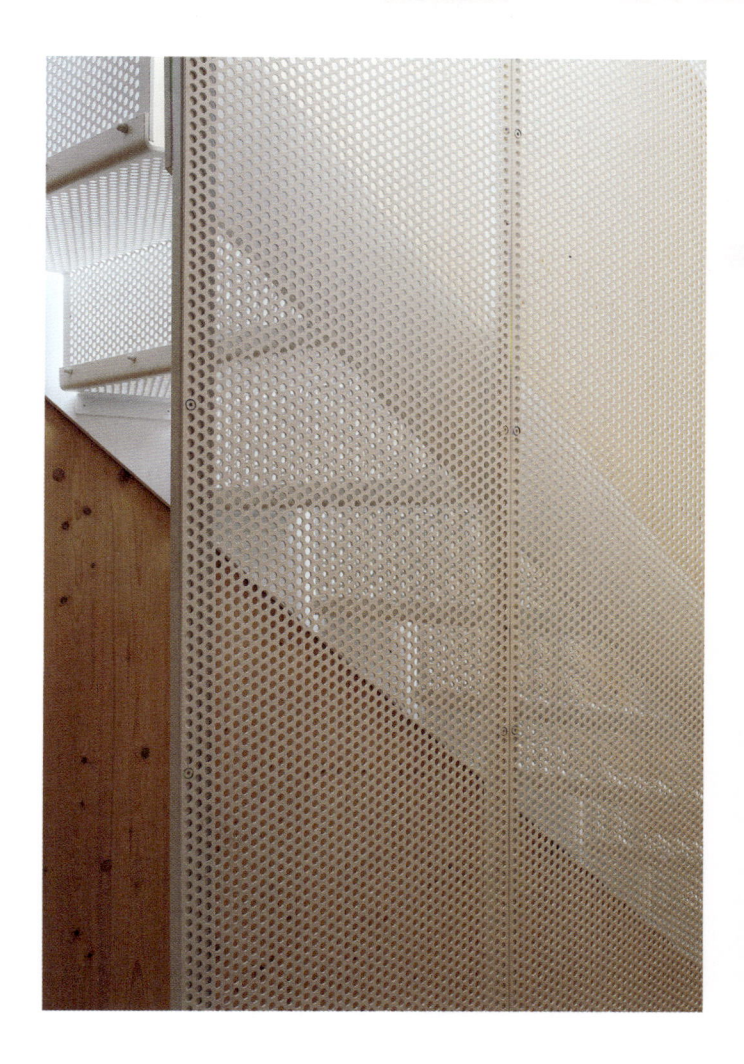

zach fluker & liz tatarintseza

the architect's house

zach fluker & liz tatarintseza

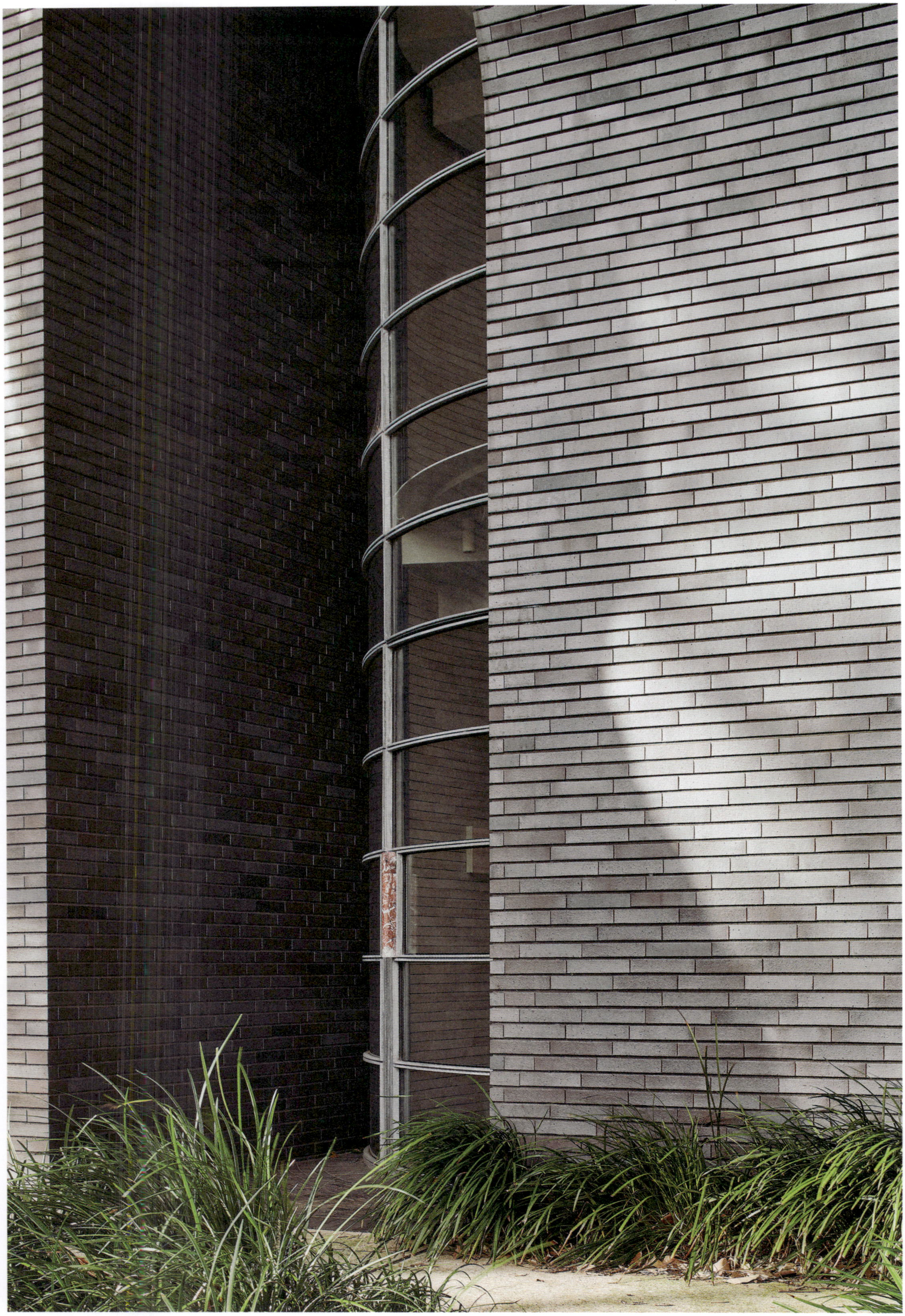

William Smart, Architect, Smart Design Studio

WAREHOUSE-STYLE HOME, ALEXANDRIA, SYDNEY

One of Sydney's leading architects, William Smart initially made his mark with a pint-sized one-bedroom apartment in the city's Kings Cross area. Decked out with one entire wall of glossy red joinery that contained numerous functions, it was described by Smart as a 'Swiss army knife'. The size of his practice and home/studio in Alexandria, is substantially larger, as are the projects his studio now works on.

Originally a 1950s warehouse used for machinery that produced sweets, and located in a heritage precinct with a number of warehouses dating from the post-war period, Smart could see the benefit of the location and the 3,600-m^2 site for a new office, as well as the opportunity to create a home for him and his partner, John Adcock, and their dog, a German pointer named Digby. Since moving to the area, other architectural practices have followed suit, with new cafés opening nearby. 'Our previous office in Surry Hills was spread across several levels and in two buildings. It just wasn't large enough or suitable for a studio in which people could collaborate easily,' says William, who, as with this new home, had included an apartment on the top floor. 'Having our home above the office means that I can work any time of the day or night and even take a quick nap at some point,' says William.

As with William's previous studio, arranged around the art of model-making, here staff are literally surrounded by maquettes, the models are made from white card that complements the pristine white walls dotted with plans and schemes. However, the new studio, with its saw-tooth roof, now features a welcoming reception area at the front along with meeting rooms located directly above. The facade and front portion of the building, occupying a footprint of 7 x 33 m, have been completely rebuilt in slim Roman-style bricks, creating a contemporary entrance that still respects the building's past.

Above this new structure, and accessed via a curvaceous staircase of pink terrazzo treads, is William and John's apartment, approximately 200 m² with two separate outdoor terraces. The first thing one immediately notices upon arrival is the long extruded barrel-vaulted ceiling that comprises a series of interlocking vaults varying in height from 2.7 m to 4 m; the lower ceiling heights are in the kitchen and study. The Roman-style bricks appear to have been fashioned on a potter's wheel, allowing light to permeate the precious vessel where it's needed. William had a certain vision in his mind soon after purchasing the warehouse, partially inspired by Carlo Scarpa's Gipsoteca plaster gallery in Possagno, 60 km north-west of Venice. Designed in the mid-1950s, the same time William's warehouse was built, Scarpa's design included a masterful use of light in the elongated museum, which was conceived for a sculpture by Antonio Canova. 'This was a starting point, but with any idea it is often about looking at the past and taking it forwards,' says William.

Designed over one level, the main bedroom and bathroom are located at one end of the apartment, with the study at the other. At the core is the open-plan living and dining area, with the kitchen nearby. 'There are no doors except the two for the toilets,' says William. 'The vaulted ceilings [four in total] loosely delineate these spaces,' he adds. To allow the space to 'read' as one, the kitchen was approached more akin to furniture rather than the usual wall-to-wall built-in joinery. The 7-metre-long island, with its Corian® benchtop and polyurethane cupboards, contains everything from the two smaller fridges to the two ovens. A 16-metre-long credenza, also finished with polyurethane joinery, connects the spaces feature stone floors throughout.

To create a seamless and holistic design, William, working with his team, created a number of the pieces of furniture, including the dining table, chairs and stools. The unusual coffee table in the lounge was conceived with a built-in television that can easily be retracted when not being used. William and John took a few pieces from their previous home, such as an Arflex sofa and a couple of chairs. The large parchment light (120 cm in height) by Davide Groppi is sculptural, as is the two-side artwork by Belgian artist Peter De Potter on one side and Australian artist Tim Richardson on the other.

As with Scarpa's masterful use of light in the Possagno museum, light enters through highlight windows at the ends of each barrel-vaulted form. This soft light against the brick walls creates a sense of calmness and tranquillity. 'It's such a reflective space; the way the light plays on the brickwork. It allows me the space that I need not only physically, but in my mind,' says William.

Unlike the previous home, which was more conventional in its layout, this one doesn't include a bath and the workings of the kitchen are not on view. The same artistry extends to the dressing area, which creates more of a physical separation to the bedroom. Attached to the dressing-room cupboards are graphic paintings by artist Mike Parr. The couple also left the brick walls and ceilings unadorned to allow their form to be an artistic work in its own right.

TIPS

We wanted this place to respond to the way we live. It was certainly not about resale or creating a home that would suit others. There's no bath here, but in the 15 years we were in our other place, we never used the bath, so why put something in just for the sake of it.

Sometimes, some of the most engaging spaces are those that are left empty. It allows for areas to breathe.

When it's your own home, why should you compromise? It should be about doing things that you like and take pleasure from.

william smart

the architect's house

william smart

229

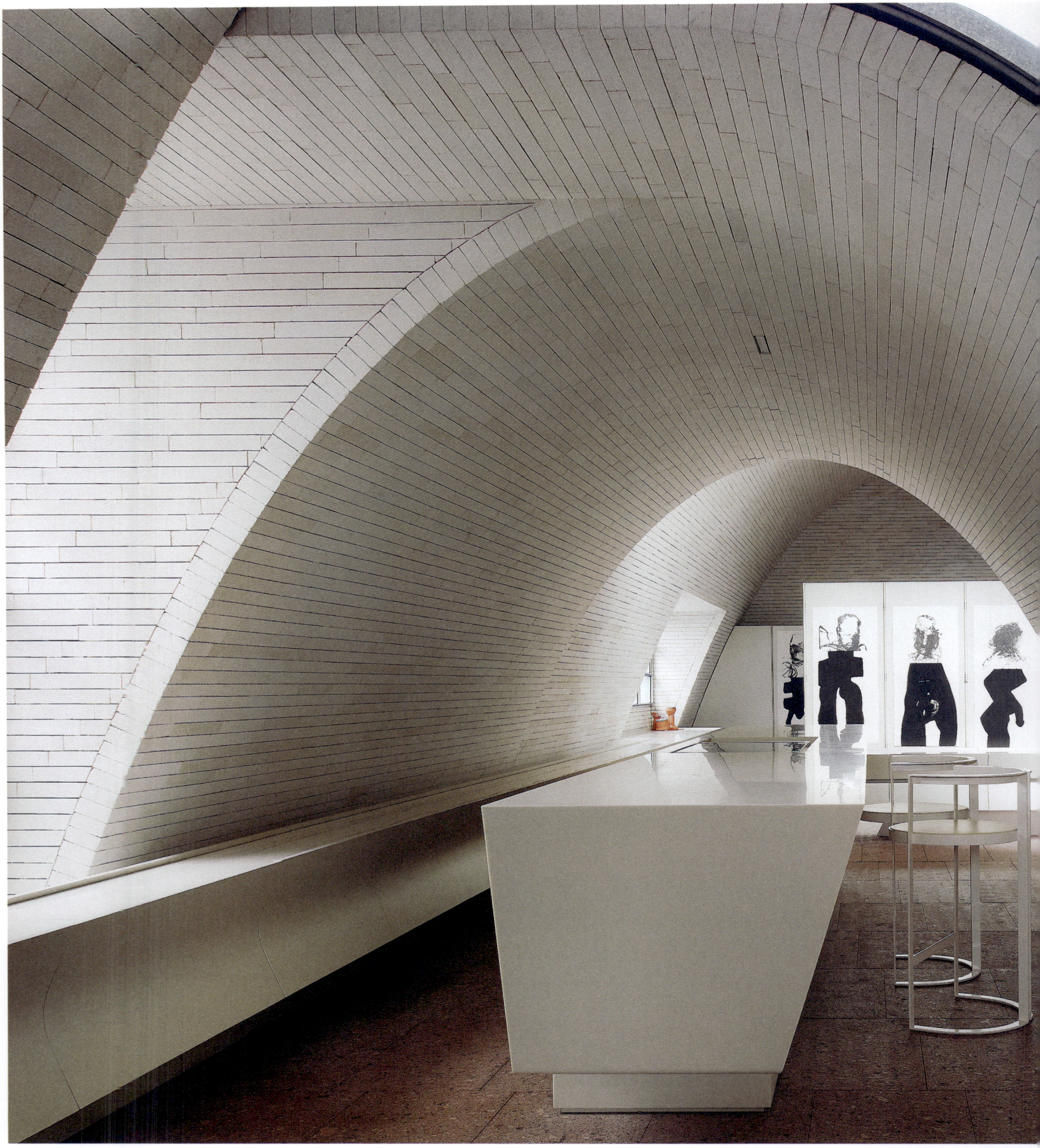

william smart

the architect's house

william smart

233

234 the architect's house

william smart

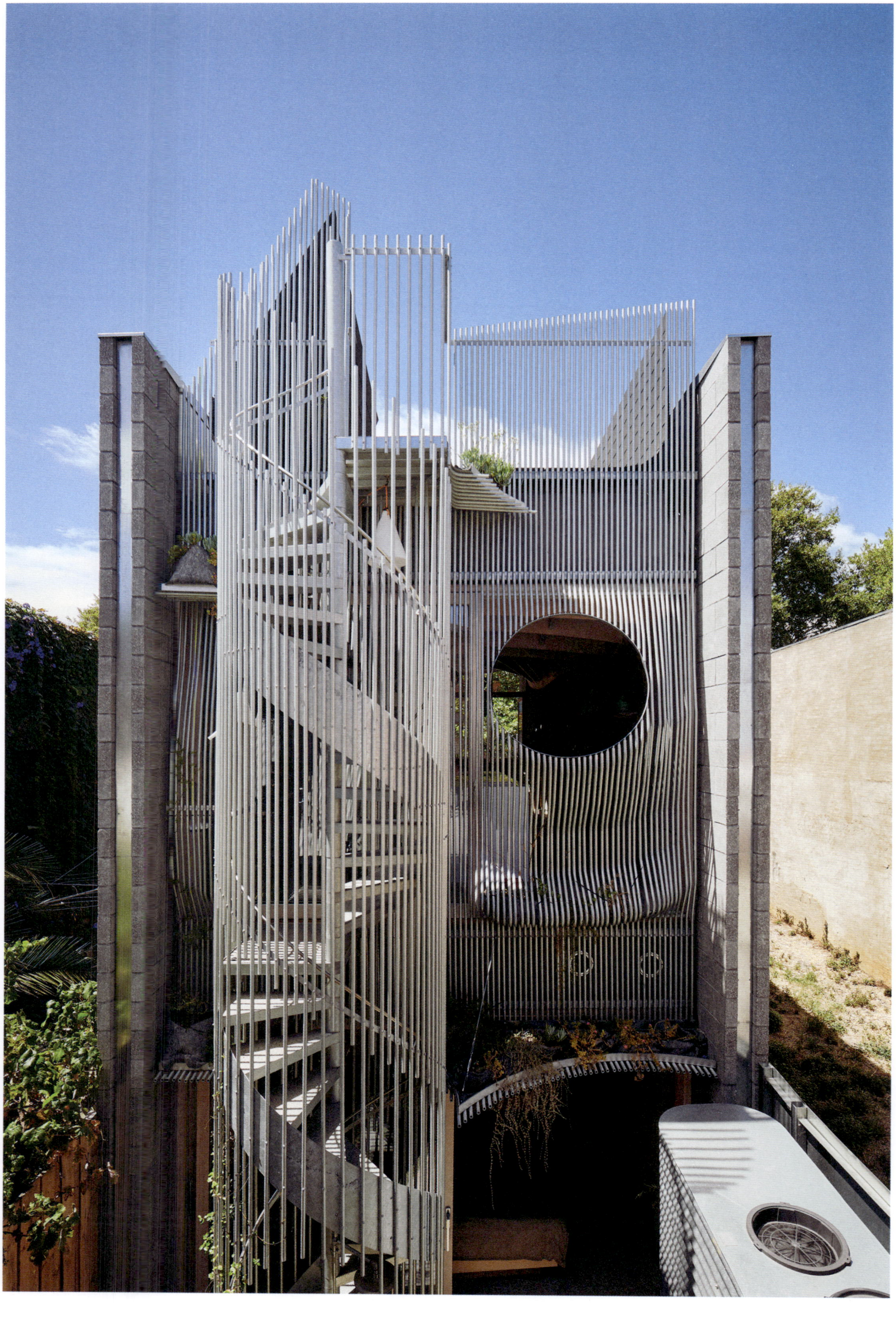

David Leggett & Paul Loh, Architects, Leggett Loh Design Studio (LLDS)

NORTHCOTE HOUSE, MELBOURNE

One neighbour refers to this home as the 'Opera House'. However, its scale is vastly smaller and its location, accessed from a laneway-like street, is at the other end of the spectrum to Sydney Harbour, where the Sydney Opera House can be found. Perhaps the home's cantilevered timber-strutted awning initiated the analogy – a grand gesture on a pint-sized block behind a row of shops.

Designed by architects David Leggett and his life and business partner Paul Loh, this new house was years in the making. The couple spent a considerable amount of time prototyping materials from their workshop in Preston, while living above the adjacent 1950s shopfront which remains the studio of LLDS. Both had studied and also worked in London and knew there was a 'project' waiting for them on their return. That project was building a new two-storey house in the rear yard of the adjoining shop, on a slither of land just over 100 m² – formerly used for tandem car parking.

Given the duo's Preston workshop is dedicated to creating Computer Numerical Control (CNC) materials and robotics-fabricated building components via machinery, the new house, shared with their pampered mini schnauzer, Merlin Junior, was always going to be a testing ground for their ideas. Like a large-scale format router, CNC fabrication can produce extraordinary results, including 'pleated' concrete walls and balustrade joinery. Producing furniture is also within its means, akin to the type of experiments used by Jean Prouvé as part of his talent for creating steel furniture.

However, it was the size of the site, a mere 4.6 m in width, that initially suggested the form for the house – a Victorian terrace-style typology that is common both in London and Melbourne. However, unlike a Victorian terrace, with ornate wrought-iron balustrades, the facade features a cantilevered timber awning, sculptured using CNC technology. And unlike the party walls of most Victorian terraces, the walls enclosing this awning are made from chunky bluestone. 'People have drawn comparisons to the work of Victor Horta as well as to architects such as Antonio Gaudí. But we see more of a connection to the work of Josep Maria Jujol, who is seen by many as being a more restrained version of Gaudí,' says Paul. The couple were inspired by Brutalist-style architecture. 'We've always admired the architecture of London-based Peter and Alison Smithson,' adds David.

Unlike many contemporary homes that are rectilinear in form and sometimes severe, the Northcote House is layered both inside and out with curves. The rear elevation, abutting the shop, features curvaceous steel poles across the entire facade, bending around windows and protruding to animate the facade and create a 'veil', providing privacy and diffusing the harsher afternoon light. 'We also wanted to frame views of the nearby church and the parapets of the stores,' says Paul. Another design cue for the house can be found in Paul's love of Issey Miyake's pleated clothing – captured in the treatment of the concrete walls that are ridged or pleated. The brass circular plugs, where the concrete wall pleats come together, form coat hooks or anything else that needs to be displayed, although the beauty of the walls is best expressed when left bare.

Although the house appears relatively spacious, it's only just over 80 m² with a roof terrace of approximately 12 m². Unlike a traditional Victorian terrace, the two bedrooms, each with its own bathroom, can be found on the lower level, along with a snug, while the top level is given over to the kitchen/dining area. Pivotal to the design are the 13 skylights, lined in brass and placed in the ceiling's alcoves, which vary in depth. 'We wanted to diffuse the overhead sunlight as well as explore what could be achieved using CNC technology,' says David, pointing out the undulations of the ceiling, as well as the bespoke Corian® bench in the kitchen, with its *izakaya*-style dining table and accompanying chairs, also designed by LLDS. Others using this technology may have simply come up with an organic-shaped form. Here, the level of detail is truly remarkable, with the textured Corian® next to the brass-lined sinks to allow water from a glass or a plate to drain. And why have flat-fronted Corian® cupboards when technology can produce crinkle-cut surfaces – opening to reveal a series of plastic Alessi appliances, also crinkle-cut.

At the heart of the design is the organic-shaped plywood balustrade that frames the curved snug. The two levels, accessed via brass-clad treads and a Stuv fireplace with a 9-m-high flue was conceived to allow both natural light and the warmth of the steel flue to permeate both levels. Also, unlike a traditional Victorian terrace, you won't find two English-style high-back armchairs. Instead, there's a pile of cushions on a rug in the middle of the concrete floor and a built-in daybed that appears to have been 'chiselled' from the wall cavity. 'We see a certain Baroque sensibility in the staircase,' says Paul, referring to the geometry of the balustrade.

Given the size of the house, most of the time is spent either in the snug/library or around the kitchen bench. But on warmer days, the couple gravitate to the rooftop garden, which is partially concealed by a berm. Accessed via a spiral steel staircase, this outdoor space becomes another room. There are also two bedrooms at the lower level, each one with its own en suite – lined in Corian® with ripple-edged floors (for grip) and ceilings that reflect the light. And given the proportions, no space is wasted. A small passage outside one of the showers that leads to the second bedroom is referred to as the drying area. Storage for both bedrooms is also kept to a minimum, with the main bedroom having only plywood built-in joinery that necessitates the folding, rather than hanging, of Paul's collection of Issey Miyake, with other items having to be stored below the bed.

But while the spaces are modest, there's a sense of joy and delight to be found at every turn, with a hand-blown glass, portal-shaped window in the main bedroom, created by artist Ruth Allen, which has an impression of pressed lips. The ceiling in the main bedroom, with its scale-like textured concrete, also shows the advances the couple have made using CNC technology. The house continually changes with the seasons and can be closed up, or opened up entirely, allowing for cross ventilation and a strong connection to the elements, both natural and man-made.

TIPS

Trust your architect and be open to new ideas. It's important not just to think about the traditional house you may have grown up in. Think about how you want to live now and in the future. Maybe ask the question, 'Do we really need four bedrooms if we only have one child?'

Be mindful of the carbon footprint you're creating. Perhaps reduce the clutter that surrounds you and look at a more minimal space, surrounding yourself with things that have meaning rather than collecting things that are rarely used, if at all.

david leggett & paul loh

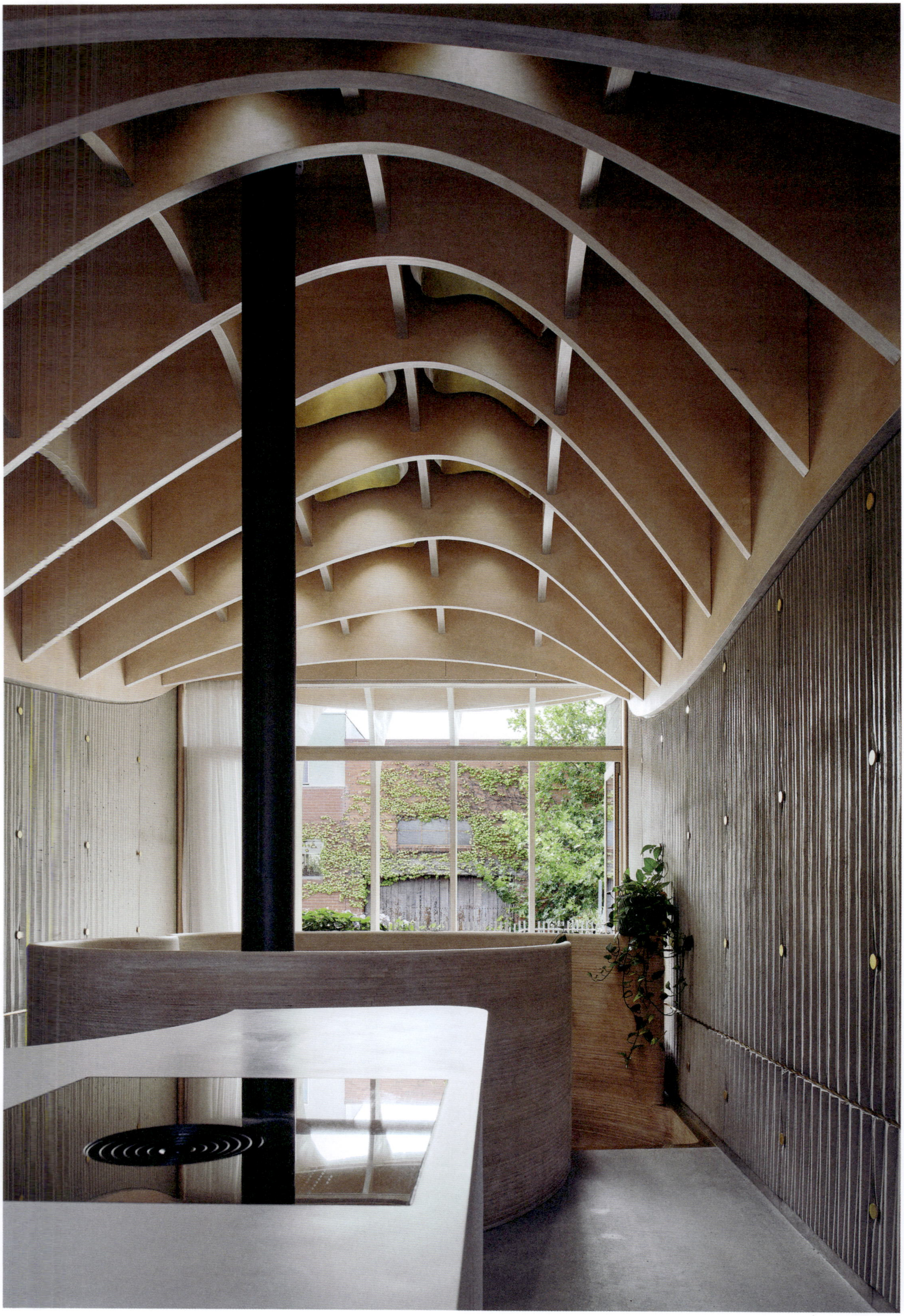

241

THE POSTCARD ART OF
GILBERT & GEORGE
1972—1986
Frei Otto
VISION

david leggett & paul loh

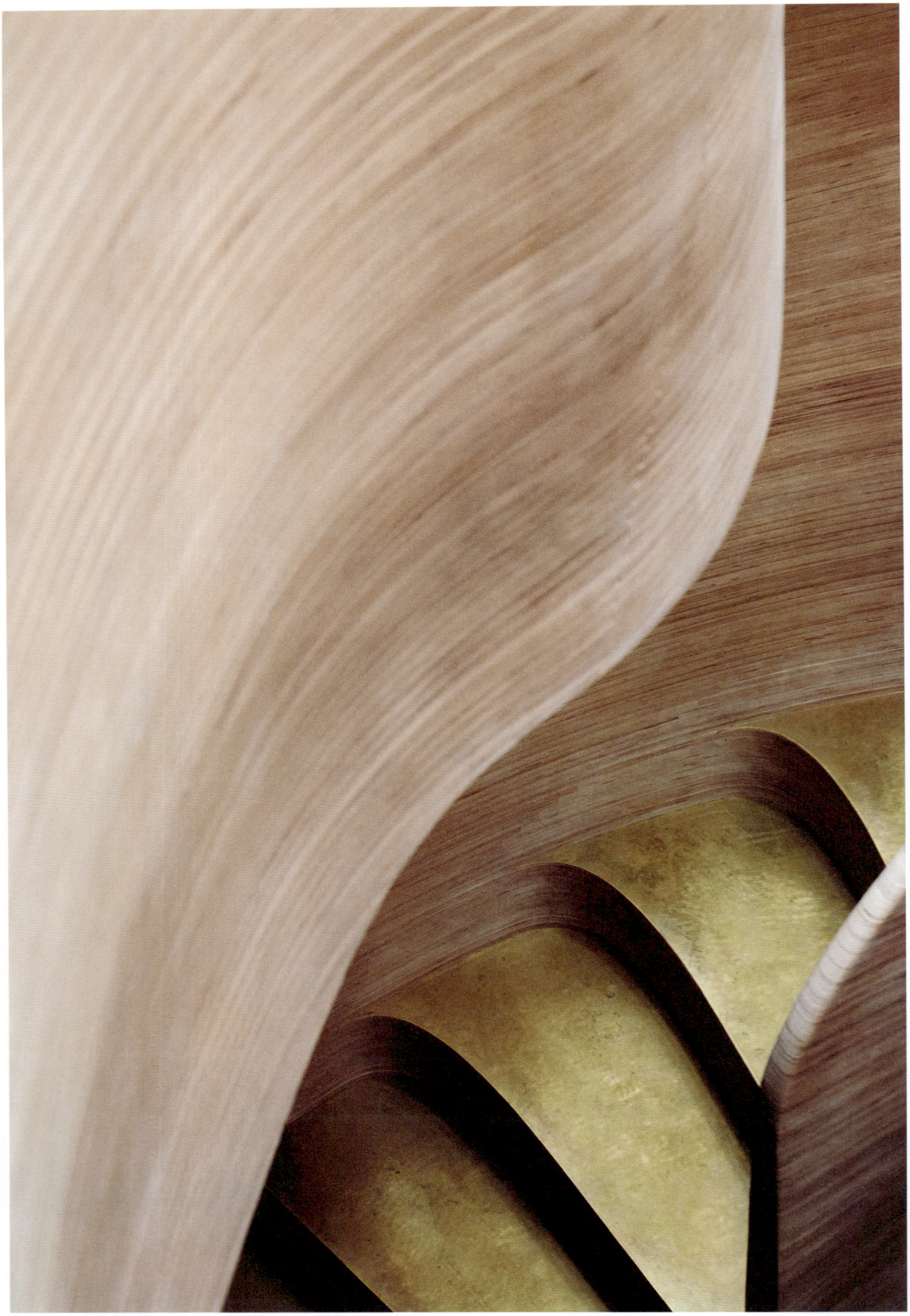

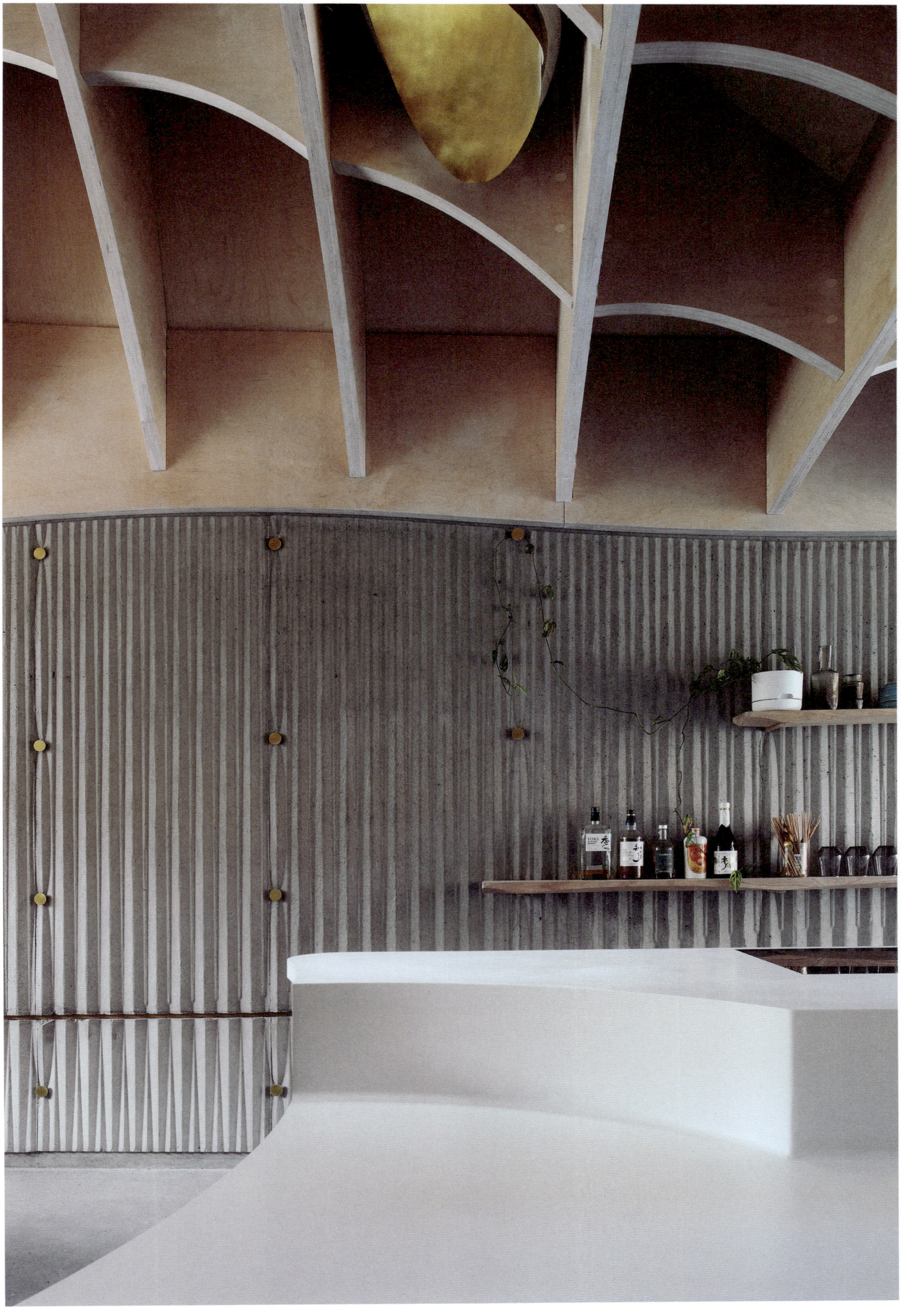

the architect's house

david leggett & paul loh

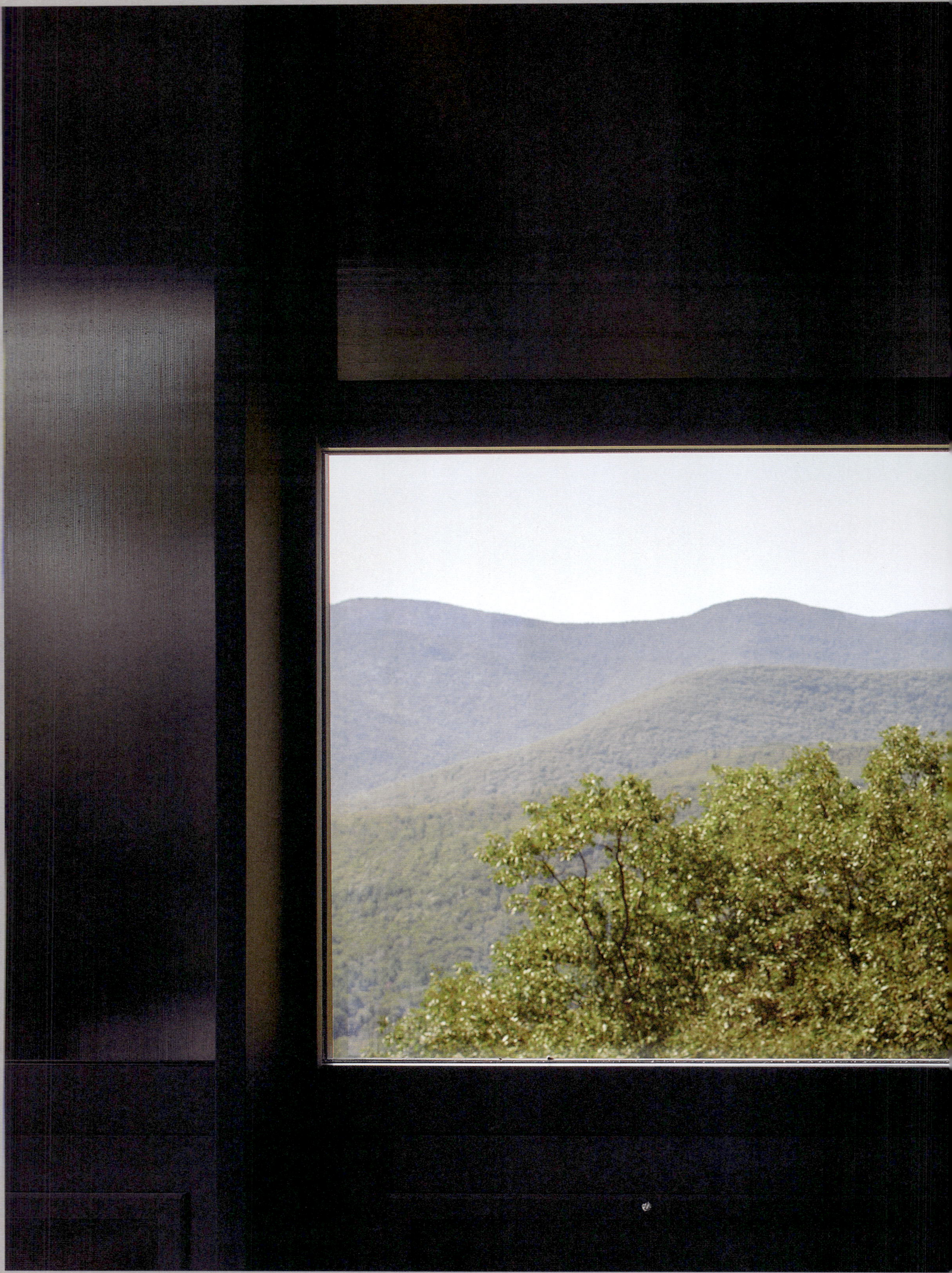

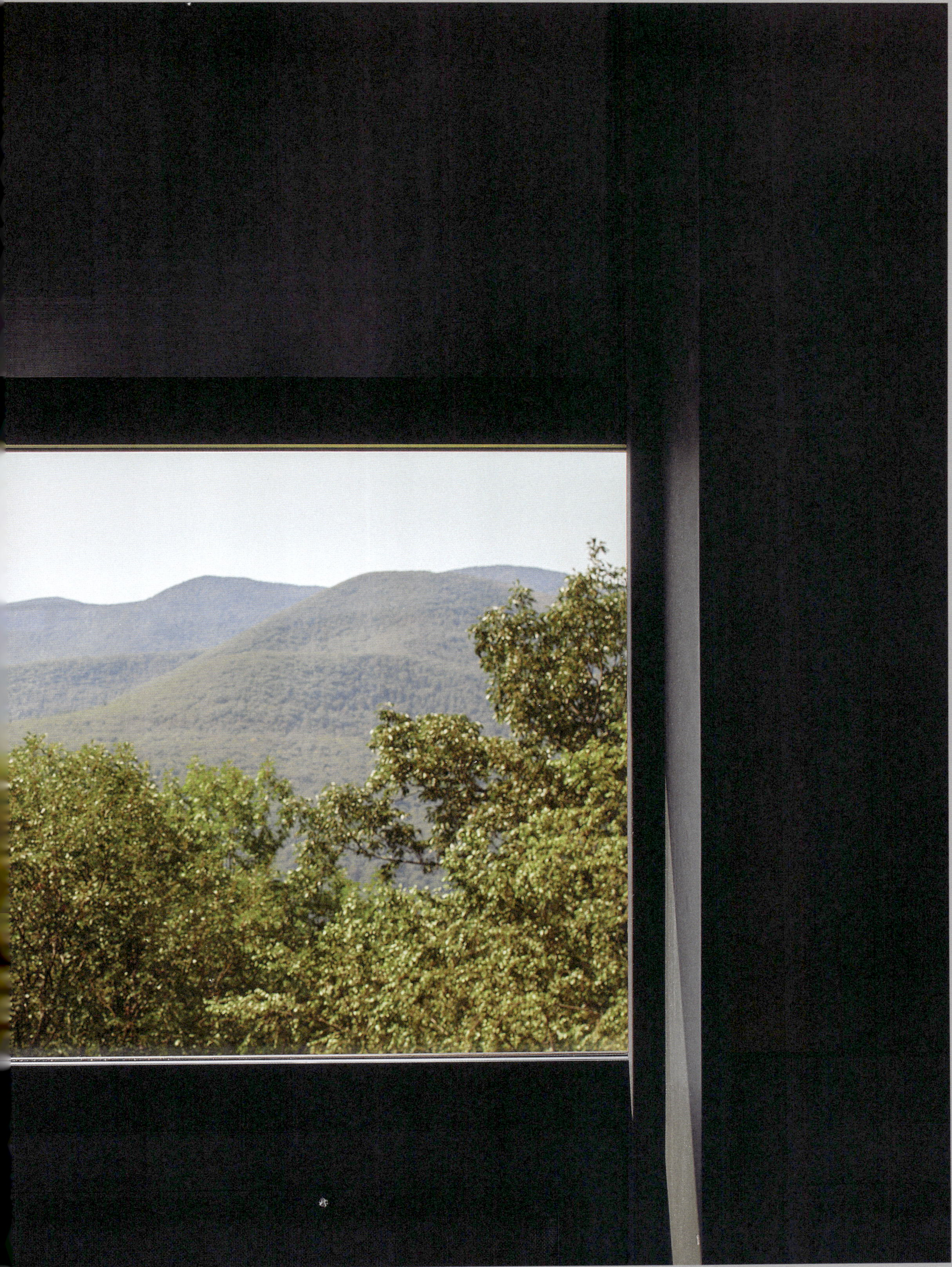

acknowledgements

I would like to thank Nicole England for both her wonderful photography and, importantly, for introducing me to Kate Pollard, my publisher at Penguin Random House. I would also like to thank Fran Madigan for casting her eye across the pages of this book. And thanks to Trisha Garner, a talented book designer, who also brought her skills to these pages, and to Erwin Schulz for his dedication and expertise in enhancing the images. Also thanks to the following who generously assisted the photographer on location: Vange Markou in Belgium, Natalie James in Melbourne and Rick Kersley in New York.

I would like to thank the many architects who are featured in the book, who have shown what can be achieved when the architect has the freedom to design their own home.

My gratitude also goes to my editor at *Wallpaper**, Ellie Stathaki and also to Sophie Lewis, my editor at *est living*, for their suggestions.

My thanks also to my partner Naomi, who has allowed me to 'live the dream' and turn what was initially a passion for architecture into a career.

251

about the author

Stephen Crafti has been writing about architecture and design for over 30 years and has produced more than 45 books. He also writes for leading newspapers and magazines in Australia and overseas. In addition, Stephen leads architecture and design tours in both Australia and overseas with leading cultural tour company Australians Studying Abroad (ASA). He also leads his own tours in Melbourne, where he resides with his partner in a home designed by architect Robert Simeoni with the assistance of furniture and lighting designer Suzie Stanford.

about the photographer

Nicole England is a Melbourne-based architecture and interiors photographer who has worked with many of the industry's top architects and designers internationally. She has an intimate understanding of light and form, and a sharp eye for composition. Her photography brings the everyday spaces we inhabit into focus, highlighting the artistry and the beauty that is often overlooked.

Nicole has published three books: *Resident Dog*, *Resident Dog (Vol 2)* and *Art in Residence*.

credits for furniture & art

Charles Wu, Polysmiths
PAGE 17
  Pendant Light by GUBI
  TMM floor lamp by Santa & Cole
  CH25 Armchair by Carl Hansen & Søn
PAGE 18
  Candlestick chairs by Ercol
  Kartell Papyrus olive green chair

Andrew Piva, B.E. Architecture
PAGES 26-7
  Eames Lounge Chair & Ottoman
  Vintage Missoni fabric on armchair
  Drawings against wall by artist Mike Parr
PAGE 28
  Vintage bentwood bistro chairs
  George Nelson light from Herman Miller
PAGE 29
  Custom-made lamp
  Bench by Meller 63
PAGE 30
  Vintage Thonet chair
PAGE 31
  Blue artwork by John Nixon
PAGE 33
  Vintage Missoni fabric on the lounge
  Pot-belly fireplace by Cheminées Philippe

Ben Ridley, Architecture for London
PAGE 41
  Sofas from Really Well Made
PAGE 38
  CH338 dining table and CH26 dining chairs by Carl Hansen & Søn

Mathieu Luyens & Julie Van De Keere, JUMA Architects
PAGE 47
  AA Armchairs by Airborne
PAGES 48-9
  Vitra Eames Plywood chair
  Eames LTR occasional table with chrome legs
  Barcelona Relax Chairs by Knoll
  Soriana sofa by Afra + Tobia Scarpa
  Coffee table by Charlotte Perriand for Cassina
PAGE 52
  Carved mask by Matthew Baker
PAGE 53
  Painting by artist Jeroen Broeckx
PAGE 52
  GUBI multi-light
  Tulip table and chairs from Saarinen for Knoll

Jay Bargmann, FAIA
PAGE 60
  Eames three-seat sofa from Herman Miller
PAGE 65
  Eames Aluminium Group Chair by Herman Miller

Sam Peeters, Contekst
PAGE 73
  Table designed by Contekst
  Frederica JGS Mogensen chairs
  Flos Toic floor lamp by Castiglioni
PAGE 74
  USM Haller table
PAGE 75
  Chairs - Vitra by Prouve
PAGE 77
  Art by Antonia Eodrian
  Sculpture in accve by Grace Woodcock
  Side chair by Taira
  Lounge owned by the family for years

PAGE 78
  Pendant light by Louis Poulsen PH
PAGE 79
  Wall print by unknown artist
  Bird sculpture by unknown artist

Peggy Hsu & Chris McCullough, HSU McCullough
PAGE 85
  Mole Lounge Armchair with Ottoman by Sergio Rodrigues
  Montauk Lounge Chair by West Elm
PAGES 88-9
  Grace Serpentine Three-Piece Sectional Sofa with brass legs by Anthropologie
  Lobby Chair by Wendelbo
  Side table - E1027 Adjustable Table by Eileen Gray
  Linden counter stool by Fyrn
PAGE 90
  Painting by artist Moses Soyer
PAGE 91
  Mosaic wall 'Tribute' by Chris McCullough

Thomas Gluck, GLUCK+
PAGE 95
  Womb Chair & Ottoman by Eero Saarinen
  Arne Jacobsen Series 7-style chair
  Flos Arco-style lamp
  Custom-designed table by Thomas Gluck
  Hans Wegner CH07 Shell-style chair
  Standard Sofa by Blu Dot
  Bench by George Nelson
PAGE 98
  Tulip-style table by Saarinen
  DKR Wire Chairs by Eames
PAGE 99
  Polywood Modern Adirondack Chair

Percy Weston, Surman Weston
PAGE 108
  Vintage dining chairs and table
  Painting by Nicolette Ismay
  Sculpture by Nicolette Ismay
PAGE 110
  Painting by Timothy Weston
PAGE 111
  Vintage chairs

Mat Barnes, CAN
PAGE 121
  Painting by Hetty Douglas
  'Bless This Acid House' by Jeremy Deller and Fraser Muggeridge
PAGE 122
  Lamp by Habitat
  Liquid Geology coffee table by CAN
PAGE 122
  Steel cabinet by IKEA
  Tapestry by Glitch Textiles
PAGE 124
  Top left image: Mudlark Chair by CAN, Vintage chairs
  Bottom left image: Art by Roger Serras
PAGES 126-7
  Angle sofa by Simon Pengelly
  Vintage armchair
  Liquid Geology side table by CAN
  Hai Chair & ottoman by HEM

Matthew Royce, M Royce Architecture
PAGE 129
  Sculpture by Lee Hun Chung

PAGES 132-3
  Slatted bench by James De Wulf
PAGE 136
  Painting of Jesus by unknown artist, purchased at a flea market in Mexico City
  Suspended wire sculpture - Ruth Asawa
PAGE 138
  Sculpture by Lee Hun Chung
  Chairs found in a vintage store

Jonathan Tuckey, Tuckey Design Studio
PAGE 144
  Far left, Two silver point on linen works by Erika Winstone
  Art by Ryan Durrant
PAGE 146
  Artist Jim Page-Roberts

Robert Simeoni, Robert Simeoni Architects
PAGE 157
  Coconut Chair by George Nelson
  Plywood chairs by Eames
PAGE 158
  Side chair by Walter Burley Griffin designed for Newman College at the University of Melbourne

Manuel Aires Mateus
PAGE 169
  "Pó" Series by Daniel Malhão Photography
PAGE 168
  Chairs, family heirlooms from the 19th century
  Baroque painting by unknown artist
  Desenho by Sergio Taborda
PAGE 169
  Chairs by Thonet
  Luz Jiménez
  Francisca Aires Mateus
PAGE 172
  Jasper Morrison Chairs - Vitra
  "PO" Series by Daniel Malho
PAGE 173
  Art by Jose Pedro Croft
  Art by Hez Wijnhorst
  Art by Eduando Chillida
PAGE 175
  Art by Richard Serra

John Friedman & Alice Kimm Architects
PAGE 179
  Chairs by Toledo Jorge Pensi for Knoll
PAGE 182
  Plywood chairs by Eames
PAGE 187
  Bed designed by John Friedman fabricated by Evan Pohimier
  Painting by Catherine Opie
  Paper lantern lamp by Isamu Noguchi

Ilze Quaeyhaegens & Gert Cuypers, cuypers & Q Architects
PAGE 190
  Chaise longues by Charles Zublena
PAGES 194-5
  Green artworks by Roeland Tweelinckx
  Vintage Eames LCM chairs from Herman Miller
  Cassina Naan table by Piero Lissoni
  265 by Paolo Rizzatto light from Flos
PAGE 196
  1960s candle holder by Hans Nagel and Werner Stoff
  Art by Panamarenko
PAGE 198
  Chairs by Habitat
  Table by Sixinch

PAGE 199
  Wall clock by George Nelson
Jeff Provan, Neometro & MA+Co
PAGE 205
  Vintage Butterfly chairs
PAGE 206
  Wiggle Side Chair by Frank Gehry
PAGE 207
  Paper Lantern by Society
  Sculpture by Bruce Armstrong
PAGE 208
  Painting on wall by Jeff Provan
  Three-piece Bend Sofa by Patricia Urquiola
  Wall light Flos 265 small
  Painting by Dennis Ropar
PAGE 209
  Masks by Ton Ton
  Painting by Matthew De Moiser
  Red paintings by Pegleg Tjampitjinpa
  Air Chairs by Jasper Morrison
PAGES 210-11
  Centre image:
  Paper lantern – Akari 33N by Akari Light
  Star Wars Walker collectable

Zach Fluker & Liz Tatarintseva, ao-ft
PAGE 219
  Drum Pouf by Softline
PAGE 223
Sunny lounge chair by Lammhults

William Smart, Smart Design Studio
PAGE 227
  Sofa by Arflex Marenco
  Peter armchairs by Flexform
  Pouf by Arflex Marenco
  Custom-designed coffee table
  Moon light by Davide Groppi
  Charcoal timber side tables by Harbour
  Artwork featured on the front of the wardrobe
    doors in the main bedroom by Mike Parr
PAGE 228
  Sculpture of bull by unknown artist,
    bought from Mao & More
  Small sculpture next to bull – Wing by
    Dung Ming-Lung
PAGE 229
  Stool – side table by Aalto
PAGE 230
  Custom-designed chairs
PAGE 233
  Double-sided work on steel stand
    by Peter de Potter
PAGE 234
  Artwork by Coen Yung

David Leggett & Paul Loh, LLDS
PAGE 242
  Stûv 30-Compact fireplace

Quadrille, Penguin Random House UK,
One Embassy Gardens, 8 Viaduct Gardens,
London SW11 7BW

Quadrille Publishing Limited is part of the Penguin Random House group of companies whose addresses can be found at global.penguinrandomhouse.com

Penguin Random House UK

Copyright © Stephen Crafti 2025
Photography © Nicole England

Stephen Crafti has asserted his right to be identified as the author of this Work in accordance with the Copyright, Designs and Patents Act 1988

Penguin Random House values and supports copyright. Copyright fuels creativity, encourages diverse voices, promotes freedom of expression and supports a vibrant culture. Thank you for purchasing an authorised edition of this book and for respecting intellectual property laws by not reproducing, scanning or distributing any part of it by any means without permission. You are supporting authors and enabling Penguin Random House to continue to publish books for everyone. No part of this book may be used or reproduced in any manner for the purpose of training artificial intelligence technologies or systems. In accordance with Article 4(3) of the DSM Directive 2019/790, Penguin Random House expressly reserves this work from the text and data mining exception.

Published by Quadrille in 2025

www.penguin.co.uk

A CIP catalogue record for this book is available from the British Library

ISBN 9781837833870

10 9 8 7 6 5 4 3 2 1

Publishing Director: Kate Pollard
Photographer: Nicole England
Retoucher: Erwin Schulz
Designer: Trisha Garner
Copy Editor: Imogen Fortes
Proofreader: Hannah Boursnell
Production Manager: Sabeena Atchia

Colour reproduction by p2d

Printed in China by C&C Offset Printing Co., Ltd.

The authorised representative in the EEA is
Penguin Random House Ireland, Morrison Chambers,
32 Nassau Street, Dublin D02 YH68.

FSC MIX Paper | Supporting responsible forestry FSC® C018179

Penguin Random House is committed to a sustainable future for our business, our readers and our planet. This book is made from Forest Stewardship Council® certified paper.